Neither Villain nor Victim

Critical Issues in Crime and Society
Raymond J. Michalowski, Series Editor

Critical Issues in Crime and Society is oriented toward critical analysis of contemporary problems in crime and justice. The series is open to a broad range of topics including specific types of crime, wrongful behavior by economically or politically powerful actors, controversies over justice system practices, and issues related to the intersection of identity, crime, and justice. It is committed to offering thoughtful works that will be accessible to scholars and professional criminologists, general readers, and students.

Tammy L. Anderson, ed., *Neither Villain nor Victim: Empowerment and Agency among Women Substance Abusers*

Mary Bosworth and Jeanne Flavin, eds., *Race, Gender, and Punishment: From Colonialism to the War on Terror*

Luis A. Fernandez, *Policing Dissent: Social Control and the Anti-Globalization Movement*

Michael J. Lynch, *Big Prisons, Big Dreams: Crime and the Failure of America's Penal System*

Raymond J. Michalowski and Ronald C. Kramer, eds., *State-Corporate Crime: Wrongdoing at the Intersection of Business and Government*

Susan L. Miller, *Victims as Offenders: The Paradox of Women's Violence in Relationships*

Susan F. Sharp, *Hidden Victims: The Effects of the Death Penalty on Families of the Accused*

Robert H. Tillman and Michael L. Indergaard, *Pump and Dump: The Rancid Rules of the New Economy*

Mariana Valverde, *Law and Order: Images, Meanings, Myths*

Michael Welch, *Scapegoats of September 11th: Hate Crimes and State Crimes in the War on Terror*

Neither Villain nor Victim

Empowerment and Agency among Women Substance Abusers

Edited by
TAMMY L. ANDERSON

RUTGERS UNIVERSITY PRESS
New Brunswick, New Jersey, and London

LIBRARY OF CONGRESS CATALOGING-IN-PUBLICATION DATA

Neither villain nor victim : empowerment and agency among women substance abusers / edited by Tammy L. Anderson.

    p. cm. — (Critical issues in crime and society)

  Includes bibliographica references and index.

  ISBN 978-0-8135-4208-9 (hardcover : alk. paper) — ISBN 978-0-8135-4209-6 (pbk. : alk. paper)

  1. Women drug addicts   2. Female offenders—Drug use.   3. Women prisoners—Drug use.   4. Female offenders—Rehabilitation.   5. Women prisoners—Rehabilitation.   6. Drug use—Prevention.   7. Drug abuse—Treatment.   I. Anderson, Tammy L.

  HV4999.W65N45 2008

  362.29082—dc22   2007019963

Visit our Web site: http://rutgerspress.rutgers.edu

Manufactured in the United States of America

This book is dedicated to all women with substance abuse problems, their supporting families and friends, and the dedicated professionals who help them. In the face of great obstacles, may your courage, strength, and hope lead you to resolution and peace.

CONTENTS

ACKNOWLEDGMENTS

THIS EDITED VOLUME was inspired by my research with female substance abusers and by my wish to offer academics, policy makers, practitioners, and students an alternative viewpoint on them as well as on the illicit drug world in general. In my published work, I have often used a gendered framework and have included males and females as research subjects, which has allowed me to make meaningful comparisons between them. My findings and my written work did not always jive with published accounts. For example, the substance abuse and criminological literatures are dominated by reports of women as poor or exploited victims who cannot function independently or live outside of considerable risk, or who are social misfits, fallen women—even monsters—bordering on the pathological. I seldom found evidence of these two images—villain or victim—in my work, yet I found few scholars willing to take me seriously when I reported different accounts. Instead, my work was met with opposition or, more often, simply trivialized, an experience common to the authors in this book and to many other feminists researching deviance, drugs, and crime.

There seem two main obstacles to gaining respect for an alternative viewpoint on women offenders and substance abusers. The first is epistemological in nature. Many scholars writing about drugs, crime, and violence believe gender is not a useful theoretical framework by which to understand any deviant phenomena, or that gender only matters when studying women. To include women as research subjects or to use gender as a framework for investigation is only necessary, this contingent holds, if women form a sufficient portion of the population in question. A second obstacle is more sociocultural in nature. It has to do with the heavy stigma women deviants carry, and with the paternalism and, at times, sexism of male and female researchers in viewing these deviants outside of the villain/victim paradigm.

In the spring of 2003, I ran into both obstacles at a department colloquium. The experience proved a turning point in my frustration and helped inspire my 2005 *Theoretical Criminology* piece and this edited volume. That spring, my department hosted a well-known sociologist who had written a classic book about inner-city drugs, crime, and violence. After his talk, I went to dinner with him and a few colleagues, and had a chance to discuss his work. At the time, I was conducting an ethnographic study of male and female offenders who had received substance abuse treatment in prison, and his work was highly relevant to my own. Over pasta, I asked him why he hadn't given gender greater attention in his work. He turned to me and said, "I don't know, but I think you should study the women, Tammy."

Throughout my career, people have responded to me in a similar fashion when I have asked them about the use of gender in their work or about making gender-based comparisons between male and female research subjects. Like our department's visiting speaker, they have missed my point about using gender as a concept or framework in drugs, crime, and violence research. To them, doing so depended on who your subjects were: the concept of gender would be relevant to studies with women subjects, but not necessarily relevant when investigating men. Additionally, as I often found, those who adopted this viewpoint on gender and research subjects also concurred with the dominant narrative of women offenders or substance abusers as either villains or victims. They often trusted other scholars to continue documenting women's plight.

At the 2003 meetings of the American Sociological Association, I gathered some notable women scholars on substance abuse (i.e., persons who are also my friends, colleagues, and mentors) for a dinner to discuss these matters, around which I was contemplating a book project. Over another pasta, Margaret Kelly, Judith Levy, Eloise Dunlap, Sheigla Murphy, and Claire Sterk complained to me about this gender gap, but especially about the pejorative and often sexist stories scholars wrote about women who abused substances. Through their many hours of fieldwork with thousands of women (and from developing hundreds of publications), my dinner companions did not think the prevailing narrative about women substance abusers was accurate. They agreed that scholars' use of gender was limited and scholars' choice of research subjects disconnected to gender. However, a bigger concern was the problematic narrative about women that viewed them as victims or monsters.

The essays presented here utilize gender frameworks in understanding women's lives. Such a framework includes instances where women adopt masculine and/or feminine identities, roles, or behaviors in negotiating criminal careers or attempting to exit from them. Although we seek to overcome the epistemological and sociocultural obstacles that have stunted research on drugs, crime, and violence, we also hope, more broadly, to offer an alternative and more useful narrative that will enable people to better understand not only women and men who abuse substances, but the very social worlds in which they live and operate.

No work of this size and scope is possible without the assistance, guidance, and support of many others. I offer them a shout-out here as a token of gratitude for their help in making this book possible.

To begin, I'd like to thank the University of Delaware and its department of sociology and criminal justice—my home. I am grateful for the professional and emotional support given me by all my colleagues, but especially by Susan Miller, Ronet Bachman, Margaret Andersen, Joel Best, and Lana Harrison. Thanks also to our department's support staff—Judy Watson, Nancy Quillen, Vicky Becker, and Linda Keen—for their assistance in administrative tasks. Finally, Theodore Davis and Gabby Mulnick, two undergraduate research assistants, deserve recognition for their administrative and background work.

There are also many people to thank outside of my department and university. Among them are my female mentors, including Judith Levy, Gay Young, and Rita Simon. Their scholarly excellence and kind tutelage has helped make me the scholar and teacher I am today. Thanks also to the pioneering work by Marsha Rosenbaum, Sheigla Murphy, Eloise Dunlap, Claire Sterk, Lisa Maher, and Jody Miller that reshaped discourse on women, crime, and substance abuse and laid the groundwork for this book's objectives and content.

Additional gratitude goes to institutional support from the Section on Alcohol, Drugs, and Tobacco of the American Sociological Association, the Drinking and Drugs Division of the Society for the Study of Social Problems, and the American Society of Criminology for consistently hosting gender-based substance abuse panels that provided an outlet for the authors in this volume and for others. Thanks also to the many federal, state, and local agencies that have funded the work in this volume.

Finally, I should like to thank my editor, Adi Hovav, at Rutgers University Press and series editor Ray Michalowski for their stellar guidance in this book's development. And I am indebted to Drew Humphries and Patricia Erickson for their thorough and very helpful review of the manuscript.

FOREWORD

Claire M. Renzetti

THE IMAGES ARE familiar, not only in popular culture but in the social science literature as well. The *female* drug addict—the gendered adjective necessary because the images conjured are so different for women than for men—is villain or victim. She is a favorite target of derision for any number of the traits imputed to her: her promiscuity, her lack of will, her neglect of her children or others close to her, her selfishness, her self-pity and self-loathing. To test the pervasiveness of these images, I asked a group of students what comes to their minds when they hear the words "female drug addict." The responses came with little hesitation, hands immediately went up: "Skinny, lazy, selfish," "Somebody who only thinks about how she's going to get high, feel good, even if it means forgetting about her kids and their needs," "A woman who would sell her own children just for a fix," "She doesn't care what she has to do to get drugs—have sex with dirty, disgusting strangers; kill somebody, maybe her mother or sister or baby," "Sick, can't help herself, vulnerable." These depictions, even the more sympathetic ones, can be encapsulated in what Tammy Anderson refers to in this book as the "pathology and powerlessness" narrative that has historically characterized popular and academic discourses about female substance abusers. Anderson is calling for a "critical re-evaluation of this narrative" in light of recent research, much of it collected here, showing far greater complexity in the lived experiences and social relationships of women substance abusers. And herein lies the significance of this book.

Anderson and the contributors to this volume clearly demonstrate through their work that the dichotomy between "good" women (those who don't use drugs) and "bad" women (those who do use drugs) is false. Also false is the dichotomy of drug-abusing women as either victims ("forced" or "led" into substance abuse and then "trapped" by it, but forgivable because they have no power to resist) or villains (addicts "by choice," who sell themselves and anything or anyone of significance for the selfish pleasure of a drug-induced high or stupor). Anderson and her colleagues seek to, as Anderson herself puts it, "shift the narrative." By deconstructing these false dichotomies they provide instead a more nuanced analysis of women in the illicit drug world, one in which women have power, agency, social capital, and social networks.

To be sure, the life histories of substance-abusing women are often chronicles of victimization from an early age—sexual abuse, parental neglect, physical battering, psychological manipulation—that took place in a context of disadvantage and a social environment peopled with substance-abusing role models (see, for example, Raphael 2000, 2004). Women's pathways to substance abuse and other offenses, the research shows, are not primrose-lined streets of childhood innocence, security, and privilege. Nevertheless, in portraying substance-abusing women as defeated pawns or narcissistic demons, social scientists and the media alike not only oversimplify the problem, but also do the women, their families, and the general public a huge disservice. For if we do not understand the complexity of a phenomenon and the multidimensional nature of the lives concerned, how can we possibly expect to effectively address the problems that spin off and ripple from the interactions and relationships involved?

Certainly, our current responses to substance abuse in general, and to substance-abusing women in particular, are ineffective at best, devastatingly harmful at worst. Our prisons overflow with captives from the "war on drugs." In prison, treatment programs are inconsistent or nonexistent. But, as Anderson and her colleagues point out in this volume, treatment programs alone cannot ameliorate substance abuse.

Such abuse is not a discreet, isolated problem. Indeed, it cannot be understand apart from its interconnectedness to other serious social problems, including gender inequality, economic inequality, and contemporary social welfare policies that punish the poor. Another dichotomy falls apart here: the separation of the "legitimate" social realm from the "illicit" social realm. Is it any wonder that substance-abusing women often have poor outcomes following release from prison (see Davies and Cook 1999)?

Anderson and the authors of this book show that substance-abusing women live simultaneously in the "legal" and "illegal" worlds and that women's involvement in the illicit drug world, like their involvement in legitimate social activities, is multifaceted and offers both positive and negative consequences. This involvement, the authors show, varies on several levels, such as willingness and ability to sell drugs, level of addiction, and commission of other offenses to support drug use. All of these behaviors involve decision making on the part of women (and men), but such decisions are made in the context of structural and personal constraints. Anderson and her colleagues take a variety of approaches to peeling back these multi-layered contexts so that we may envision more effective, more gender-sensitive policies and practices toward substance abuse and abusers. They toss out the question that has historically dominated the criminal legal system—i.e., how can we better fight the war on drugs?—asking instead how we can better respond to drug-involved offenders and their families to ameliorate the negative consequences of drug use, to assist in recovery, and to promote successful reentry following incarceration. Their answers suggest that there are alternative, humane solutions. Our collective future depends on our willingness to implement these.

REFERENCES

Davies, S., and S. Cook. 1999. "Neglect or punishment? Failing to meet the needs of women post-release." In S. Cook and S. Davies, eds., *Harsh Punishment: International Experiences of Women's Imprisonment*. Boston: Northeastern University Press, 272–290.

Raphael, J. 2000. *Saving Bernice: Women, Welfare, and Poverty*. Boston: Northeastern University Press.

———. 2004. *Listening to Olivia: Violence, Poverty, and Prostitution*. Boston: Northeastern University Press.

Neither Villain nor Victim

Introduction

Tammy L. Anderson

SINCE THE APPEARANCE of scholarship on women's substance abuse in the last quarter of the twentieth century and the early twenty-first century, academics, policy makers, and practitioners have been engaged in a vibrant and important discussion about how a historically neglected population has altered our understanding of and response to one of the most important social problems of our time. Gender-oriented substance abuse research in the 1970s and 1980s initiated this awakening with studies on women's heroin, marijuana, and psychotropic drug use (Prather and Fidell 1978; Gomberg 1982, 1986; Rosenbaum 1981) and its impact on parenting, health, and well-being. This pioneering work documented the daily lives and experiences of a group of substance abusers (and offenders) that the fields of sociology and criminology knew little about. From this work, we learned not only about the unique drug experiences of women, but also about the overall social organization of the illicit drug world.

By the 1990s, inquiry on women and drugs expanded to other substances (e.g., crack and powder cocaine) and issues: pregnancy, HIV, violence victimization, mental illness, and prostitution. During this period, different perspectives emerged and began to outline a debate not only about them but also about the role of gender in understanding the substance abuse experience in many social contexts. The debate was and remains, however, focused on women's plights (e.g., their victimization) and their failure to perform female roles (e.g., motherhood) due to involvement with drugs. Such thinking has led to what I (Anderson 2005) and others (e.g., Maher 1997; Moore and Devitt 1989) call the "pathology and powerlessness" perspective. Like the old "good woman/bad woman" dichotomy, today's discussion about women substance abusers classifies them as either villains or victims.

This pathology and powerlessness perspective, which has dominated research about women substance abusers, emphasizes themes of dysfunction, moral depravity, dependence, powerlessness, exploitation, and victimization in women's experiences in the illicit drug world. It discusses women's drug experiences as a set of female-specific problems, and consequently denies women's activities or agency in negotiating the world. It also fails to recognize how women balance conventional pursuits with illegal ones. Consequently, by studying women's substance abuse as a set of problems among marginal women, the fields of sociology and criminology have not thoroughly considered how women's experience and agency helps us understand the world and our society as it pertains to drugs, crime, and deviance. Moreover, such limitations in perspective neglect the fundamental ways in which gender shapes deviant and illicit social contexts.

Alternatively, a more feminist perspective on women drug users emerged in the 1990s. For example, studies by Ettorre (1992), Maher (1997), and Miller (1995) challenged claims that women drug users' lives could be solely understood from stories about pathology and powerlessness. These authors found women often occupied the gray area between villains and victims, powerful or powerless, good and bad. For example, Maher's (1996; 1997) work in Bushwick, New York, with heroin- and crack-using women documented "novel" phenomena for the fields of criminology and substance abuse studies, such as that most drug-using sex workers operated outside of pimping relationships and controlled their own clientele and money. Of course, Maher also noted they experienced harm, did fairly reprehensible things, and were not achieving equality with men as others contended (Bourgois 1995). Maher's (1996, 1997) work was significant in challenging many studies consistent with the pathology and powerless perspective; however, she was unable to move the debate significantly past the victim-based approach she sought to challenge. Fraser and Valentine (2005, 123) recently observed: "These aspects of life in the streets—enjoying the sex work; wielding the power of the employer over some men—are fascinating in their departure from the main picture, and would add much to Maher's formulation of agency, yet they remain unexamined."

The purpose of this volume is to carry on this more feminist tradition by exploring the connections among power, empowerment, and agency among women in the illicit drug economy. In doing so, we hope to shift discussion about women substance abusers to one centered on their agency (i.e., abilities, competencies, and actions that benefit the self and others) in shaping their lives and the world around them. This perspective renders the villain/victim dichotomy shortsighted by revealing the complexities of women substance abusers' lives. Simply put, we contend that shifting to a more empowered approach allows a better reflection of women's real-world experience. This change will require significant reconceptualization of not only women's experiences and activities in the illicit drug economy, but also those of men, boys, and girls. Therefore, this book promises to stir intellectual curiosity and invite controversy, because its central themes challenge our understanding about the illicit drug world.

WHY SHIFT THE NARRATIVE?

To some, additional attention to women's issues—the smaller portion of the drugs and crime population—only diverts attention and precious resources away from the "real" problem: male substance abuse, crime, and deviance. Scholars, policy makers, and practitioners taking this position often fail to see the utility of gender-oriented frameworks in understanding drugs and crime problems among both women and men. The field's relative isolation from its parent discipline, sociology, exacerbates this matter.

Others more sympathetic to women may argue that documenting women's power and agency in illegal contexts and activities will only derail efforts to obtain resources for these women. In other words, showing women's power and agency in illegal endeavors will diminish sympathy for assisting them in securing better lives. To their credit, "powerlessness and pathology" frameworks have succeeded in elevating academic attention to women and in raising support and resources for them.

We, however, believe that shifting the narrative to power and agency is critically important, for numerous reasons. First, latter-twentieth-century "war on drugs" policies increased the proportion of women drug users under criminal justice jurisdiction to a size researchers and policy makers cannot ignore. Even a cursory look at official statistics (see, for example, Harrison and Beck 2005) shows a growing portion of female arrestees and inmates in the criminal justice system, a portion that disabuses claims about their insignificance. Although such policies have increasingly criminalized women, they have not necessarily reduced the drug problem or improved the lives of those involved. Thus, an alternative narrative is warranted.

Second, we question the more conceptual and policy-oriented claim of the dangers in breaking from narratives about women's plight to narratives detailing their power and agency. After many years of research with women substance abusers, the authors in this book believe and demonstrate that a limited focus on themes of pathology and powerless among women substance abusers is detrimental to theory, research, and policy.

To begin, persistent focus on women's victimization and/or the consequences they encounter in criminal contexts denies not only an understanding of the benefits they obtain from illicit drug world interaction but also how they exercise agency and mobilize resources to achieve a sense of control in their lives. Many essays in this book illustrate what many may think a contradiction—i.e., that costs and benefits simultaneously exist and that an important part of any story is how people adapt to dire situations to preserve themselves and those around them. Understanding how women exercise agency and experience power can facilitate improved interventions with better results over the long term. Thus, we contend that the benefits and consequences all people experience from illegal activities must be addressed directly if we are to successfully combat crime and other social problems, a point Renzetti has made here in the foreword.

More important, our knowledge about illicit drug world organization and experience may be flawed by a misunderstanding about how gender shapes everyday life. This shortcoming, we argue, begins with the narrow conception of power dominating the drugs and crime field. Many studies in this field use *power-over* or *dominance* types of definitions that highlight structural position and personal possession (e.g., Anderson 1999; Bourgois 1995; Jankowski 1991). Men emerge as the most important subjects of study because they enjoy this type of power more often and are socialized to pursue it and value it over other forms; they are viewed as the most salient actors in the illicit drug economy, with women having far less impact and importance. Empowerment and agency, the types of power women are more likely to possess, are undervalued or overlooked.

The use of power-over and dominance definitions helps feed the pathology and powerlessness narrative, often constructing women as subordinates and/or exploited victims of more powerful males. Whether concerning drug selling, drug financing (e.g., sex-for-drugs exchanges), meeting or retaining basic sustenance needs (e.g., housing), securing treatment and/or succeeding in abstinence, the literature consistently tells stories about how men wield power over women and over the opportunities women encounter. Such power-over orientations obscure the reality of drug-world organization and the experiences of all involved. The essays included here illustrate an alternative reality.

TOWARD A MORE EMPOWERED PERSPECTIVE ON WOMEN, DRUGS, AND CRIME

Given this history and the book's objectives, some basic ideas for a new perspective about women substance abusers may now be outlined. This approach frames the scope of women's illicit drug experiences in terms of five types of agency that return relational and structural (autonomous) power: (1) survival/instrumental agency, (2) symbolic resistance, (3) leisure and recreational activities, (4) expressive and/or revenge-based agency, and (5) political activism and social change. The chapters in this volume describe how women substance abusers use these types of agency in illegal and legal pursuits.

Before describing these forms of agency, it is essential to point out that women reap both benefits and consequences, often simultaneously, from exercising them, suggesting more complicated life situations than previously documented. Thus, the link between agency and power in people's lives and the role of agency and power in shaping criminal worlds must be understood at the outset. The description of types of agency throughout this book will likely enable researchers, policy makers, and practitioners to better address the dynamics that shape individual lives as well as the contexts of crime and deviance.

First, survival or instrumental agency pertains to competencies, abilities, and activities geared toward the provision of basic human needs or the adaptation to harsh circumstances or negative events. When people talk about engaging in sex work to raise money for food, clothing, and shelter, they are speaking of instrumental agency. In this book's epilogue, for example, Carol Tracy tells a compelling story about instrumental agency among a family she encountered early in her professional career. The survival/instrumental form of agency is well-documented in the literature, yet its importance has been undervalued. Few have viewed it as a positive or potentially empowering thing for women.

Each of the authors here—especially Anderson, Hartwell, Mullins, Kelley, Malloch, and Coontz and Griebel—illustrate how women use survival or instrumental agency in various areas of their lives. For example, Hartwell and Kelley show how some of the most troubled and highly stigmatized women substance abusers (e.g., the mentally ill and codependent) employ it in relationships, even when these are dysfunctional, to shore up support for themselves and those around them. Moreover, Saum and Grey's chapter illustrates how women offenders maximize community-based interventions like drug courts for improved reentry prospects, better than do their male counterparts.

Survival and instrumental forms of agency likely return relational power rather than structural power. Sex work, drug dealing, minor hustles, caretaking, and providing emotional support are examples of how women take care of themselves and others in the face of great obstacle. They are capable actors who take charge of their lives while negotiating the illicit drug world. Thus, they likely can continue doing so during the transition toward conventional lifestyles.

Second, when women actively reject stigma, derogatory images, and undesirable expectations by managing and creating alternative identities, they are engaging in a type of agency I call "symbolic resistance." Instead of conforming to subordinated or traditional identities, women substance abusers often construct new images or selves, or carefully manage existing ones, in an attempt to convey power and secure desired outcomes. They do this with people in their families and neighborhoods as well as with criminal justice and social service professionals. The chapters by Anderson, Mullins, and Baskin and Sommers report instances of symbolic resistance.

Adopting more intimidating and socially respected identities works for women in the illicit drug world in many of the same ways it works for men; it enables them to manage consequences and accrue structural power (i.e., larger and quicker incomes, advanced positions in drug markets, and valuable social capital) that can protect them from consequences. To date, very little research and policy has acknowledged this form of women's agency, although British scholars using critical cultural perspectives on crime and deviance have discussed it, albeit mostly with males (see Brake 1985; Willis 1977). In addition, there have been many studies on stigmatizing offenders (the reverse of symbolic resistance) using labeling theory, a theory that has had a stronghold in studies of drugs, crime, and deviance.

A third style of agency pertains to leisure and recreation. It is a form of structural power since it focuses on independent and autonomous desire and pursuits. Deviance yields reward and is, at times, pleasurable for men, adolescents, and women and mothers. This lies at the core of Ettorre's postmodern focus on women's drug-using bodies and is what Mullins is referring to when he writes that women experience "life as party" on the streets.

Too often, stigma and interventions are geared toward reinforcing women's roles in the family, leaving nothing independently pleasurable or rewarding for them. Both Anderson and Ettorre note that policy initiatives should acknowledge this when fashioning interventions for women substance abusers. We must find ways to assist women in securing conventional forms of pleasure and leisure to offset the lure of drugs and crime. Participation in pleasurable activities returns self-fulfillment, a basic human need for all people.

A fourth form of agency is expressive or revenge-based aggression. It features violent competencies and activities for exploitation and intimidation. This violence is motivated by hedonism, materialism, dominance, and power. It usually returns structural power or is performed in attempts to acquire such power. Expressive violence provides still another significant challenge to the pathology and powerlessness approach. Consider Sonya, Stephanie, and Rhonda from the Baskin and Sommers chapter. Sonya uses violence to intimidate and successfully market drugs, while Rhonda understands that violence returns power. Thus, women's drug-using violence is like men's, at times—expressive and about reputation and bravado—but different on other occasions.

Expressive or revenge-based violence by anyone undermines public safety and creates serious problems for the criminal justice system. Although research has shown that males routinely engage in it (Bourgois 1995;

Anderson 1999), little work acknowledges women's use of it. Instead, violent acts by women have been more often constructed as self-defense (consistent with the pathology and powerlessness perspective), not as expressive or as revenge-oriented. "Self-defense" explanations deflect responsibility for women's aggression, and a narrow view of self-defense as the only motivation for women's violent crime may undermine public safety. At least four chapters in this volume—those by Anderson, Katsulis and Blankenship, Mullins, and Baskin and Sommers—recommend that criminal justice officials take greater measures to hold women responsible for expressive or revenge-like violent and criminal agency.

A fifth and final type of agency documented here is political activism and advocacy. Consider that women substance abusers may be motivated by their illegal experiences and run-ins with social control agents to change or alter social institutions to improve their lives and those of women like them. Such agency likely returns both relational and structural power since it helps them mend ties to those around them and gain resources for their own and others' well-being. Berger's chapter describes this form of agency brilliantly with a socially scorned group: HIV-positive female substance abusers.

Although previous research may not have identified political activism and advocacy as an important type of agency among illicit drug users, it has documented the value of peers in helping others desist from drugs and crime. For example, some HIV outreach models utilize former addicts and HIV-positives to get others actively using drugs to test for the virus and use HIV risk reduction practices (Levy and Anderson 2005; Levy et al. 1995). These non-using addict peers advocate harm reduction strategies to active addicts. In addition, therapeutic community drug treatment programs use former addicts as peer counselors for those trying to get off drugs (see DeLeon 2000 for a complete description). Both of these peer models advocate positive agency on an interpersonal level, which yields desirable outcomes among all parties. In the process of empowering former addicts and HIV-positives to educate and advocate for themselves and others, interventions are improved.

Categorizing agency into these five forms and documenting examples among women substance abusers will assist researchers in explaining crime, and policy makers and practitioners in combating it. The book permits this objective by primarily focusing on agency and its relationship to power, rather than on the havoc of criminal behaviors. It emerges from the idea that when we study agency in its manifold forms, we learn more about a broader range of experience.

Each of the five types of agency described here could help pinpoint improved explanations to assist theoretical development. For example, deviance and crime resulting from survival or instrumental agency is likely under-stood with "strain and opportunity" theories that focus on criminal adapta-tions to economic stress or resource deprivation. Symbolic-resistance forms of agency can be addressed with "cultural reproduction and labeling" theo-ries that articulate the identity stances (rejection or acceptance of a deviant label) or consequences (e.g., stigma) resulting from illegal activities. Lifestyle criminology or postmodern theory—much of which is based in the United Kingdom—can assist knowledge of leisure and recreational agency, given their focus on leisure and desire. Models of personal risk are also helpful. Low self-control and social psychology theories of power and self-esteem are adequately suited to understand expressive and violent agency; political activism and advocacy might glean insights from Marxist or feminist theo-ries. Thus, by shifting our focus regarding women substance abusers to the types of agency they employ, we sharpen our ability to better theorize and combat crime and deviance.

In closing, focusing on these five forms of agency and their connec-tions to relational and structural power attempts to outline a new perspec-tive on women substance abusers that will hopefully shift the narrative away from the pathology and powerlessness perspective, and reveal that these women are not solely villains or victims. The chapters in this volume are not, however, the only reports substantiating this more modern view-point; other studies also exist. Notable examples include Valdez, Kaplan, and Cepeda's (2000) study of the heroin careers of Mexican-American women and Straus and Falkin's (2001) study of women methamphetamine users and sellers. This growing empowerment and agency literature will likely move us toward a new vision of women substance abusers, well into the twenty-first century.

The book is divided into three parts. Part I deals with the many ways women negotiate the illicit drug world, highlighting their modern roles in drug marketing. Part II focuses on how women substance abusers man-age the more intimate aspects of their lives while they try to exit the drug world and achieve abstinence. Part III focuses on understanding how ex-tant policies and practices undermine women's empowerment and agency, and calls for a dramatically different approach.

REFERENCES

Andersen, Margaret L., and Patricia Hill Collins, eds. 2004. *Race, class, and gender: An an-thology.* 5th ed. Belmont, CA: Wadsworth.
Anderson, Elijah. 1999. *Code of the street.* New York: W. W. Norton.
Anderson, Tammy L. 2005. "Dimensions of women's power in illicit drug economy," *Theoretical Criminology* 9, no. 4: 371–400.

Bourgois, Philippe. 1995. *In search of respect: Selling crack in El Barrio*. New York: Cambridge University Press.

Brake, Michael. 1985. *Comparative youth culture*. London: Routledge and Kegan Paul.

De Leon, G. 2000. *The therapeutic community:Theory, model, and method*. New York: Springer Publishing Co.

Ettorre, Elizabeth. 1992. *Women and substance abuse*. New Brunswick, NJ: Rutgers University Press.

Fraser, Suzanne, and Kylie Valentine. 2005. "Gendered ethnographies: Researching drugs, violence, and gender in New York," *Australian Feminist Studies* 20, no. 46: 121–124.

Gomberg, Edith. 1982. "Historical and political perspective:Women and drug use," *Journal of Social Issues* 38, no. 2: 9–23.

———. 1986. "Women, alcohol, and other drugs," *Drugs and Society* 1, no. 1 (Fall): 75–109.

Harding, Sandra. 1986. *The science question in feminism*. Ithaca, NY: Cornell University Press.

Harrison, Paige M., and Allen J. Beck. 2005. *Prisoners in 2004*. Washington, DC: U.S. Bureau of Justice Statistics, U.S. Department of Justice.

Jankowski, Martin. 1991. *Islands in the streets: Gangs and American urban society*. Berkeley and Los Angeles: University of California Press.

Levy, Judith A., and Tammy L. Anderson. 2005. "The Drug Career of the Older Injector," *Addiction Theory and Research* 13, no. 3: 245–258.

Levy, Judith A., Chuck P.Gallmeier, and W. Wayne Wiebel. 1995. "The outreach assisted peer support model for controlling drug dependency," *Journal of Drug Issues* 25, no. 3: 509–527.

Maher, Lisa. 1996. "Hidden in the light: Occupational norms among crack-using, street-level sex workers," *Journal of Drug Issues*, 26, no. 1: 143–173.

———. 1997. *Sexed work: Gender, race, and resistance in a Brooklyn drug market*. London: Oxford University Press.

Mauer, Marc. 2001. "The causes and consequences in prison growth in the United States," *Punishment and Society* 3, no.1 (January): 9–20.

———. 2004. "Race, class, and the development of criminal justice policy," *Review of Policy Research* 21, no.1 (January): 79–92.

Miller, Jody. 1995. "Gender and power on the streets: Street prostitution in the era of crack cocaine," *Journal of Contemporary Ethnography* 23, no. 4: 427–452.

Moore, J. W., and M. Devitt. 1989. "Addicted Mexican-American mothers," *Gender and Society* 3: 53–78.

Prather, Jane E., and Linda S. Fidell. 1978. "Drug use and abuse among women:An overview," *International Journal of the Addictions* 13, no. 6: 863–885.

Rosenbaum, Marsha. 1981. *Women and heroin*. New Brunswick, NJ: Rutgers University Press.

Strauss, S.M., and G. P. Falkin. 2001. "Women offenders who use and deal methamphetamine: Implications for mandated drug treatment," *Women and Criminal Justice* 12, no. 4: 77–97.

Valdez, A., C. D. Kaplan, and A. Cepeda. 2000. "The process of paradoxical autonomy and survival in the heroin careers of Mexican American women, *Contemporary Drug Problems* 27 (Spring):189–212.

Willis, Paul. 1977. *Learning to labor*. London: Saxon House.

PART ONE

⊚ *Empowered Negotiation of the Illicit Drug Economy*

PART I OF this book includes chapters by Anderson, Ettorre, Baskin and Sommers, and Mullins. They focus on how women are involved in and negotiate the illicit drug world, mainly through drug selling or marketing activities. These chapters cover the modernized roles women now play in illicit drug world social and economic organization, and the styles these women use to complete that work. The various types of agency the women use can be quite empowering, earning them both structural and relational power, even though also yielding consequence.

Over time, scholarship has been slow to acknowledge women's participation in illicit drug distribution. The first published accounts about women heroin users, in the late 1970s and early 1980s, described them as being lured into drug use by domineering men and having no significant role in any aspect of drug distribution. This picture would change with the onset of the crack cocaine epidemic in the mid- to late 1980s. Studies about women crack cocaine users—by scholars such as Maher (1996, 1997), Miller (1995), and Fagan (1993, 1995) showed women's movement into supporting roles in drug marketing and in low-level dealing. As a result of these studies, controversy followed and polemics formed.

One side likened women's 1990s drug selling to earlier feminist predictions about women and crime: women were gaining ground on men and so becoming like them as criminals. The other side disputed any structural gains by women and claimed they remained relatively powerless in drug marketing and continued being victimized.

The chapters in Part I depict still another era in women's involvement in the drug economy, depictions that may also prove contentious. For example, chapters by Anderson and Ettorre elaborate on four core activities women perform that sustain the illicit drug world and those involved in it. These activities include women's provision of housing and sustenance needs to others, drug purchasing, subsidizing male dependency, and marketing activities. One of Anderson's main premises is that women's illicit drug-world agency facilitates their own and their family's survival in addition to spurring the legitimate economy in numerous ways—something Coontz and Griebel elaborate on in Part 3. Like other authors in this book, Anderson maintains that such instrumental and survival-based agencies (forms of relational power) provide important experiences that can and should be redirected to conventional pursuits.

Ettorre reads these activities another way: as pursuits of pleasure and leisure. Thus, whereas Anderson shows how women drug users today are survival-oriented and economically motivated, Ettorre claims that bodily desires and recreational interests also motivate women's illegal activity. This position is provocative, for it proposes that pleasure and fun, not simply survival or self-defense instincts as commonly claimed by the pathology and powerlessness perspective, inspire women's drug involvement. Ettorre maintains (as do others in this volume) that the pleasure and recreation women get from illicit drugs must be taken into account when fashioning effective interventions.

The chapters by Baskin and Sommers on modern-day drug dealing by women, and by Mullins on women's use of violence in illegal drug market business, illustrate still other forms of agency not typically assigned to women: expressive and revenge-based violence. For example, both Baskin and Sommers and Mullins show that women use violence or commit crime to achieve a certain end (e.g., stealing from drug dealers to obtain money), exact revenge (e.g., "getting back" for being victimized or for a damaged reputation), resist social expectations (e.g., acting in a particular way to avoid gender norms), or show off or achieve identity (e.g., shoring up a desired image). In short, women commit criminal and violent acts for many reasons, not simply in response to being victimized by more powerful and abusing males. Both Baskin and Sommers and Mullins show that a portion of female offenders use violence in ways similar to men, i.e., as bullies and predators. Scholars, policy makers and practitioners must acknowledge this to enhance interventions and public safety.

Finally, each chapter in Part I substantiates Anderson's premise about women's agency as relational and autonomous. Women sometimes act from duress or pressure by males, and at other times they do not. Even when women engage in crime or violence with men, they often do so as partners in nonexploitative relationships; women criminals rely at times on male comrades for street justice. This partnership challenges the one-dimensional stance of the pathology and powerlessness approach, which views male/female crime partnerships as male exploitation or corruption of women.

Further, women's criminal enterprise does not always assist their families. The women live what Mullins calls "life as party," one driven by desire and pleasure, as Ettorre also contends. The women enjoy the freedoms that independence and autonomy bring to all; they commit crime and violence for lifestyle reasons, and enjoy its fruits independently.

To sum up, women are more equitable players in the illicit drug world today; their activities are fundamental to its social and economic organization. They are not entirely different from or subordinate to men (as prior research had claimed). Their motives for criminal involvement are wide-ranging and include survival, instrumental action, self-actualization, independence, and leisure.

CHAPTER 1

Dimensions of Women's Power
in the Illicit Drug Economy

Tammy L. Anderson

INTRODUCTION

The purpose of this chapter is to advance our understanding of the gendered social and economic organization of the illicit drug world by articulating several dimensions of women's power.[1] A central premise is that females routinely perform four core activities (providing housing and other sustenance needs, purchasing drugs, subsidizing male dependency, and participation in drug sales) that not only demonstrate their power in and contribution to the illicit drug world, but also emphasize that its organization is fundamentally gendered. Thus the paper offers an important alternative to the leading "pathology and powerlessness" narrative in the "drugs and crime" discourse. Articulating this view additionally promises new directions for social policy and related interventions.

UNDERSTANDING POWER

The argument requires a broadened definition of power. Power has traditionally been defined as having dominance and control over others (Connell 1987), or as a possession one does or does not have or can or cannot obtain. Some (Allen 1999) have called this version "power-over." This type of power is structural in nature, something unequally distributed in society, especially by gender, race/ethnicity, and class.

Discourse on problems related to the illicit drug world often presupposes the power-over definition. Further, it employs a dualistic construction of hegemonic masculinity and emphasized femininity (Connell 1987, 2005), where men's dominance over women is presumed in the organization and routine activities of the illicit drug economy.

Feminist conceptualizations of power surpass "dominance and control" versions and must be embraced here to understand the chapter's objective.

These conceptualizations focus on forms of power that are transformative and relational (Allen 1999) rather than dominating and autonomous. Power is transformative when it is purposed toward accomplishment and change. Its relational nature pertains to a utility for the self and others (e.g., children, loved ones, or a more communal entity), instead of for the self alone. To comprehend women's experiences with this more transformative and relational concept of power, one must focus on ability or competency in achieving desired ends. Feminists often call this power-to or empowerment (Allen 1999). It is often nested in connections to others.

Drug-world organization features multiple, interdependent types of power. At a bare minimum, they include structural (i.e., possession of resources, domination, and control) and relational or transformative (i.e., empowerment of the self and others) types. Men retain more structural power; women boast a more relational or transformative power, routed in empowerment (i.e., the ability and competence to influence and achieve desired outcomes) and agency (action) that benefits the self and others.[2]

A point repeatedly made here is that men's greater possession of structural power (power-over) in drug markets is, to a considerable extent, made possible by women's agency and the types of relational or transformative power ("power to" and empowerment) the women wield. In other words, women's more relational power assists male's accumulation of structural power and is, therefore, fundamental to "successful" (i.e., stable and lasting) illicit drug-world organization. Men's and women's power are thus interdependent.

Many women, especially lower-class blacks and Hispanics, living in inner-city neighborhoods have successfully demonstrated both relational and autonomous agency. For example, single mothers who attempt to care for children and run the household have historically and increasingly shown agency, as a result of large-scale economic change that has decimated legitimate work opportunities in urban areas, and of punitive social policies that have institutionalized large portions of males. Thus, the assumption that males active in the inner-city drug economy are those with power and status effectively obscures a more gender-intertwined reality where women share that power and also accrue capital from exercising agency.

More appropriately, ability and competence (examples of empowerment) in the drug world are patterned by gender into routine interactions. Men and women share some experiences but differ in other, important ways. Their unique qualities, roles, and undertakings are interdependent and facilitate the drug world's existence. Therefore, a fuller understanding of the gendered organization of power in the illicit drug economy is possible by analyzing the connection between women's activities and the forms of capital they produce for themselves and others. It is only through a reorientation to this broader conceptualization that we can understand the dimensions of women's power and the gendered social and economic organization of the illicit drug world.

FOUR DIMENSIONS OF WOMEN'S ECONOMIC POWER

To reiterate this chapter's central premise, women routinely perform several core activities (e.g., providing housing and other sustenance needs, purchasing and selling drugs, and subsidizing male dependency) that are fundamental to the social and economic organization of the illicit drug world. All are instances of empowerment and agency that satisfy the needs of a woman and those around her while simultaneously securing the organization of the illicit drug economy. These contributions earn the women important forms of capital, which can aid more conventional lifestyles in the future. Themes of responsibility, risk management, and stability permeate these activities, making resultant forms of capital more reliable and transferable than the high-risk activities or more unstable capital that their male counterparts amass.

Women's Control of the Household

The first dimension of women's power in the illicit drug economy pertains to providing housing and/or controlling the household. It is one example of how women contribute resources to the illicit drug economy while at the same time keeping themselves, and their families, anchored in conventional society.

Dunlap et al. (2000) were among the first to discuss the role of grandmothers in providing housing to drug-using family members. Their work helped elucidate the power, capital, and importance of older women's contributions not only to the lives of others but also to the stability and solidarity of the family as an institution. Additional work by Hardesty and Black (1999), Murphy and Rosenbaum (1999), and Sterk (1999) also remind us that women, including those living in inner-city drug markets, remain committed to the responsibilities of running the household despite considerable risk (e.g., victimization or financial exploitation) and consequence (arrest or dislocation). None of these scholars discussed providing housing as a form of empowerment for women. In fact, few researchers[3] have taken such a perspective. Research on inner cities consistently shows high concentrations of female-headed households, with grandmothers, mothers, and other female relatives securing and maintaining residences for family members (McNeil 1998). Both non-using and using women are more likely today than ever before to be financially responsible for the financial costs of the household. For example, using U.S. Census data, McNeil (1998) showed that female-headed households with children and no spouse grew dramatically between 1969 and 1996, during the period when illicit drug use became an "epidemic" and rose to national prominence. Older non-using grandmothers typically provide shelter in inner-city, drug-infested neighborhoods (Anderson 1999; Dunlap et al. 2000; Maher et al. 1996; Wilson 1993), and, according to the U.S. Census (Casper 1996), single females over sixty-five years of age are more than twice as likely than their male counterparts to run households nationally.

A perusal of ethnographies (e.g., Anderson 1999; Bourgois 1995; Dunlap and Johnson 1996; Dunlap et al. 2000; Sterk 1999) on the illicit drug world provides consistent evidence that both male and female drug users and sellers often reside in both nuclear and extended family households controlled by women. In fact, drug-involved family members remain in or return to older female relatives' homes well into adulthood (see, for example, Anderson et al. 2002).

Women were able to retain control of the household despite considerable financial challenge in the twentieth century. This was due, in large part, to their qualification for rental support (e.g., Section 8 certificates and public housing residency), their purchase of homes via assistance programs (especially in the past), and their subsequent commitment to paying household rents or mortgages. Most important, however, the ability is an outcome of women's continued commitment to the family (see Dunlap et al. 2002 and 2000; Dunlap and Johnson 1996; Hardesty and Black 1999; Maher et al. 1996).

Housing provisions are critical to the accumulation of capital, not only for household heads but also for dependents living with them. This is true for all members of society, not only those in illicit drug worlds. Women's maintenance of the household provides household members with safety, sustenance needs, identity empowerment, accessibility to employment and educational opportunities, and job search networks (Bratt 2002); all are examples of social, human, and personal capital. In turn, female heads gain social and personal capital for themselves by demonstrating considerable commitment to household responsibility and stability; their agency empowers their own futures and those of persons dependent on them.

This is especially the case for poor African American and Latino families, which have historically provided needed assistance, child rearing, and care for adult as well as juvenile household members. The black family protects members from life obstacles and provides needed support unavailable in major social institutions (Hill 1993; Nobles 1997; McAdoo 1997; Dunlap et al. 2000).

Housing and Drug Market Success

Although sociologists have previously acknowledged such contributions of women, few have considered how these are vital to the economic and social organization of the illicit drug world. For example, the opportunity for young males to attain a powerful position in the drug trade and to accumulate financial capital is facilitated, one could argue, by women's control of the household and women's responsibility for the family's basic sustenance needs.

Private residences enable dealers to bring the product to market (by providing a place to prepare and package the product and store commodities and supplies—see Wilson 1993 and Maher 1997). In addition, the ADAM survey shows that more than 60 percent of arrestees made their last drug purchase indoors (ADAM 2002), suggesting the importance of residential properties as a place of sale. Moreover, housing reduces the costs of business, by guarding against law enforcement or other social control agencies (for instance, police must obtain search warrants to enter private residences) and against victimization (see also Jacobs 1999 for more on this point). Finally, housing provides a consistent or stable way for people to contact the dealer or locate one for a potential transaction or business deal. Cell phones and pagers are today also used for communication, but having a secure residence enables one to always be located by customers or associates.

To sum up, women's autonomous and relational agency in providing housing and sustenance needs for themselves and others helps earns important forms of capital for themselves and their dependents, and helps organize the drug world, enabling both men and women to excel in drug selling. Dealers are able to eschew the financial demands of complete independence and responsibility that setting up and running a conventional business would require, thus promoting their attainment of structural power positions in the market. Such independence calls for much more capital than most dealers typically possess (see Jacobs 1999; Bourgois 1995).

Although numerous social, economic, and political factors have positioned women as the predominant heads of households in the inner city, latter twentieth-century and early twenty-first-century anti–drug policies threaten to invalidate their positive agency and to destabilize neighborhoods. Consider, for example, landlord–tenant anti-drug policies that evict household owners or heads for drug arrests (*Daily Business Review* 2002): this provides a powerful example of how power and consequence coexist for women in the illicit drug world.

Women Drug Users' Purchasing Power

Control of the household may more often be a dimension of power among non-using women, but this section elaborates more directly on the economic power of specifically drug-using women. A second critical dimension of women's power in the illicit drug world can be found in spending on drugs and related products.

To begin, the capability to consume is fundamental to personal existence and to the growth of capitalist economies. This principle applies to all individuals, even those engaged in illegitimate activities. Women's ability to generate money and their subsequent spending on drugs increases dealers' profits. Further, it expands illicit markets by providing additional and stable revenue sources, thus contributing to the U.S. and global mainstream economies[4] (ABT Associates 2001). In other words, women's ability to generate and spend money is a good example of relational agency that further empowers them in attaining their desired goals and helps males achieve structural market power,[5] even if the activity is not intended to do so.

Women's spending on illicit drugs is typically not discussed in this fashion, although a recent study by Murphy and Arroyo (2000) has opened dialogue about the power and control women possess as consumers. Ethnographers (Maher 1997; Sterk 1999) have noted that women have considerable income to spend. Consider, for example, recent findings that show women's drug expenditures approximate (ONDCP 2000) or surpass those of men (Fagan 1993; Lovell 2002). Too often, this empowerment point gets lost in the pathology narrative highlighting women's drug-related misery—that is, their decline into sex work, where they settle for crack instead of money capital (Bourgois and Dunlap 1992; Inciardi et al. 1993; Ratner 1993). The paragraphs that follow articulate the centrality of women's spending to the capital accumulation of male dealers, the social organization of the drug world, and the economic vitality of the drug market and the larger society.

The purchasing power of the female user and addict comes from numerous avenues, many of which introduce new and stable sources of income into the market, allowing it to thrive and expand. I consider two here: sex work and employment in the secondary labor market.

First, sex work engaged in by women drug users provides a constant infusion of financial capital into illicit markets. For example, May et al. (2000) found that the survival of drug markets is largely dependent on women sex workers. This is especially the case with crack cocaine and, to a lessor extent, heroin. Profits for male dealers can be maximized not only from the money that drug-using women sex workers spend on drugs for themselves and others, but also from the money their clients spend. Previous work on crack-abusing sex workers (e.g., Bourgois and Dunlap 1993; Inciardi et al. 1993; Ratner 1993) maintained that most transactions were for drugs instead of cash[6] or were controlled by male pimps. Maher's (1996,

1997) study of women drug abusers in New York, Miller's (1995) work in Columbus, Ohio, and Sterk's (1999) research in Atlanta found the opposite; most sex work featured cash exchanges with women operating independently of "pimping" relationships.

Sex workers bring new sources of revenue (i.e., money from outside clients) into illicit drug markets (May et al. 2000). Revenues from drug-using female sex workers are abundant and stable because of the everpresent desire for sex (see Coontz and Greibel, this volume, for more on this point). The women deliver new financial capital infusion into the drug world via sex-for-money exchanges (with non-using "johns" who pay for sex and get more heavily involved in drugs). Thus, women are central to the growth of the illicit and licit economies; the market is dependent on their agency—yet it disallows their accumulation of structural power.

A second source of women's purchasing power can be found in their employment in the secondary labor market. Deindustrialization and uneven international economic development in the latter twentieth century worsened the financial status of inner-city males and females (see Marable 2000; Sassin 2002; Wallerstein 2004; Wilson 1996). However, women's willingness to seek and maintain employment in the secondary labor market (Browne 1999; Browne and Kennelly 1999) not only assisted them in assuming family responsibilities, but has also provided them with a third source of reliable money capital available for drug purchasing. Women have had much more experience with these sorts of jobs (Reskin 1999), using them to support themselves and their families over time. Money earned from secondary labor market employment is meager, often not enough to elevate an individual or family out of poverty. Still, this money is valuable in the drug world. It is easy to obtain such jobs because fast food restaurants and other service-sector employers have high turnover rates and low human capital requirements. For numerous reasons, many having to do with gender socialization, women are willing to seek and stay employed in these workplaces. This work commitment earns them capital (financial, human, social, and personal) in the illicit drug world.

Unlike the more stable sources of revenue that women have for spending on drugs, men's financial capital often is less valuable or more problematic. For example, male drug abusers' revenue more often comes from illegal activities at greater risk of social control (e.g., major and minor theft, some violent crime). Thus, the men's income tends to be more sporadic even though it can, at times, be larger than women's.

Men are also reluctant to seek employment in the secondary labor market for the same reason—gender socialization—that women embrace it. This is especially true for young African American males in the inner city, who are routinely confronted with numerous symbolic disincentives to seek and remain employed in service-sector jobs (that is, these jobs contradict core masculine values and identities—see Anderson 1999; Dunlap 1992; Bourgois 1995; Wilson 1996). There is some indication, however, that this pattern might be shifting (see, for example, Bourgois 2003) toward greater participation in the secondary labor market by inner-city minority males.

In sum, women are powerful economic actors, contributing stable and reliable income that facilitates growth in the illicit drug and conventional economies. At least two of women's income sources—sex work and secondary labor market employment—earn them financial capital that is more stable overall than are their male counterparts' sources of funds. In their financial negotiations of the illicit drug world, women demonstrate empowerment and agency to earn important forms of capital.

Although it is true that their economic power is, at times, manipulated or exploited by others, dealers understand their value as customers, and family and friends continue to rely on them as providers. Further, even though most participants in the drug world do not retain financial capital over the long term, women's experience in raising revenues for family support and drug purchasing earns them some level of independence, thereby highlighting the interplay between relational and autonomous agency among women. This experience will help them with more pro-social undertakings, including providing for themselves and others (that is, economic independence and money management) and securing positive and fulfilling relationships.

Women Subsidizing Male Dependency

A closely related third source of women's economic power is subsidizing male drug users and addicts: their consumption of drugs, their sustenance needs, and their lifestyles. Again, this is an example of relational agency, because women drug users often use their economic resources to pay for drugs for themselves and their dependent male partners.

Consistently, both large-scale surveys and smaller ethnographic studies have shown adult males' rates of abuse and addiction to be considerably higher than females'. For instance, the most recent National Household Survey of Drug Abuse (NHSDA 2002) reported that men are twice as likely as women to abuse or be dependent on alcohol or illicit drugs. Although there are no official estimates of how many male sellers, users, and addicts there are in the inner city, the recent ADAM (2002) data show that despite a proportionately larger pool of female arrestees for drugs, male arrestees in large urban areas were more often heavy drug users and heavy drinkers; therefore, it stands to reason therefore that the pool of drug-abusing and addicted men is quite large, outpacing the group of non-using male sellers.[7]

In addition, studies by Anderson and Levy (2003), Bourgois et al. (1997), Duneier (1999), and Waterston (1993) have shown just how capricious and unforgiving the world of drug sales can be to male abusers, especially those who are older. This larger pool of men is vulnerable, like the women, both in the conventional economy and within the drug world. Consequently, many seek support from bread-winning females.

The idea of women drug users as breadwinners, supporting the drug habits and lifestyles of male partners, is alien not only to the study of drugs and crime but also to the discipline of sociology. Discussions in sociology of breadwinners and financial dependency often emanate from the economic dependency model; to date, very few articles concern women breadwinners, and even fewer investigate men's economic dependency on women. However, knowledge about economic dependency can also help explain the gendered organization of the illicit drug world.

To begin, the economic dependency model presumes a dichotomized division of labor between financial support and domestic work. Traditionally, men provide financial support for the household through paid work in the external labor market, and women provide unpaid labor in the form of household maintenance and childcare. In this model, women become economically dependent on men (Brine 1994). When, alternatively, women drug users finance men's drug use, this action challenges the basic tenets of the economic dependency model by reversing women's role to that of financial head of household.

The notion that bread-winning women provide for dependent men also departs from early drug abuse studies of the 1960s to mid-1980s, which characterized female heroin users as needing a man to support their drug consumption (File 1976; File et al. 1974; Hser et al. 1987)—though the reverse is true with crack cocaine (see Sterk 1999; Maher and Daly 1996). As major breadwinners and providers, women drug users (especially those involved in sex work) who support drug-addicted male partners assume the more powerful economic role while their male dependents fall into economic subordination. In short, this is a very compelling case of women's empowerment and agency, which past research has neglected.

Work by Anderson (1990, 1999), Bourgois (1995), Jacobs (1999), and Jankowski (1991) has largely ignored addicted men and their economic vulnerability within the illicit drug world. However, lower-class men's economic dependence on women is likely to continue as the twenty-first century goes on. For example, male drug abusers are likely to become dependent on others as they age; research has shown they get shut out of the most lucrative hustles and often suffer injury and illness from their more violent and risky lifestyles (see Anderson and Levy 2003; Bourgois et al. 1997;

Waterston 1993). The elimination of some forms of social welfare (such as Supplemental Security Income, or SSI, for drug and alcohol abuse—see Goldstein et al. 2000) and increased social control policies (arrest and incarceration) may also increase men's economic dependency on women. Finally, as Anderson (1999) and Bourgois (1995) noted, men's willingness to work or stay employed in many service sector and secondary sector jobs lags behind that of women.

What do women obtain from supporting addicted men who contribute very little to their relationships or the household? To begin, when women breadwinners (both those who use and those who do not use drugs) support men's alcohol and drug use and sustenance needs, they secure and retain a companion in an era when men, especially minority men, are becoming a scarce commodity as a result of increased social control policies. This helps keep the women anchored in conventional roles and identities, and aids preservation of the family. Such agency, consequently, has utility in both the illicit drug world and conventional society.

Although this companionship can be problematic (see Kelley, this volume, for an example), it meets a basic human need. Moreover, the degree to which women gain personal capital from managing these relationships may promote their economic independence and enable them to secure more fulfilling relationships in the future. A woman drug user with competence and know-how (empowerment) in achieving economic independence will be better equipped to successfully reenter conventional society should she be incarcerated for a criminal offense or to attempt to terminate a career in drug use.

Women's Role in Drug-Dealing Activities

The last dimension of women's power to be discussed here focuses on women's role in drug dealing. Over the past decade or so, there has waged a vigorous debate about the level and nature of women's participation in drug-dealing activities—the most coveted jobs in the illicit drug economy, and a central concern for policy makers. The debate centers on structural power: how many women are involved in drug selling, where they are located in the hierarchy, and whether they are gaining ground on men. In criminology, the so-called gender question in the marketing of drugs or in drug-world organization has arisen only recently as the level of women's participation in sales has climbed.

Rather than engage this debate, I call attention instead to those styles women employ in these activities that demonstrate empowerment and agency, resulting in all types of capital accumulation. Again, this style can be characterized by responsibility (to oneself and others), risk avoidance, and stability. Two examples illustrate my point, and consideration of these phenomena may help counter the focus on women's pathology and power-lessness that currently stymies sociological discourse and social policy.

"Style" and Empowerment. Recent scholarship has shown that women bring a unique style to drug dealing that rewards them with respectable and stable social and financial capital (see Baskin and Sommers, this volume, for recent examples). Research (Dunlap et al. 1997; Jacobs and Miller 1998) has revealed that women are more cautious than men in their drug-deal-ing activities. Although most business models would propose that such an approach would limit profits, at least two benefits may be more valuable, including the reduced threat of arrest and victimization.

Perhaps the clearest and most recent example of this point can be found in the work of Jacobs and Miller (1998). Their ethnography in St Louis, Missouri, detailed the risk-avoidant strategies women drug dealers used to protect themselves from arrest (thus enhancing their ability to remain in the community and available, to some extent, to family) and to reduce their victimization and that of others (in an example of stabilizing often volatile drug sales).

The growing literature on females gangs further supports this claim, along with others made here. For example, works by Brotherton (1996), Brotherton and Salazar (2003), and Kontos, Brotherton, and Barrios (2003) show that gangs made up of "independent" females are tightly bonded enti-ties that exercise relational power in taking care of one another other and one another's families. Principles of community and equity characterize their drug selling and other illegal activities. Adoption of a "smartness" ethic in doing business, similar to the tactics described by Jacobs and Miller (1998), enables them to avoid confrontation, detection, and social control.

Positions Women Hold. A second illustration of women's empower-ment and agency in drug sales pertains to their excelling in the roles of drug-purchasing middlewomen (e.g., "steerers" or "touts"—see Furst et al. 2001). Maher (1997), Furst et al. (2001), and Sommer et al. (2000) found that when women are involved in drug dealing, they are most often middlewomen. It is currently not possible to estimate how many middle-men and middlewomen are operating in illicit drug markets or what pro-portion of them are female. Despite the extent of their presence, however, the middlewoman represents another important dimension of women's economic power.

To begin, middlewomen are usually drug users/abusers, indigenous to inner-city drug markets, making a living and financing their drug use by purchasing drugs for less knowledgeable customers, novices, or outsiders. In short, middlemen and middlewomen purchase drugs for others not familiar with the market. Their fees for this risky activity range from 25 percent to 100 percent of the base purchase, or a portion of the drugs. The position thus epitomizes the ethic of relational power discussed here. Agency is performed for both self and others.

The value of middlemen and middlewomen to the vitality of the illicit drug market cannot be overstated. First, these persons play a direct role in expanding the profits of the market, by ushering in new revenues and safely negotiating transactions; this activity produces new and stable financial capital into the illicit drug economy. Second, they help neutralize the violence that can often accompany sales, by placing familiarity and competence into transactions that would otherwise be fraught with suspicion, fear, and ineptitude. This earns these actors considerable social capital among dealers, users, and even some community members not involved in drug activities.

TRANSFERRING POWER AND CAPITAL INTO CONVENTIONAL ACTIVITIES

This section elaborates on a few general ideas that support this point. My focus is on the utility of the "empowerment and agency" argument to social policy, not on specific types of interventions that could redress drug-related problems.

First, by employing a "power-to" rather than a "power-over" definition, we have learned that empowerment and agency are about transformation (the essence of offender reentry). When women demonstrate empowerment and agency, they are embracing the idea of change. Thus, they may be more comfortable with the idea of transformation when presented with strategies to desist from drug use and criminal activity. Men's focus on power-over forms, on the other hand, leaves them preoccupied with possession and loss, and may disadvantage them in embracing "change" opportunities encountered in the community or in institutions (such as prison). Criminal justice interventions should therefore acknowledge the different orientations and experiences with power and agency between men and women, and work to channel the agency of each into more conventional activities.

Second, the notion that illicit drug-world participation and work can translate into valuable forms of capital in the conventional world or even improve the chances of escaping negative pursuits seems implausible given the dominant narrative and current discourse. Nevertheless, this chapter has shown it is a possibility, and important to understand. For example, women's role in providing housing not only helps to organize the drug world and to allow more consistent financial capital accumulation by dealers (especially males); it contributes to individual and family well-being.

The benefits of women's commitment to the household will be realized for generations to come. However, latter-twentieth-century policies regarding drug activity and drug-related evictions threatened capital accumulation, increased homelessness, and destabilized inner-city families.

Experience and success in economically based activities furnish women with personal capital for future conventional pursuits, such as providing for themselves and their children and perhaps enabling them to secure more fulfilling, nonabusive relationships. Also, women's competence as bread-winners can help ease poverty in low-income families, where often a second income is absent. Cutbacks in treatment programs and social supports (such as cash assistance, women's shelters, and violence prevention programs), and continued punitive responses (including incarceration) may impede the re-alization of these more pro-social goals. An approach favoring increased social support may be a wiser course of action.

The motherhood identity is one that consistently anchors women drug users into mainstream society and can provide them with a source of em-powerment outside of drugs. Because inner-city drug-using and drug-selling males are largely absent from parenting and lag behind women in embracing employment in the secondary labor market, they have fewer resources for identity empowerment outside the illicit drug world. This gendered link between illegal and conventional worlds not only impacts people's lives today, but also promises to influence the next generation.

Third, although women gain empowerment and capital from doing for others, too often they are pressured to channel their energies into others' benefit. For example, many intervention programs seek to restore women as effective mothers or to prepare them to become effective mothers in the future. This focus denies women a complete self-fulfillment or existence outside of family. We must be careful not to channel all women's agency and sense of empowerment into the benefit of others (perhaps fostering codependency). Interventions should also help women find ways to use em-powerment and agency for their own fulfillment.

CONCLUSIONS

Two major theoretical points about illicit drug world organization can be gleaned from this chapter. First, the accumulation of structural forms of power (more often held by men) requires empowerment and agency by others. Since the illicit drug world is patriarchicly organized, men con-tinue to dominate the marketing hierarchy. However, there can be no doubt that their ability to do so is highly reliant on women's empowerment and agency. The illicit drug market is best characterized as a web of social, financial, and interpersonal relationships among men and women, focusing

on the exchange of illicit goods. Thus drug world organization is fundamentally gendered. Future discourse and policy would be highly negligent
to ignore this point.

Second, the view of women as pathological, powerless, and sexualized
objects denies not only their reality, but also that of drug-world organization. This point should raise new questions about other possible contributions of women. Here, I have focused almost exclusively on the economic side of drug marketing activities. However, there are many other
issues about experience in the drug world that could benefit from a more
feminist-empowered viewpoint. Other chapters in this book highlight
some of these matters.

NOTES

1. This chapter is a version of a paper published under the same title by the author
   in *Theoretical Criminology* 9, no. 4 (2005): 371–400. It is reprinted here with permission from Sage Publications.
2. Empowerment and agency can and often do have a reciprocal relationship. Task
   performance and other forms of agency or action is made possible by feelings
   and perceptions of ability and competence; agency can also generate increased
   perceptions of empowerment. This paper uses the term *empowerment* to describe
   feelings and perceptions of ability and competence, whereas *agency* is used to define action. Taken together, the terms allow for a broader conception of power,
   one that is seldom employed in drugs and crime research.
3. The value of women's provision of a stable residence to the drug trade and to
   the criminal success of its actors was discussed by Wilson (1993) and raised again
   by Maher (1997). Wilson (1993,188) claimed that "the mesh between women's
   provision of a home base and their lack of mobility and men's lack of a home base
   but high mobility may be a combination that works well for a sexually integrated
   drug network." Wilson argued that women's control of the household contributed to their criminal involvement, enabling them to reach parity with men.
   Thus, Wilson located the provision of housing within the traditional discourse
   on women deviants. Maher (1997) challenged her by showing that women have
   yet to reach parity with men in the drug world.
4. U.S. residents are estimated to have spent about $63.8 billion on illicit drugs in
   2000. Approximately $400 billion per year, a significant portion of the GDP of
   the United States and other countries, enters the world's legitimate economy via
   the illicit drug trade (see ABT Associates 2001).
5. This is a good example of the reciprocity between empowerment and agency.
6. A recent ONDCP study (2000) reported that, when work is exchanged for drugs
   instead of cash, men and women do the work with equal frequency.
7. Jacobs' ethnography (1999) in St Louis, Missouri, indicates, however, that most
   young male drug dealers (including crack dealers) use drugs (often "blunts"—
   marijuana soaked in PCP, crack, etc.), and that more young male dealers become
   abusive or addicted to crack than are willing to admit the fact. Anderson and
   Levy's work in Chicago with older drug addicts (Anderson and Levy 2003; Levy
   and Anderson 2004) revealed that most males had commenced drug dealing
   careers while not using their supplies, but that over time they became addicted,
   which damaged their dealing careers.

REFERENCES

ABT Associates. 2001. *What Americans Spend on Illicit Drugs: 1988–2000.* Washington, DC: Office of National Drug Control Policy.

Adler, Freda. 1975. *Sisters in Crime: The Rise of the New Female Criminal.* New York: McGraw-Hill.

Allen, Amy. 1999. *The Power of Feminist Theory.* Boulder, CO: Westview Press.

Anderson, Elijah. 1990. *Streetwise: Race, Class, and Change in an Urban Community.* Chicago: University of Chicago press.

———. 1999. *Code of the Street.* New York: W. W. Norton.

Anderson, Tammy L., and Judith A. Levy. 2003. "Marginality among older injectors in today's illicit drug economy: Assessing the impact of aging," *Addiction* 98: 761–770.

———, Caitlin Shannon, Igor Schyb, and Paul Goldstein. 2002. "Welfare reform and housing: Assessing the impact to substance abusers," *Journal of Drug Issues* 2, no. 1: 265–296.

ADAM. 2002. *Drug Use and Related Matters among Adult Arrestees, 2001.* Washington, DC: Bureau of Justice Statistics, National Institute of Justice.

Bourgois, Philippe. 1995. *In Search of Respect: Selling Crack in El Barrio.* New York: Cambridge University Press.

———. 1996. In Search of Horatio Alger: Culture and Ideology in the Crack Economy," *Contemporary Drug Problems* 16, no. 4: 619–649.

———. 2003. *In Search of Respect: Selling Crack in El Barrio.* 2nd ed. New York: Cambridge University Press.

———, Mark Lettiere, and James Quesada. 1997. "Social misery and the sanctions of substance abuse: Confronting HIV risk among homeless heroin addicts in San Francisco," *Social Problems* 44, no. 2: 155–173.

Bourgois, P[hilippe], and E. Dunlap. 1993. "Exorcising sex-for-crack: and ethnographic perspective from Harlem." In M.S. Ratner, ed., *Crack pipe as pimp: An ethnographic investigation of sex-for-crack exchanges,* 97–132. New York: Lexington Books.

Bratt, Rachel G. 2002. "Housing and family well-being," *Housing Studies* 17, no. 1: 13–26.

Brines, Julie. 1994. "Economic dependency, gender, and the division of labor at home, *American Journal of Sociology* 100, no. 3: 652–688.

Brotherton, David C. 1996. "'Smartness,' 'toughness,' and 'autonomy': Drug use in the context of gang female delinquency," *Journal of Drug Issues* 26, no. 1: 261–277.

———, and Camilla Salazar-Atias. 2003. "Amor de reina! The pushes and pulls of group membership among the Latin queens." In *Gangs and Society: Alternative Perspectives,* ed. Luis Kontos, David Brotherton, and Luis Barrios. New York: Columbia University Press.

Browne, Irene, ed. 1999. *Latinas and African American Women at Work.* New York: Russell Sage Foundation.

———, and Ivy Kennelly. 1999. "Stereotypes and realities: Images of black women in the labor market," Pp. 302–326 In Irene Browne, ed., *Latinas and African American Women at Work.* New York: Russell Sage Foundation.

Casper, Lynne M. 1996. *Who's Minding Our Preschoolers?* Current Population Reports, Housing Economic Studies. Washington, DC: U.S. Department of Commerce, Bureau of the Census.

Connell, R. W. 1987. *Gender and Power.* Stanford, CA: Stanford University Press.

———. 2005. *Masculinities.* 2nd ed. Berkeley and Los Angeles, University of California Press.

Daily Business Review. 2002. "U.S. Supreme Court OKs public housing drug evictions," [Miami, FL] *Daily Business Review,* v76, no. 201 (March 27), A9.

Duneier, Mitchell. 1999. *Sidewalk.* New York. Farrar, Straus and Giroux.

Dunlap, Eloise, Andrew Golub, Bruce D. Johnson, and Wesley Damaris. 2002. "Intergenerational transmission of conduct norms for drugs, sexual exploitation, and violence: A case study," *British Journal of Criminology* 42, no. 1: 1–20.

Dunlap, Eloise, and Bruce D. Johnson. 1996. "Family and human resources in the development of a female crack-seller career: Case study of a hidden population," *Journal of Drug Issues* 26, no. 1: 175–198.

Dunlap, Eloise, Bruce D. Johnson, and Lisa Maher. 1997. "Female crack sellers in New York City: Who they are and what they do," *Women and Criminal Justice* 8, no. 4: 25–55.

Dunlap, Eloise, Sylvie C. Tourigny, and Bruce D Johnson. 2000. "Dead tired and bone weary: Grandmothers as caregivers in drug-affected inner city neighborhoods," *Race and Society* 3, no. 2: 143–163.

Fagan, Jeffrey. 1995. "Women's careers in drug use and drug selling," *Current Perspectives on Aging and the Life Cycle* 4: 155–190.

———, ed. 1993. *The Ecology of Crime and Drug Use in Inner Cities,* New York: Social Science Research Council.

File, Karen. 1976. "Women and drugs revisited: Female participation in the cocaine economy," *Journal of Drug Issues,* 24: 179–225.

———, Thomas W. McCahill, and Leonard D. Savitz. 1974). "Narcotics involvement and female criminality," *Addictive Diseases: An International Journal,* 1: 177–188.

Furst, R. Terry, Richard S. Curtis, Bruce D. Johnson, and Douglas S. Goldsmith. 2001. "The rise of the middleman/woman in a declining drug market," *Addiction Research* 7, no. 2: 103–128.

Goldstein, Paul, Tammy L. Anderson, Igor Schyb, and James Swartz. 2000. "Modes of adaptation to termination of the SSI/SSDI addiction disability: Hustlers, good citizens, and lost souls," *Advances in Medical Sociology* 7: 215–238.

Hamid, Ansley. 1990. "The political economy of crack-related violence," *Contemporary Drug Problems* 17, no. 1: 31–78.

Hardesty, Monica, and Timothy Black. 1999. "Mothering through addiction: A survival strategy among Puerto Rican addicts," *Qualitative Health Research* 9, no.5: 602–619.

Hartsock, Nancy. 1985. *Money, Sex, and Power.* Boston: Northeastern University Press.

Hill, R. 1993. *Research on the African American Family: A Holistic Perspective.* Westport, CT: Auburn House.

Hser, Yih Ing, M. Douglas Anglin, and Mary W. Booth. 1987. "Sex differences in addict careers: Part 3: Addiction," *American Journal of Drug and Alcohol Abuse,* 13: 231–251.

Inciardi, J.A., D. Lockwood, and A. Pottieger. 1993. *Women and Crack Cocaine.* New York: Macmillian.

Jacobs, Bruce A. 1999. *Dealing crack: The Social World of Streetcorner Selling,* Boston: Northeastern University Press.

Jacobs, Bruce, and Jody Miller. 1998. "Crack dealing, gender, and arrest avoidance," *Social Problems* 45, no. 4: 550–569.

Jankowski, Martin Sanchez. 1991. *Islands in the Street: Gangs and American Urban Society.* Berkeley and Los Angeles: University of California Press.

Kontos, Luis, David Brotherton, Luis Barrios, eds. 2003. *In Gangs and Society: Alternative Perspectives.* New York: Columbia University Press.

Levy, Judith A., and Tammy L. Anderson. 2004. "Older injecting drug users' careers," forthcoming in *Addiction Theory and Research*.

Lovell, Anne M. 2002. "Risking the risk: The influence of types of capital and social networks on the injection practices of drug users," *Social Science and Medicine* 55: 803–821.

Maher, Lisa. 1996. "Hidden in the light: Occupational norms among crack-using, street-level sex workers," *Journal of Drug Issues* 26, no. 1: 143–173.

———. 1997. *Sexed Work: Gender, Race, and Resistance in a Brooklyn Drug Market*. London: Oxford University Press.

———, and Kathleen Daly. 1996. "Women in the street-level drug economy: Continuity or change?" *Criminology* 34, no. 4: 465–491.

Maher, Lisa, E. Dunlap, B. Johnson, and A. Hamid. 1996. "Gender, power, and alternative living arrangements in the inner-city crack culture," *Journal of Research in Crime and Delinquency* 33, no. 2: 181–205.

Marable, Manning. 2000. *How Capitalism Underdeveloped Black America: Problems in Race, Political Economy, and Society*. Cambridge, MA: South End Press.

May, Tiggey, Michael Hough, and Mark Edmunds. 2000. "Sex markets and drug markets: Examining the link," *Crime Prevention and Community Safety* 2, no. 2: 25–41.

McAdoo, H. P., ed. 1997. *Black Families*. 3rd ed. Thousand Oaks, CA: Sage Publications.

McMahon, Thomas J., and Bruce J. Rounsaville. 2002. "Substance abuse and fathering: Adding poppa to the research agenda," *Addiction* 97, no. 9: 1109–1115.

McNeil, John. 1998. *Changes in Median Household Income: 1969–1996*. Current Population Reports. Washington, DC: U.S. Department of Commerce, Bureau of the Census.

Miller, Jody. 1995. "Gender and power on the streets: Street prostitution in the era of crack cocaine," *Journal of Contemporary Ethnography* 23, no. 4: 427–452.

———. 2001. *One of the Guys: Girls, Gangs, and Gender*. London: Oxford University Press.

Murphy, Sheigla, and Marsha Rosenbaum. 1999. *Pregnant Women on Drugs*. New Brunswick, NJ: Rutgers University Press.

Murphy, Sheigla, and Karina Arroyo. 2000. "Women as judicious consumers of drug markets." In *Illegal Drug Markets: From Research to Prevention*, ed. Manzai Natarajan and Mike Hough. Monsey, NY: Criminal Justice Press.

NHSDA. 2002a. *Substance Abuse or Dependence*. Washington, DC: Substance Abuse and Mental Health Services Association, Office of Applied Studies.

———. 2002b. *Substance Use among Persons in Families Receiving Government Assistance*. Washington, DC: Substance Abuse and Mental Health Services Association, Office of Applied Studies.

Nobles, W. 1997. "African American family life: An instrument of culture." In *Black Families*, ed. H. P. McAdoo. Thousand Oaks, CA: Sage Publications. 83–93.

Ratner, M. S., ed. 1993. *Crack Pipe as Pimp: An Ethnographic Investigation of Sex-for-Crack Exchanges*. New York: Lexington Books.

Reskin, Barbara F. 1999. "Occupational segregation by race and ethnicity among women workers," In Irene Browne, ed., *Latinas and African American Women at Work*, 183–206. New York: Russell Sage Foundation.

Sassen, Saskia. 2002. *Global Networks, Linked Cities*. New York: Routledge.

Simon, Rita J. 1975. *Women and Crime*. Lexington, MA: Lexington Books.

Sommers, Ira, Deborah Baskin, and Jeffrey Fagan. 2000. *Workin' Hard for the Money: The Social and Economic Lives of Women Drug Sellers*. Huntington, NY: NOVA Science Publishers.

————. (1996). "The structural relationship between drug use, drug dealing, and other income support activities among women," *Journal of Drug Issues* 26, no. 4: 975–1006.

Sterk, Claire E. 1999. *Fast Lives: Women Who Use Crack Cocaine.* Philadelphia: Temple University Press.

Wallerstein, Immanuel. 2004. *World-Systems Analysis: An Introduction.* Durham, NC: Duke University Press.

Waterston, Alice. 1993. *Street Addicts in the Political Economy.* Philadelphia, PA: Temple University Press.

Wilson, N. K. 1993. "Stealing and dealing: The drug war and gendered criminal opportunity." In *Female Criminality: The State of the Art,* ed. C. C. Culliver. New York: Garland Publishing.

Wilson, William J. 1996. *When Work Disappears.* New York: Vintage Books.

CHAPTER 2

Seeing Women, Power, and Drugs through the Lens of Embodiment

Elizabeth Ettorre

INTRODUCTION: TOWARD A FEMINIST EMBODIMENT APPROACH IN THE DRUGS FIELD

The emergence of the body as an academic concern is a relatively recent development within the social sciences. Specifically, feminists working on women's health during the 1970s helped to demonstrate the body as a key area of theoretical interest—albeit their views tended to draw attention to the constraints and/or inequalities of the body culture. In recent years, feminist scholars offered critiques of these earlier views and introduced the notions of agency and subversion into feminist scholarship on the body (Davis 1997,12). Within feminist sociology, bodies have been viewed as cultural and social entities where we shape normal as well as stigmatized identities. Bodies have also been seen as focal points for struggles over power, and as sources of our identities. For drug users with stigmatized identities, these ideas have had a particular impact, given that an individualistic, mechanistic view of bodies ("bodies are machines") emerging from medical and legal paradigms (Turner 1992) is upheld in the drugs field. Also, although biological principles have been used as a basis for constructing body questions, it is difficult for drug theorists to move from asking, "What do drug-using bodies do?" to "How are drug-using bodies socially and culturally constructed?" We find that the gendered body is taken as a given, although the body is usually the point at which drug theorists begin their analysis, especially with regard to the effectiveness of drug treatment (see, for example, Arfken et al 2002; Baker 2000).

For years, the sorrows and joys in the lives of women drug users have remained veiled. Long-established assumptions have been that men are *the* socially dominant and active subjects in the drug-using culture and that women are socially subordinate and relatively passive. Although such assumptions define drug users in a variety of ways, male drug users have been seen to occupy the cultural space of *dominant user,* and female users have become the targets of societal rage (Kandall 1996, 285). In recent years, these sexist assumptions and what we can term regulatory practices have been challenged by women scholars (see, for example, Ettorre 2004,1992; Measham 2002; Evans et al. 2002; Raine 2002; Murphy and Rosenbaum 1999; Sterk 1999; Henderson 1996; and Anderson 1995, 1998, and 2005) within a feminist perspective that develops new types of identities and potential embodiments for women (Measham 2002; Hammersley et al. 2002; Ettorre 2004).

For example, Henderson (1996) suggests a type of sensual hedonism for female drug users whose recreational use is marked by personal agency and pursuit of pleasure: "feminizing drug use"; these users combined activities such as fashion-seeking, clothes consumption, music, and dance into a cultural space demarcated by *fun* (Henderson 1993). Anderson (1998, 2005) contends that women appear in the drug world differently than do men, and subtle connections between women's pursuits in the illegal and conventional worlds need to be made. Focusing on empowerment, as well as suggesting new identities and embodiments for women, Anderson (2005) contends that women drug users perform core activities—such as providing shelter, housing, and other sustenance needs, purchasing and selling drugs, and subsidizing or promoting male dependency—fundamental to the social and economic organization of the drug world. Although all of these embodied activities can be seen to aid more conventional lifestyles in future assimilation into the conventional world, the responsibility, risk management, and stability implicit in them are also transferable to the conventional world.

In this chapter, I analyze through a feminist lens new forms of female embodiment in the drugs field. I ask the question "How can women drug users' bodies be seen as social constructions by what they do in the illegal drugs world?" Focusing specifically on Anderson's (2005) "core activities," I scrutinize the effects of these core activities on women's drug-using bodies. My assumption is two-fold. First, a feminist embodiment approach brings together the notions of gender, the body, and power in a refreshing perspective that challenges outdated views on so-called deviant gendered bodies views that have become entrenched in the drugs field. Second, a feminist embodiment approach is needed for us to understand the sorts of cultural tensions and social fears that the female drug-using body evokes.

Implicit in this approach is a deep awareness that no gendered body exists neutrally outside the process of making meaning produced by culture, the subject, and the expert (Bordo 1993). Within the drugs field, there has been a glaring absence of work that employs a feminist embodiment approach, with rare exceptions (see Campbell 1999, 2000). By exploring in this chapter the links between the female body, the technologies of drugs use, and the performance of core activities, I present a feminist embodiment approach as well as offer a clear understanding of the contested nature of gendered representations of drug use. My interpretation of Anderson's (2005) core activities is that control of the household and consuming drugs hint at the norms-making processes required of women—processes that are the effect of regulatory practices shaping most female bodies engaged in them as "normal." Although subsidizing men's use and dealing are not "normal," they imply a legitimating process. It is important for women drug users to be able to convert their deviant lifestyles to more conventional ones and to convert their shrewdness to a more so-called normal lifestyle. On the other hand is the notion that core activities must allow for a level of resistance, incoherence, and instability in finding female empowerment through alternative activities such as pleasure-seeking, self-determination in promoting harm reduction, and self-governance in doing drugs.

This chapter includes four main discussions. First, I define three contemporary notions: gender, the body, and power. Second, I outline selected theories that bring together these respective notions. Third, I examine how women's core activities overlap with the gendered body culture of the drug-using world. Drug cultures are not only gendered, body cultures but also spaces where the female body emerges as a site for the commonplace acts of resistance and rebellion as well as of conformity. This polluted body becomes a metaphor for failed femininity, emotionality, sexuality, and the breaking down of self-risk management (Malloch 2004). Fourth, I ask "Where do we go from here?" and suggest further developments for a feminist embodiment approach to women drug users.

GENDER, EMBODIMENT, AND POWER

Recently, I (Ettorre 2004) clarified differences between a classical and a postmodern perspective in the drugs field and argued that a clear benefit of the latter perspective is its conceptual fluidity and expansive methodology toward all things social and cultural. This perspective develops workable ideas on gender and the body, and a thorough understanding of both concepts, gender and body, aids our understanding of women drug-users' lives. In the following discussion, I summarize my ideas on gender and the body and include my thinking on power—three notions essential for a feminist embodiment approach. I will then look at gender-sensitive theories of embodiment and make links with the drugs field. A postmodern perspective not only facilitates a feminist embodied approach but also allows us to consider drug use as a form of embodied deviance.

Gender

Judith Lorber (1994) has explored gender as both a process and an institution. As a process, gender shapes the meaning of *female* and *male, masculinity* and *femininity*, on cultural, political, and economic levels. It affects the social groupings of men and women, and divisions between the private and public arenas of social life. As an institution, gender is a component of culture and a persistent form of inequality. In this sense, gender regulates and disciplines. It is a moralizing system that exerts social control on individuals via a set of norms centered on the activities of individuals marked by "differences" in being male and female as well as masculine and feminine.

Judith Butler (1993, 1990) argues that gender is performed, which is another type of coercion; performing gender forcefully shapes the body along narrow constraints of gender differences (McRobbie 2005). These ideas expose the importance of analyzing how gender regulates us as well as the possibilities of flexibility and change issuing from performing gender. This work shows gender's *embedded-ness* in the lives of drug users.

The Body

Behavior always reveals itself through the body. The body is a means of expressing who we are and can become. How our bodies move in societies is shaped by complex cultural values. Further, the body has become a fundamental feature of taste and distinction (Turner 1992) in which bodily management is an important part of physical and cultural capital (Bourdieu 1984)—meaning the body gathers status as it moves. The body can be seen as the end-product of a whole system of power relations (Armstrong 1987). Embodiment scholars, such as Turner (1996) and Shilling (1993), imagine the human body as politically shaped by histories and practices of control. The body provides the focus for regulatory practices (medical and legal surveillance, etc.) carried out on the individual as a material person who uses drugs.

Power

The body is the product of power relationships. It is an object of power that is controlled, managed, and reproduced (Turner 1996). Embodiment theorists argue that power manifests itself through bodily disciplines or technologies of the self and through regulatory practices targeting specific populations. Since the Enlightenment, the body has been the focal point of practices of surveillance and rational control. The body has been constructed at the center of controlling discourses. It has been sexualized and medicalized, and this happens through a new type of power, *biopower* (Bradotti 1994). Biopower is all about making bodies normal and conforming in society. Biopower is the social force producing and normalizing bodies to serve relations of dominance and subordination in society. Ultimately, biopower aims for total control over humans (Braidoti 1994). For drug-using bodies, the notion of normalization is consistently operational in their own deviant lifestyles.

EMBODIMENT THEORISTS: "ABSENCE," "BECOMING," AND "ETHICS"

Three useful embodiment theorists, Turner (1992, 1996) Braidotti (1994, 2002) and Frank (1991, 1995, 2004), offer views linking gender, embodiment and power. Bryan Turner (1992) contends that the absence of the body from social theory poses major problems for the formulation of a sociological perspective on the human agent, agency, and human embodiment. Also, he argues that "if sociology is the study of action, we require a social theory of the body because human agency and interaction involve far more than knowledgeability, intentionality, and consciousness" (35). In this view, the body is brought into culture as a "potentiality" (emerging entity) managed and developed through the processes of aging and gender differentiation.

Within what she calls a materialist theory of becoming, Rosi Braidotti (2002) exposes a strained relationship between bodies and the use of discourses that uphold oppressive ideas on the body. She contends that the body is fragmented in these discourses, particularly in the biomedical one. On the one hand, biomedicine upholds the metaphysical unity of the body based on a careful balance of oppositions between body and mind. On the other hand, other discourses besides biomedicine (law, religion, criminal justice, etc.) take the body as their target (1994, 46).

Arthur Frank (1995) argues that we must ensure that the stories we tell reflect the lives of people we study. Such behavior on our part forms our ethical work. There is a need for an ethics of the body shaping a sociology of the body. Bodies need to be in relationship to others—especially those that are viewed as wounded bodies. His "communicative body" is the ethical ideal for wounded bodies that speak in stories or in what he refers to as illness narratives. Frank contends that wounded women's bodies silenced through illness and pain must break their silence, turn silence into action, and become communicating bodies—bodies not afraid to share their suffering with others who respond with compassion or empathy.

EMBODIED DEVIANCE

The above ideas help to create a politics of embodiment bringing into focus the complex relationship among gender, the body, and power, and are linked to drug use. Although the body is an essential part of our social identity, and the means for self-expression (Davis 1997), in our consumer cultures the body is a means to construct complex lifestyles. Scientists, policy makers, law makers, and physicians have been unwilling to deal with this material body; the idea that the body is a machine has predominated. Ideals of the body are formed by ideas from history, science, medicine, and consumer interests (Urla and Swedlund 1995) and we assess bodies according to what has been called "benchmark man" (Brook 1999); all these processes are embedded in the drugs field.

To make links with the drugs field, I introduce the concept *embodied deviance,* defined as the scientific and lay claim that bodies of individuals classified as deviant are marked in some recognizable way (Urla and Terry 1995). Deviant social behavior always manifests itself in the substance of the "deviant's" body. Individuals who deviate from social norms are viewed as socially and morally inferior; their social and moral troublemaking is embodied. As a form of "embodied deviance," drug use *marks* bodies of individuals, determining their low status and lack of moral agency. A drug-using body becomes a vehicle for solving a variety of problems that all bodies, especially young ones (Patton 1995), face. But these problems become magnified because drugs involve bodies in risk cultures (Monaghan 1999) and there are specific gendered norms, styles, and rules of engagement in the drugs world (Morgan and Joe 1996; Friedman and Alicea 2001). Women drug users are clearly at a disadvantage in relationship to men. Traditionally, in drug cultures, what is male or defined as masculine takes priority over what is female or defined as feminine (Perry 1979), reflecting the institution of gender embedded in drug-using cultures and treatment systems. Even though both women and men drug users will experience the damaging effects of these gendering processes, women are disadvantaged because masculinist, patriarchal, or paternalistic, rather than gender-sensitive, epistemologies predominate (Ettorre 1994). These epistemologies permeate all theories and practices.

SEEING WOMEN'S CORE ACTIVITIES
THROUGH THE LENS OF EMBODIMENT

Returning to Anderson's four core activities, I ask how the notion of gendered embodied deviance intersects with them. In answering, I hope to demonstrate how gender can be a template for gathering important knowledge on drug use. Gendered practices are used to construct the stigmatized drug-using female body in such a way that the drug use of any woman, viewed as a type of female embodiment, is disciplined in relationship to others and to her reproductive body (Campbell 1999). Within biomedicine, the symbol of the age of biopower is the reproductive body, the body of a woman capable of producing babies under the benevolent guise of medicine. I noted earlier that biopower is all about making bodies normal and conforming in society. The marking of female bodies as reproductive has been a crucial way in which biopower produces and normalizes female bodies to serve prevailing gender relations. Women's bodies are shaped by reproduction, and the discourse of reproduction is shaped by the workings of women's bodies. Female bodies are set up alongside *nature* and *irrationality*; male bodies are the stronghold of reason. With the rise of Cartesian ideas (e.g., the mind-body split), there has been a deprecation of bodies, with a patriarchal assault on nature and all things feminine. As women's bodies, including drug-using bodies, are pressed into the service of reproduction, their social agency is defined and valued by how well they reproduce. Of course, for drug users, reproduction is a problematic issue (Murphy and Rosenbaum 1999).

The female drug-using body embodies deviance and is a politically shaped body, formed by practices of suppression and restraint. Although the construction of *the body* is, as we have seen earlier, an effect of endless circulation of power and knowledge, the female drug-using body provides the focus for regulatory practices targeting an individual perceived as a shameful, unfeminine, and irresponsible person. A major assumption supporting women's engagement in core activities is that the female body is normalized as life-giver and reproducer, an assumption taken as a biological given.

The Domestic Body: Control of the Household

Anderson (2005) notes that one dimension of women drug users' "power" pertains to the housing that drug-using women provide to members of inner-city drug worlds. Calling attention to a woman's control of the household, Anderson notes that this activity points to organizing the variety of physical, intimate spaces that provide refuge, emotional labor, and cultural sustenance for a woman's significant others. For a drug-using woman, the domestic body is the domesticated, instrumental, useful body. Even though many discourses (e.g., biomedical, legal, media, drugs) regulate her body as a deviant one, various technologies of the self (providing a visible space for significant others, collecting material goods for her and other's subsistence, etc.) are at work in her desire for drugs. Her domestic and deviant embodiment disrupts dualistic thinking. First, such a female body is not imprisoned temporally and spatially in the restricted area of a prison—where those in the criminal justice machinery would place this body if it were visible to them. Second, the household is designated as a social space demarcated more by female than by male bodies. A hybrid domestic masculinity (McDowell 2003) exists, but a female drug user is unable to challenge the naturalized view of her regulated body within this domestic space.

In the drugs field, domesticated drug-using bodies, whether men or women, may move freely between the public and private spaces of their lives. To be successful domesticated bodies, women maintain connections between what is viewed by society as their respectable or responsible embodied activities (e.g., relations with their significant others, such as a partner or children) and their disrespectful or irresponsible embodied activities (e.g., drug use). But criminal justice and medical personnel do not bestow respectability on women drug users—even on those who are respectable or responsible within their domestic spaces. In the hierarchies of social values (Skeggs 1997), women drug users remain outside of respectability and are more easily classified as dangerous, bad, or risky bodies. Gaining respectability while doing drugs is problematic, as shame or disconnection is embedded easily in these women's domestic lives (Dale and Emerson, 1995).

But female drug users embody dependability by attending to intimate household spaces and making provisions for others' bodies and bodily needs. Yet their own bodies are somewhat fluid. This is shown by the negative consequences of their bodily addiction (as in drug use). Domestic space is seen as tainted by these female bodies embedded in deviant lifestyles. In discourses focusing on who is normal, these bodies are emblematic of recklessness, lack of responsibility, and failed femininity. Regardless of these women's ability to embody dependability and to provide opportunities for their partners to accumulate resources, the women are never far from the grasp of biopower and are continually pressed into the service of normality.

Anderson (2005) notes the core activity of household control provides important forms of capital for women and their dependents, enabling successful drug careers. But this success is based on female bodies culturally constructed in opposition to social authority and as a challenge to the continuity of male property and power. Drug use is experienced as a bodily or corporeal style; however, women's domesticated bodies epitomize the dual aspects of dependency (Ettorre 1992): others are dependent upon them and they are dependent upon drugs. These bodies are constructed to serve prevailing gender relations, yet the bodies are produced outside the realm of gender respectability. In effect, dependency itself is a bodily style for these female bodies, as their domestic spaces are central to the social and economic organization of drugs and related embodied activities.

The Consuming Body: Female Purchasing Power

Women drug users are consumers, and their ability to raise finances for the purchase of goods and services helps stimulate both illegal and legal economies (Anderson 2005). Rather than look specifically at the income sources—sex work, social transfer payments, and secondary labor market employment—I look generally at drug-using women as consumers of drugs and as "powerful economic actors."

In contemporary society, consumer culture is where the reproduction of social inequalities and reinforcement of normality thrives. Consumer culture actively creates the self as of prime importance and oriented toward self-indulgence rather than self-denial (Howson 2004). The consumption of drugs flourishes within a society "addicted itself to the sorry tension between individual excess and social control" (Ferrel and Sanders 1995, 313). Although drug use may be viewed as criminal consumption, designated as deviant and serving mainly male interests or male street cultural capital (Collison 1996), the consuming body of the female drug user may be seen as able to gain competence, control, and power (Murphy and Arroyo, quoted in Anderson 2005).

This drug-consuming body is both cultural construction and social resource. It is constructed by burdensome social and moral discourses—although resistance to the social vulnerability of one's body is possible. The cultural adages that "Drug use is anathema to women's bodies as reproducers" or "Women who consume drugs fail in their social responsibility to be the guardians of morals" are refrains emerging from these discourses. Although female users may control economic resources, they may also embody resistance when they break traditional norms by being drug dealers in drug-consuming spaces. This resistance *is,* regardless of the fact that some women may be ill-equipped to handle the violence necessary to maintain their dealing in an environment of security and control (Fagan 1994).

For all women, consuming health is a social imperative (Doyal 2002). Within biomedical discourses, drug use is not indicative of a body consuming health (Ettorre and Miles 2001). Nevertheless, these consuming bodies create opportunities for embodying themselves as strong and coping. The moral outrage against women drug users is a powerful way in which women's bodies are stigmatized, but this can be an occasion for female bodies to access reserves of emotion and understanding, consume actively, and create a lifestyle that has traditionally remained repressed in a drug-using environment. For Ahmed (2004) such resistance is all about "deviant bodies" favoring a "performance of disgust" (i.e. drug use) and challenging social beliefs about who is normal. To consume drugs is to expose oneself to risk (Collison 1996). However, the female drug-consuming body creates space for an imaginative form of femininity: criminal pleasures may become escapes from powerlessness and domination in everyday life, and illicit pleasures such as drug use, consumptions of desire.

The Female Laboring Body: Women Subsidizing Men's Use

Related to the consuming body is the female laboring body. In discussing sources of women's economic power, Anderson (2005) notes that subsidizing male drug users, their consumption of drugs, sustenance needs, and lifestyles is a core activity for women users. The female body has no clear or established history, and the value put on it has been constant only in being constantly less than the value given the male body (Shildrick 1997, 22). This statement is true in the drugs field, where women's needs are reconstructed as risks, and when these women are viewed as undeserving of the status of victim or of citizen (Malloch 2004). To see the real value of gendered bodies, especially drug-using, female laboring bodies, we must look at these bodies in relation to others. When women financially support men's drug-using activities, their bodies become "relational resources" whether or not their relationships are marked by risky behaviors (e.g., unsafe sex, drug use, injecting), victimization, violence, or exploitation.

Both female and male users engage in embodied risk relationships, and love and intimacy may play a large part in managing these relationships. For women to be successful as laboring relational bodies, they need to learn about difficult embodiments and complex, gendered rules of engagement in intimate relationships. For example, drug-using, female sex workers are confronted with not only the risks associated with work relationships but also with changing drug fashions (from crack cocaine to powder cocaine to ecstasy, etc.) (Green et al. 2000). These women are aware of the risks and benefits associated with these changing drug fashions and the ways different drugs feature in relationships among workers, clients, managers, and dealers. Although some drug-using women may thrive economically in this environment, others may become increasingly desperate and find their bargaining power so reduced that they accept a fraction of the money they once received for their services (Willis and Rushforth 2003). Green et al. (2000) found that it was difficult for sex workers to separate "professional," work-related drug use from recreational drug use. They experienced their bodies as occupational resources, shaped by different relationships with "working" and with "private" partners, much as did other women who relied on their bodies to produce income (Evans et al. 2002). Here, drugs and risky sex cut across both the public and private boundaries of work and leisure. As laboring bodies supporting partners, female users of all ages, sexual orientations, classes, and ethnicities, like non–drug-using women, experience their own bodies as relational investments—useful physical capital or resources (Bordo 1993).

The Female Body "in Commerce": Dealing Drugs

The number of women involved in drug selling, and their location in the pecking order vis-à-vis men, remain burning issues (Anderson 2005). When women drug users become engaged in dealing drugs, their bodies are shaped by culture in the commercial world through the business of doing drugs. Bodies are contextualized by gender, race, ethnicity, sexual orientation, and class as well as by culture. Denton and O'Malley (1999) describe the ways the illicit drug market is fragmentary and competitive, lending itself to small business entrepreneurs. They contend that this business structure makes women's success more practicable in this illicit economy. Further, the lack of a clear authority structure, and capacity to absorb new dealers, mean fewer barriers for women dealers to overcome. Significant others in women dealers' family networks become a stable operational base for the women to become successful drug entrepreneurs. The deviant embodiment of these women reveals a balance between well-disciplined, financially focused bodies and supposedly undisciplined bodies who neglect their families.

Here, the embodiment discourse exposes that whose drug dealing bodies we are talking about makes a difference. In the past, the standard core of the body in commerce, whether drug-using or not, was a white, male, middle-class body—the norm for all. The embodiment discourse exposes that gender, race, and ethnicity as well as class make a difference, and shows differential accounts of female and male agency. Female embodiment in the form of drug dealing is incorporated particularly easily in the disciplinary machinery of the illicit drug economy when this activity is supported by intimacy, trust, and primary relationships (Denton and O'Malley 1999). Drug dealing is a bodily style. The drug-dealing female body shows the ways that restrictive masculinist assumptions about the character of the procedures and skills involved in drug dealing can be overturned; nevertheless, we must be cautious in assuming that women have greater participation than before in the drug distribution business. Maher and Daly show that women are often recruited into drug sales because police are less likely to search them; once police are on to this scheme, however, women are not as likely to be recruited to sell drugs (Friedman and Alicia 2001). Here, the disciplining of law (Moran 2001) enacted by the policing of drugs is organized around masculinist assumptions about which bodies should deal drugs. But when female bodies are recruited into this activity and become bona fide dealers, there is a chance that their defiance of traditional expectations may remain invisible while their legitimacy as dealers becomes somewhat tenuous, if not denied. Whether or not dealing drugs is an empowering embodied experience for these women (Friedman and Alicia 2001), involvement in this activity inevitably has bodily consequences for significant others around them. This is demonstrated, for example, when Marilyn, a forty-year-old dealer interviewed by Friedman and Alicia (2001, 135) says: "There was this thing with the Filas [expensive name-brand shoes]. I explained to them [her children] either Mom uses, deals drugs and you have Filas or I don't use, I'm in treatment and you have Payless shoes. I told them you have a choice . . . use, don't use, deal, treatment, Filas, Payless . . . They chose the Payless shoes. They wanted me around."

Perhaps these reflections suggest a communicative body (Frank 1995), a woman who attempts to speak in painful but healing narratives.

WHERE DO WE GO FROM HERE?

As implied in this chapter, being a female drug-using body is neither stable nor secure in society. Through a feminist embodiment approach, we have seen that this deviant body is shaped over time in various disciplin-ing public and private spaces and established through empowering "core activities" in the illegal drug world. Although drug use may be a mark of cultural difference for women (Ettorre 2007), this is not the full picture. We need to include in both our theoretical and our empirical studies how female embodiment shapes successful social and financial engagement in domestic, consuming, laboring, and dealing spaces (O'Malley and Valverde 2004). The feminist embodiment approach offered in this chapter has illus-trated women drug users' attempts at stability in the physical and temporal spaces constructed around and through their bodies. This approach has exposed the precariousness of the act of taking drugs, and has also revealed women drug users who resist gendered identities and oppressive roles that target such women as more domesticated and deviant, and less financially able than men.

In the drugs field, the body should be seen as a central element in the construction of the social. Given that we need more precise conceptualizing in the drugs field (Reinarman 2005), the drug-using body should be seen as the template upon which cultural identities are fashioned and emotions played out. In the context of the gendering and problematic nature of drug use, the task of feminist scholars is to bear witness to this form of embodied oppression. Bodies are where narratives of risk, respectability, identity, con-flict, anxiety, and social management converge (and not as gender-, race-, class-, and age-neutral, nondeterminate systems).

We know that biomedical and legal discourses on the body have be-come embedded in contemporary drug research cultures. Thus we need to be cognizant of how those working in the fields of biomedicine and law continue to devise ways to transform the boundaries of drug-using bodies. Whether sick or healthy, deviant or normal, able or disabled, black-skinned or white-skinned, etc., all drug-using bodies are viewed as empirical objects to be tested, managed, quantified, and classified. Through an awareness of the complexities of the workings of gender, the body, and power, we are able to understand the embodied experiences of gendered subjects living in drug-using communities.

By making women's bodies central in the drugs discourse, recognizing discourses which target this body, and making space for a communicative body, I have exposed the importance of developing a feminist embodiment approach.

In conclusion, we should continue to utilize this sort of approach as a way of bearing witness to women drug users. When developing theories, we must include ideas on gender, the body, and power, especially if we wish to expose *deviant bodies* as cultural constructions that go against the norms of conventional society.

REFERENCES

Ahmed, S. 2004. *The Cultural Politics of Emotion*. New York: Routledge.

Anderson, T. 1995. "Toward a preliminary macro theory of drug addiction." *Deviant Behavior* 16: 353–372.

———. 1998. "A cultural identity theory of drug abuse." *The Sociology of Crime, Law, and Deviance* 1: 233–262.

———. 2005. "Dimensions of women's power in the illicit drug economy." *Theoretical Criminology 9, no. 4: 371–400*.

———, and J. A. Levy. 2003. "Marginality among older injectors in today's illicit drug economy: Assessing the impact of aging." *Addiction* 98:761–770.

Arfken, C. L., N. Borisova, C. Klein, S. di Menza, C. R.Schuster. 2002. "Women are less likely to be admitted to substance abuse treatment within 30 days of assessment." *Journal of Psychoactive Drugs* 34, 1: 33–38.

Armstrong, D. 1987. "Bodies of knowledge: Foucault and the problem of human anatomy." In G. Scambler, ed., *Sociological Theory and Medical Sociology*, 59–76. London: Tavistock.

Baker, P. 2000. "'I didn't know': Discoveries and identity transformations of women addicts in treatment." *Journal of Drug Issues* 30, 4: 863–880.

Bordo, S. 1993. *Unbearable Weight: Feminism, Western Culture, and the Body*. Berkeley and Los Angeles: University of California Press.

Bourdieu, P. 1984. *Distinction: A Social Critique of the Judgement of Taste*. London: Routledge.

Braidotti, R. 1994. *Nomadic Subjects: Embodiment and Sexual Difference in Contemporary Feminist Theory*. New York: Columbia University Press.

———. 2002. *Metamorphoses:Towards a Feminist Theory of Becoming*. Cambridge: Polity.

Brook, B. 1999. *Feminist Perspectives on the Body*. London: Longman.

Butler, J. 1990. *Gender Trouble: Feminism and the Subversion of Identity*. New York: Routledge.

————. 1993. *Bodies That Matter.* New York: Routledge.

Campbell, N. 1999. "Regulating 'maternal instinct': Governing mentalities of late twentieth century U.S. illicit drug policy." *Signs: Journal of Women in Culture and Society* 24, 4: 895–923.

————. 2000. *Using Women: Gender, Drug Policy, and Social Justice.* New York: Routledge.

Collison, M. 1996. "In search of the high life: Drugs, crime, masculinities, and consumption." British Journal of Criminology 36, 3: 428–444.

Dale, B., and P. Emerson. 1995. "The importance of being connected: Implications for work with women addicted to drugs." In C. Burck and B. Speed, eds., *Gender, Power and Relationships,* 168–184. London: Routledge.

Davis, K. 1997. "Embody-ing theory: Beyond modernist and postmodernist readings of the body." In K. Davis, ed., *Embodied Practices: Feminist Perspectives on the Body,* 1–23. London: Sage.

Denton, B., and P. O'Malley. 1999. "Gender, trust and business: Women drug dealers in the illicit economy." British Journal of Criminology 39, 4: 513–530.

Doyal, L. 2002. "Gender equity in health: Debates and dilemmas." In. G. Bendelow, M. Carpenter, C. Vautier, and S. Williams, eds., *Gender, Health, and Healing,* 183–197. London: Routledge. .

Ettorre, E. 1992. *Women and Substance Use.* Houndsmills, Basingstoke, UK: Macmillan, and New Brunswick, NJ: Rutgers University Press.

————. 1994. "What can she depend on: Substance use and women's health." In S. Wilkinson and C. Kitzinger, eds., *Women and Health: Feminist Perspectives,* 85–101. London: Taylor and Francis.

————. 2004. "Revisioning women and drug use: Gender sensitivity, embodiment, and reducing harm." *International Journal on Drugs Policy* 15: 327–335.

————. 2007. "Women, drugs, and popular culture: Is there a need for a feminist embodiment perspective?" In P. Manning, ed., *Drugs and Popular Culture: Drugs, Identity, Media, and Culture in the Twenty-First Century,* 227–238. Cullompton, Devon: Willan Publishing.

————, and Miles, S. 2001. "Young people, drug use, and the consumption of health." In S. Henderson and A. Petersen, eds., *Consumption of Health,* 173–186. London: Routledge.

Evans, R. D., C. Forsyth, and D. K. Gauthier. 2002. "Gendered pathways into and experiences within crack cultures outside the inner city." *Deviant Behavior* 23: 483–510.

Fagan, J. 1994. "Women and drugs revisited: Female participation in the cocaine economy." *Journal of Drug Issues* 24, 2: 179–225.

Ferrel, J., and C. R. Sanders. 1995. "Toward a cultural criminology." In J. Ferrel and C. R. Sanders, eds., *Cultural criminology,* 297–326. Boston: Northeastern University Press.

Frank, A. 1991. *At the Will of the Body: Reflections on Illness.* Boston: Houghton. Mifflin.

————. 1995. *The Wounded Storyteller: Body, Illness, and Ethics.* Chicago: University of Chicago Press.

————. 2004. *The Renewal of Generosity: Illness, Medicine, and How to Live.* Chicago: University of Chicago Press.

Friedman, J., and M. Alicea. 2001. *Surviving Heroin: Interviews with Women in Methadone Clinics.* Gainesville: University Press of Florida.

Green, A., S. Day, and H. Ward. 2000. "Crack cocaine and prostitution in London in the 1990s." *Sociology of Health and Illness* 22, 1: 27–39.

Hammersley, M., F. Khan, and J. Ditton. 2002. *Ecstasy and the Rise of the Chemical Genera-tion*. London: Routledge.

Henderson, S. 1993. "Fun, frisson, and fashion." *International Journal of Drugs Policy* 4: 1–9.

———. 1996. "E Types and dance divas: Gender research and community prevention." In T. Rhodes and R. Hartnoll, eds., *AIDS, Drugs, and Prevention: Perspectives on Indi-vidual and Community Action*, 66–85. London: Routledge.

Howson, A. 2004. *The Body in Society: An Introduction*. Cambridge: Polity.

Kandall, S. R., with the assistance of J. Petrillo. 1996, 1999. *Substance and Shadow: Women and Addiction in the United States*. Cambridge MA: Harvard University Press.

Lorber, J. 1994. *Paradoxes of Gender*. New York: Yale University Press.

Malloch, M. 2004. "Not 'fragrant' al all: Criminal justice responses to 'risky women.'" *Critical Social Policy* 24, 3: 385–405.

McDowell, L. 2003. *Redundant Masculinities: Employment Change and White Working-Class Youth*. Oxford: Blackwell.

McRobbie, A. 2005. *The Uses of Cultural Studies*. London: Sage.

Measham, F. 2002. "Doing gender—doing drugs: Conceptualizing the gendering of drugs cultures." *Contemporary Drug Problems* 29, 2: 335–373.

Monaghan, L. 1999. "Challenging medicine? Bodybuilding, drugs, and risk." *Sociology of Health and Illness* 21, 6: 707–734.

Moran, L. 2001. "The gaze of law: Technologies, bodies, and representation." In R. Hol-liday and J. Hassard, eds. *Contested Bodies*, 107–116. London: Routledge.

Morgan, P., and K. Joes. 1996. "Citizens and outlaws: The private lives and public life-styles of women in the illicit drug economy." *Journal of Drug Issues* 26, 1: 125–142.

Murphy, S., and M. Rosenbaum. 1999. *Pregnant Women on Drugs: Combating Stereotypes and Stigma*. New Brunswick, NJ: Rutgers University Press.

O'Malley, P., and M. Valverde. 2004 "Pleasure, freedom, and drugs: The uses of 'pleasure' in liberal governance of drug and alcohol consumption." *Sociology* 38, 1: 25–42.

Patton, C. 1995. "Between innocence and safety: Epidemiologic and popular construc-tions of young people's need for safe sex." In J. Terry and J. Urla, eds., *Deviant Bodies*, 338–357. Bloomington: Indiana University Press.

Perry, L. 1979. *Women and Drug Use: An Unfeminine Dependency*. London: Institute for the Study of Drug Dependence.

Raine, P. 2001. *Women's Perspectives on Drugs and Alcohol: The Vicious Circle*. Aldershot, UK: Ashgate.

Reinarman, C. 2005. "Addiction as accomplishment: The discursive construction of dis-ease." *Addiction Research and Theory* 13, 4: 307–320.

Shildrick, M. 1997. *Leaky Bodies and Boundaries: Feminism, Postmodernism, and (Bio)Ethics*. London: Routledge.

Shilling, C. 1993. *The Body and Social Theory*. London: Sage Publications

Skeggs, B. 1997. *Formations of Class and Gender: Becoming Respectable*. London: Sage.

Sterk, C. E. 1999. *Fast Lives: Women Who Use Crack Cocaine*. Philadelphia: Temple Uni-versity Press.

Turner, B. 1992. *Regulating Bodies: Essays in Medical Sociology*. London: Routledge.

———. 1996. *The Body and Society*. London: Sage Publications. 2nd ed.

Urla, J., and A. C. Swedlund. 1995. "The anthropometry of Barbie: Unsettling ideals of the feminine body in popular culture." In J. Terry and J. Urla Eds., *Deviant Bod-ies: Critical Perspectives on Difference in Science and Popular Cultures,*, 277–313. Bloomington: Indiana University Press.

Urla, J., and J. Terry. 1995. "Introduction: Mapping embodidied deviance." In J. Terry and J. Urla, eds., *Deviant Bodies: Critical Perspectives on Difference in Science and Popular Cultures,* 1–18. Bloomington: Indiana University Press.

Willies, K., and C. Rushforth. 2003. "The female criminal: An overview of women's drug use and offending behaviour." *Trends and Issues in Crime and Criminal Justice,* no. 264 (October 2003),. Canberra: Australian Institute of Criminology. http://www.aic.gov.au/publications/tandi2/tandi264.html (accessed May 31, 2005).

CHAPTER 3

Demonstrating a Female-Specific Agency and Empowerment in Drug Selling

Deborah R. Baskin and Ira Sommers

INTRODUCTION

In the late 1980s through the early 1990s, we engaged in research to understand women's participation in the drug economy. We did in-depth life history interviews with 156 women who sold drugs in two New York neighborhoods: Washington Heights in Manhattan, and Bushwick in Brooklyn. Both neighborhoods had active heroin markets in the 1970s and were the flash points for the growth of cocaine and crack markets a decade later.

Women were contacted in two ways: as street samples recruited through "snowball" procedures, and through active caseload lists of women incarcerated for drug sale convictions at state and city correctional facilities. Both sets of women came from the two neighborhoods. Forty percent of the interviews were conducted with active drug dealers, the rest in institutional settings.

The typical woman was either African American or Latina, in her early thirties, had dropped out of high school, possessed limited legal work experience, and had two children. The youngest respondent was sixteen, the oldest forty-eight; the mean age was thirty. The women were engaged in a wide range of criminal and deviant activities. Of the 156 women we interviewed, 38 percent reported committing robbery, 17 percent reported involvement in burglary, 33 percent had committed assault, and 44 percent were at some time involved in prostitution. The women sold multiple drugs. Many diversified or changed their products over time. Most (81 percent) sold crack. The average age of initiation into dealing was younger than twenty-five. Most of the women had been selling for at least five years.

A life-history approach was used to describe initiation into dealing and involvement with drugs, the social processes of selling and drug use, income sources from both legitimate and illegal activities, and non–drug criminality. Through these interviews, the women were able to represent a level of activity, creativity, and human agency that might otherwise not have been attainable. The interviewing permitted us to understand how their experiences, relationships, and other processes structurally and experientially established the choices they faced and how such choices were then defined. In this way, we were better able to understand how embedded the women's criminal careers were within larger social worlds, which by and large reinforced their involvement.

THE CHANGING FACE OF DRUG MARKETS

I just got out of prison and I asked my sister how much it would cost to start a business. She said $500. I got a grand from my husband. I bought two ounces of cooked up crack. Opened this place at one of my sister's friend's house. She was strung out on crack. I already mastered a plan for it. I just paid the girl in crack. I didn't have to pay her cash for the apartment. I just started making good money. I wasn't using crack at the time. I did begin to use it about a year later. Soon after, me and my sister was smoking $1500 worth of crack a day. It wasn't even hurting the profits.

I had a crew. About eight of us: seven women. I always had a dream to have an all-women crew. Whether people realize it or not, women sell drugs more easily than men. More people approach you because you are a woman. Usually women don't like to be known selling drugs so sometimes they have a male front. There are a lot of women drug dealers. They have males to front off for them, to keep attention off of them. You have to have some type of protection over yourself, a man who they believe is the boss. (Denise)

Denise, like many other female drug dealers with whom we spoke, suggested that women create substantial roles within drug markets, roles that are not subordinate to males. This perception contradicts a fair amount of research and conventional wisdom. Research in this area argues that women's drug activities are heavily linked to male partners. Women are portrayed as occupying assistant roles, helping male drug dealers by touting products, by steering customers to them, or by holding drugs or related illegal paraphernalia (Adler 1985; Mieczkowski 1986).

However, during the late 1980s, we noticed a phenomenon that had been emerging in major urban centers: the growth of direct female involvement in drug selling. Clearly, women were not taking over drug markets. But they were entering distribution settings in greater numbers and in more ways than existed previously.

Women's roles and experiences in drug selling moved from adjunct selling–hustling roles to more systematic and sometimes high-stakes forms of participation. As a result, women were able to buy some protection from exploitation in sex markets. Some women were even able to avoid prostitution altogether, while others were able to leave it (Baskin et al. 1996, 401–417)—in many ways because of the new opportunities afforded women in the 1980s drug markets.

By and large, three factors that emerged during the 1980s changed the dynamics and contexts of drug use and selling for women.

First, the increased availability of inexpensive cocaine products, especially smokeable cocaine, made possible serious drug use without the risks of injection or physiological addiction. The expansion of cocaine markets and the lower price of cocaine created new forms of drug selling for both men and women. Easier access to cocaine accelerated the developmental progression from "gateway" use of alcohol and marijuana to serious drug use among both men and women, and may have contributed to more prevalent and frequent cocaine use in inner cities.

Second, significant structural shifts in the social and economic compositions of inner cities changed the organization of drug use and selling. The loss of millions of manufacturing jobs in large cities following the 1960s led to dramatic shifts in the gender/age composition of inner-city neighborhoods. The proportion of adult males to females declined sharply from 1960 to 1980, and the proportion of female-headed households substantially increased (Wacquant and Wilson 1989, 8–25). Many of these households had incomes below the poverty line (Jencks 1991), and participation in the growing informal economy became part of the diverse network of income sources for poor women (Sassen-Koob 1989). The influences of "female old heads" on young women also weakened, as neighborhoods grew poorer and poorer (Anderson 1990). With the expansion of the drug economy and its opportunities for "crazy money" (Williams 1989), street-smart girls (and boys) rejected the "old heads'" lessons about life and the work ethic.

Third, the demand for cheap cocaine products in the 1980s exceeded the capacity of existing drug distribution systems. This created new opportunities for both men and women to buy cocaine and other drugs (Goldstein 1991). The growing cocaine economy improved access to supplies, expanded entry-level roles in drug distribution, made possible entry into drug selling with a small capital investment, and generated controlled selling territories with guaranteed incomes (Williams 1989). Thus, the cocaine economy of

the 1980s opened the doors for scores of women to enter into criminal enterprises and street networks in new ways and in greater numbers.

OPPORTUNITY STRUCTURES OF URBAN COMMUNITIES

Most explanations of women's involvement in drug markets are situated in the heroin era, the twenty-year period beginning in the early 1960s.
Rosenbaum's (1981) study showed how involvement in heroin typically
narrowed the options for income production and social interactions among
women. Other studies of this period continued the age-old tradition of de-
picting deviant women (in this case, heroin users) as emotionally unstable
and sexually promiscuous (Colton and Marsh 1984; Stephens 1991; Erickson and Murray 1991). In these portrayals, women's involvement in drug
markets cut off their participation in conventional economic activities and
in traditional social circles.

Nevertheless, drug selling in heroin markets was a highly gendered activity (Adler 1985; Williams 1989). Women were rarely active in street selling for long periods, and domestic arrangements often mediated women's
participation in both drug use and drug selling (Rosenbaum 1981). The
women's main roles were limited to being "holders" or being peripheral
members of male-dominated dealing groups (Goldstein 1979). Their own
drug habits were the prime reasons for involvement in distribution activities. As their drug use increased and their ability to engage in legal work
decreased, women turned to an array of income sources, doubling up in
drug dealing and prostitution. However, as involvement in heroin continued to increase, the gendered world of drug distribution made it difficult
for women to make sufficient money to supply their drug needs (Hser et al.
1987, 33–57). Access to supplies and viable roles in selling were difficult for
women (Johnson et al. 1985). Although dealing provided access to small
supplies of drugs, it provided little money for other needs. It was a less attractive economic choice than hustling, fraud, theft, or prostitution.

By 1980, heroin use stabilized and even declined in inner cities. On the
other hand, cocaine use rose. Crack emerged in New York in 1985 and in
other urban areas shortly afterward (Belenko et al. 1991, 55–74). In New
York City, street drug markets expanded from a small number of cocaine distribution points that oftentimes resembled festive bazaars (Zimmer 1987).

As cocaine use supplanted heroin as the most widely used "serious"
drug (Kleiman 1992), the development of a cocaine economy among street
drugs changed the contexts and dynamics of women's involvement. The
unfolding of the crack era brought changes in two dimensions that had
shaped women's drug involvement in the past: the social contexts of drug
use, and the drug itself.

COCAINE, CRACK, AND DRUG MARKETS

In terms of drug use, the psychoactive and physiological effects of cocaine are quite different from those of heroin. Cocaine is a short-acting central nervous system stimulant. Its effects are relatively short-lived, and the declining stimulation of pleasure centers leads to anxiety, edginess, and depression (Warldorf et al. 1991). Users can ward off the effects of this "crash" by using more cocaine. Thus, cocaine sessions often entail binges of many hours of repeated use where sleep is obviated. This is similar, yet more intense, for crack, and therefore crack use requires multiple purchases in a short period of time. Such a drug is different from heroin, for which sales and psychoactive effects are limited in volume. Cocaine and crack are also more attractive to users than heroin since the methods of administration do not require needles. Therefore the risk of HIV transmission is reduced. Further, cocaine and crack were, for many years, portrayed as "safe" drugs that did not interfere with social activities and were also more easily controllable than heroin. Accordingly, these attractions made possible women's entry into what they saw as a safer form of intense drug use.

In terms of distribution, cocaine products became widely available as drug selling points. Organizations grew to meet the expected demand. The low per-unit cost and the ease of use fueled the expansion of these markets.

Thus, the interaction of the changing social circumstances of women in inner cities, the weakening of the dominance of males in street networks, and the expanded opportunities for cocaine use made possible the initiation of larger numbers of women into serious drug use and distribution than in earlier drug eras.

Drug selling became an attractive income option for women with low educational levels and job skills. Women had several options within these new markets, as was not the case with heroin distribution: support roles (lookout, tout), manufacturing (cutting, packaging, weighing), or direct street sales. Once cocaine and crack sales become institutionalized in New York City, their distribution became a common and visible feature in many neighborhoods. They were sold in storefronts, on street corners, and in crack (or "freak") houses. These markets were relatively easy to enter, requiring only a few dollars to create a product with a seemingly endless demand

For women, drug selling was facilitated by the expanded circle of users and opportunities. It was easy and cheap for women users to add cocaine and crack to the repertoire of drugs they used and traded socially, and to their already routine involvement in a variety of hustles. Thus, drug selling was often an extension of illegal careers and an opportunity for increasing crime incomes. As retail cocaine and crack markets were unregulated, many individual entrepreneurs were able to operate small businesses with many short-term employees. The deregulation and decentralization of drug distribution removed many gender barriers to selling.

The women sellers we interviewed show little of the passive vulnerability that characterized women in earlier drug eras. For the women we interviewed, becoming a drug dealer was an opportunistic extension of earlier life experiences. All of the women were already participating in quasi-criminal lifestyles (e.g., drug use, shoplifting, fraud, robbery). Driven by choice, necessity, or both, the women perceived drug dealing as an excellent way to "get over." In this regard, the women reflected a choice pattern quite similar to that seen in previous studies of males.

Women also entered drug distribution through the expansion of at least one existing product line (Murphy et al. 1991, 321–343) Almost a quarter of the women started selling such drugs as marijuana and learned many aspects of dealing before moving on to cocaine and crack. These women had already developed selling skills and established a network of active customers for illicit drugs. Denise described how she expanded her product line:

> I was still running my business, my old business; but it wasn't lucrative enough 'cause people weren't . . . there wasn't a whole lot of dope . . . it was like crack then. So I got turned on to it. I had to look at it like well how can I like turn this into money. And, uh, this old man from Manhattan came out and taught me how. He taught me how to cook up coke, how to bottle it, and how to sell it.

> Yeah, we bought powder, and cooked it up. And for a little while, for the first month or so, I only made like, just about $1000. Just enough to re-up. And that wasn't good enough for me. I put the word out that I had quality. Before I knew it I was sellin' . . . I was making $6500 per week if not better. Then I got workers. I had workers in the street and at night I had another house that they'd work out of, uh, as long as I paid the girl's rent, which is only $250. They sold out of her house. I had ten people that worked for me. I had four runners. Four muscles, very strong and capable men. Myself and two people that sat in the house. Except for the muscle, all the others were women. Girls I went to school with. Girls I trusted. Girls I did shit with.

Denise and her workers quickly learned that crack-selling rates were far higher than selling rates for other drugs. Clearly, the dynamic nature of the crack market and its profitability contributed to the immersion of women into selling roles.

Organizational Roles

Like other businesses, cocaine selling is hierarchically organized with higher incomes concentrated among a small number of managers. The bulk of drug sellers worked for hourly wages and, occasionally, drugs. Our women sellers did manage to achieve roles in distribution that were different from the support roles that typified their involvement in heroin sales. The roles suggest an active involvement in selling that required handling money or drugs in direct selling transactions. Most (98 percent) were involved in direct sales in either curbside or outdoor locations, a relatively rare role in the heroin markets of the 1970s (Johnson et al. 1985).

The following accounts epitomize the typical selling experiences of the women:

April: Sometimes, I would be up two or three days in a row because the money would be coming so fast that I'd be, I wouldn't want to go to sleep because I knew if I would go to sleep, I would miss money. On a typical day, I would wake up in the morning. Somebody would probably wake me up wanting to buy drugs and that was how my day started. They would call or beep me, and, uh, then I would be on the run all day. And sometimes my run would last two or three days. Uh, I used drugs to keep me motivated, to [keep] me moving. And I felt powerful.

Darlene: Madness, pure madness! You wake up, you know. You be behind a steel door—workin' from under the door. Me, I would smoke crack first. I seen a good thousand people a day, you know. Maybe the same people over and over, but a thousand people a day.

L.G.: A typical day would be wake up, uh, take the first hit, get wide open, and begin selling—all day into the night. Sometimes into the next morning till 3, 4, 5 in the morning. It would be pretty busy on Friday and Saturday nights—Thursdays, too. Sunday morning the crack business would be booming—people coming constantly. Working people, people coming all times of night, all night long until they're dead broke. Yeah, it sad, but that's the way it is.

In general, the women had several roles. In addition, they often occupied more than one role at any one time. Some (42 percent) had management roles that involved supervising other sellers, distributing drugs for resale, or collecting money. A significant number of the women (53 percent) were involved in important roles, such as "scale boys" who weighed and distributed packages of cocaine powder. Others provided service-oriented roles including "steering"—that is, directing users to a dealer. Patricia spoke about her relationships with her customers:

The main way I make money is takin' people to cop drugs. I got maybe eight or nine different customers. They are mostly white people from Long Island who can't afford to get busted or they're too clean cut to go on the block or scared to death to go on the block. Usually, I would cop a bundle or better. Dope, coke, both. When they come from Long Island they don't come down here to buy less than a bundle. A bundle of each. That's $150. Usually, I'll get a bag of dope, a bag of coke and twenty dollars.

Most of them are older than me (34). Most of them are [in their forties], 38, somewhere around there. They mostly have good jobs. They all got their own houses. All of them have nice cars. There's two of them who take the train, but they have a house out in Long Island.

I have one female customer from Long Island, used to be a top, top supervisor with Sony's, you know, top name TV brand. I mean, I'm talkin' about top dollars. Sometimes she comes twice a week. Sometimes she comes once a week. She buys two bundles of dope and two bundles of coke. She gets off up here. Sometimes she buys syringes from me, but if I don't have any I'll go to M—— and I get it from him. She'll buy four or five at a time. She hooks it up in the gallery. She gives me a shot from it. She gives me my own one. But she needs me to hit her though. I'll hit her in her arm. She can't hit herself at all. I'll hit her before I do any drugs.

Thus, the expansion of drug markets in the cocaine economy provided new ways for women to escape their limited roles, statuses, and incomes. Denise's account that follows illustrates the varied entrepreneurial skills involved in running a drug organization, skills that require knowing how to keep books, pay bills, manage inventory and cash flow, calculate profit margins, and deal with competitors and unpredictable employees and customers:

I would get up at seven. I would work out, have breakfast, shower, decide what I'm gonna wear—call around to see who got what. Everybody was meetin' at my house to count out money, and we'd have a little coffee, a small brunch, count out money and see where everybody's at. Then I'd have to make a run. But before that I went down to my closet where I kept the files on who's short and how often. Then, on my way out, I would stop and give the kids in the neighborhood $10. I'd sit up on my little fuckin' Benz and I'd talk shit to the niggers all day and play the radio and maybe go for a ride. If it was a day when someone had been short four or five times, then I'd have to take care of them. If they smokin' my stuff, I take care of them. I whoop their fuckin' ass and I'm cuttin' their shit up. Same goes for rival dealers—I'd go shoot your shit up. I'd go tear your place up. I'd stick up your workers. I'd cut up their clothes. I'd take your shit and I'd do it everyday until you either moved or you came to work for me. I like nines. I like Barringers with nickel-plated handles. I like style and something that works well. A woman can catch a bad one if she ain't prepared. I have rules—don't steal from me—ask me for something and I'll give it to you but don't steal from me. I have this one West Indian girl and I pay her $750 plus anything she want to eat. If she saw an outfit she wanted, she got it. She never skimmed from me, and she never took from me neither. When it's all done, I settle in and smoke—about $1000 per day. That's a typical day; on a rampage, I smoke more.

DEALING AND VIOLENCE

Involvement in crack distribution markets did not come without significant risks. Although women generally have low rates of violence (Baskin et al. 1993), their entry into drug use or selling increased the risks of violence. Sonya spoke of her use of violence to protect her drug dealing turf:

> I was involved in a lot of violence, a lot of physical violence. Sometimes I used weapons, a gun, a knife; with me it didn't matter, anything in my hand was a weapon. Somebody would get in my territory, I'd shoot at them and tell them to get off the corner, you know—that's how it is generally done. It became too much for me to handle alone, so I incorporated my boyfriend into my crew. Sometimes we had weapons. Usually women don't like to be known selling drugs so sometimes they have a male front. There are a lot of women drug dealers. They have males to front off for them, to keep the attention off of them. You have to have some type of protection over yourself. A man who they believe is the boss.

Stephanie described the necessity for violence as self-defense:

> I was selling up and down the block and these two guys went to rip me off. Right, they both approached me, and they kept askin' me what I had. I told them what I had. They kept sayin' let me see, let me see, like they were gonna take whatever I showed them, and I wouldn't. So I was grabbed from behind, and the guy that was standing in front of me, he grabbed my collar. And I was already high and paranoid. And I slashed him. I slashed him with a razor. When I slashed him, his blood shot out. The other guy released me. There was blood everywhere. They let me go. Because of the sight of blood. And then most people didn't expect that type of thing from a person like me. That's why they tried.

Evelyn's use of violence was for the purpose of social control:

Well, there was this one girl. I had . . . it was coincidence. I happened to meet up with her here. I had taught her, ya know, 'cause she was selling drugs and the guys used to take advantage of her and I didn't like that. I despised that. So I took her home with me and I told her, "Look, this is what you're gonna do." And I was teaching her well. One day she went out and it was something she wasn't doing. She wasn't getting high. She came to me and she was $40 short of my money. And I asked her, "Where is my money?" She said, "Ma, look. I was hangin' out and they stole my money." And I got angry with her because of the fact that they played her out for her money. It wasn't the fact that she was short the $40, because I always give her more than that to take home. It was the fact that she let another crackhead come and play her out, when she should know their game. That's exactly why I bust her ass. Because I wanted her to learn.

Fights with buyers and sellers over bad drugs, and robberies of buyers and dealers were the most prevalent forms of systemic violence. Val described an incident over buying bad drugs:

One time, one time, I went uptown to get some. I went to this spot all the time. What happen was, my man that I always get it from, wasn't there. When I say my man, I mean the regular dude that I buy it from, not my man. So we went down this block to this other kid, it was like three o'clock in the morning. He sold us the wrong kind of blow. He sold us some sniff and blow. Sniff and blow, you can't do that. You can't cook that cuz it dissolves. We waste a lot of money. We spent a G that night. Three o'clock in the morning, we go all the way back to Staten Island, cuz we had a cab, try to cook it up, and our shit was just fucked up. You know we was mad. Me and my old man. So we went back up there, got strapped. This was 3:30, now this was all through the same time in the morning. Boom, they was gone. So we came up there the next day. Now mind you, I sell drugs outside every day. So customers be looking for me. So imagine how much money I lost. We's caught up with them and shot one sucker, and the others ran and got away.

Rhonda told a similar story:

I made it my power. If you fuck with me, I am going to screw you. You know. The one guy did owe me some money. This guy, right, I knew he had top notch shit. One Sunday morning, I was thirsty. I went to Jimmy, man, you got some. I said bags. I bought two bags with my last $20. Get back home, the shit was bullshit. I went back to Jimmy, what the fuck is this? I went up in the guy's face and said I want my mother-fucking money.

He jumped back in my face and I cut the mother-fucker. I said don't sell me that shit again. 'Cause I'll stomp your face and ruin your rep.

At times, violent interactions were an outgrowth of neighborhood resistance to drug dealing. Barbara described one incident with a neighbor:

I was selling drugs in Manhattan, out of an apartment building. I was going downstairs when this guy says what are you doing here? He starts hassling me and pushes me. He says "We don't want drugs in this building." I never saw him before. He seemed high. I saw a knife in his hand. I had a .25 caliber. I was shot twice while selling and I was robbed once. They were always users. I always carry a .25. I shot him in the shoulder.

Viewing women's involvement in drug markets in economic and career terms suggests an active role in decision making. The women considered both economic (wages) and nonpecuniary (status) returns from work in the secondary labor market. Further, they realistically assessed their chances of obtaining economic and social support from domestic arrangements. Recognizing their constrained options, these women opted for illicit work, which to them seemed to represent a rational choice.

Stephanie's account reflects this weighing of options:

Well I've been working off and on in different cashiers and stuff like since I'm 15 years old. I always knew that a woman couldn't depend on a man to take care of her. I grew up on public assistance [PA]. I saw how it affected my mom when we were on PA. People always coming to check up on your home. And then I remember going all the way down somewhere, someplace she had to be interviewed for something, but I remember her sitting in front of these people and she began to cry. And, and I just couldn't understand why they were putting her through all this. And I know it was about money. It was about money for her children. And that hurt me, I never liked going through that. I hated having to go to the "face-to-face." I hated even the phrase.

So, I knew that I would have to get a career or something. But work was just menial jobs to me, and they really didn't matter. I never liked, really liked, clerical work and the sittin' down jobs. I left after about two years and did hair. But that was not getting me anything.

Shoplifting was a real big, a big high for me. Even after a day of work and making good tips, I still shoplifted. Occasionally, I forged a few checks. But shoplifting basically was like, that was just, that became in the blood after a while. I really got high off of getting over in stores and things; and many times I had plenty money in my pocket, and I would still go and steal things. People noticed how fine I was looking. People also noticed my talent for taking stuff. I was getting a reputation, respect, on the street.

But then I saw that dealing drugs was a way to make real money. I wasn't going to be on PA. I started freelancing. I purchased coke from a guy that I used to cop for myself. He had a lot of influential people used to come and cop drugs from him. So I began to bring people to him. So at first I was like a steerer. But since I still had a job . . . in the hair business there's a lot of drugs flowing. So I used to buy in large quantities and sell to people at work. I sold to people I knew, who I knew were into drugs. They would get it from me right then and there. And this went on during the course of the day. When I got off from work, I usually went to a friend's house that I know got high. I sat and got high with them, and I usually sold to whoever was in their home.

For Stephanie and many of the other women, criminal career choices provided higher incomes than were reachable by their peers in conventional careers. Further, their involvement and success in the criminal career trajectories placed them in contexts offering status, excitement, and commodities.

Dealing also helped women avoid or exit from the types of street hustling, including prostitution, that characterized women's illicit income-generating strategies. It freed some of the women from oppressive domestic partnerships and provided new ways for women to expand their traditionally limited roles, statuses, and incomes in the street economy.

THE CONSEQUENCES OF FAST LIVING

One of the unintended consequences of dramatically increased access to drugs was an uncontrolled spiral toward addiction. Most women with whom we spoke agreed that having constant cheap supplies on hand increased the danger that they would consume their profits and develop more serious drug-related problems. The highly disciplined drug seller who avoided drug abuse seemed rare and elusive. Instead, a pattern of drug abuse developed as part of the social processes within these neighborhoods and among people involved in local drug markets. The resulting lifestyle was one that was totally out of control.

When I first started dealin' I used to go shopping, buy clothes, buy jewelry, buy my brother and sister stuff. I wasn't doing anything but smokin' reefer. Smokin' crack changed everything. I would shoplift for clothes. Rob, burglarize, deal. I used to carry a .38. I thought all of this was a joke. It all was part of more money and more reputation, and more drugs.

Although Jocorn had her own organization, increased drug use compelled her to look for additional income-generating hustles:

> I was running the organization. I had to find out from my people on the streets if anything was up, if they needed more drugs, or if they didn't have much money, or if it was too hot to deal. Once they were off and running for the day, I would do other things. I was a crook. I would steal cars, take from department stores, write bad checks, or use some of the credit cards I would steal. Sometimes, I would get together with some people and we'd break into apartments. I was always down with crime.

Over time and for a majority of the women, the problem of maintaining an addiction took precedence over all other interests and over participation in other social worlds. The women became enmeshed in deviance, and alienated, both socially and psychologically, from conventional life. Their lives became bereft of conventional involvements, obligations, and responsibilities. The excitement of the lifestyle that may have characterized their early drug dealing gave way to a much more serious and grave daily existence.

The following accounts illustrate the uncertainty and vulnerability of street life. Even for Denise, who ran her own drug organization, street life took its toll:

> I was in a lot of fights. So I had fights over, uh, drugs, or, you know, just manipulation. There's a lot of manipulation in that life. Everybody's tryin' to get over. Everybody will stab you in your back, you know. Nobody gives a fuck about the next person, you know. It's just when you want it, you want it. You know, when you want that drug, you know, you want that drug. There's a lot of lyin', a lot of manipulation. It's, it's, it's crazy! It also got frightening.

Much the same was true for Gazella:

> I'm 34 years old. I ain't no young woman no more, man. Drugs have changed, lifestyles have changed. Kids are killing you now for turf. Yeah, turf, and I was destroyin' myself. I was miserable. I was . . . I was gettin' high all the time to stay up to keep the business going, and it was really nobody I could trust. Things kept getting worse and worse. Everything was spoiling around me.

Thus, regardless of how the women were initiated into drug dealing, the majority ended up in the same role—as street addicts. The women became immersed in their addiction to the exclusion of almost anything else. Here, they describe their descent to rock bottom.

Stephanie: My last year of living on the street, I went through massive changes. I began to sink. My self-esteem sank lower. I became pregnant in the street—as a hooker. I had a baby at this hospital. The baby was born deformed. The baby died. I was havin' no respect for myself. No one else was respecting me. Every relationship I got into with a man, it was constant disrespect and it came to the point of almost getting me killed.

Denise: I didn't have a place to live. I was so tired of living on the streets. My kids had been taken away forever. I was constantly being harassed by the police, like three days out of the week by TNT. I was so depressed. You know how you look bad and feel bad. Before, I had an apartment and other things. But now, nothing. I lost everything. I was at rock bottom. I was so tired of being tired.

April: Oh, my appearance went down. I lost a lot of weight. I was about one hundred pounds. I wasn't eating. Sometimes I wouldn't eat for two or three days. A lot of times, I wouldn't have the time, or I wouldn't want to spend the money to eat—I had to use it to get high).

Monica: I was living in a homeless hotel. I looked tired. I weighed like ninety-two pounds. Everyday I got up with a hangover.

Alicia: So, I had gotten evicted again. I went to live in the park and I cried for six months. I didn't want to be bothered with people. I was always lyin', schemin', and stayin' in abandoned buildings in Bushwick. I got a bad depression 'cause I was sittin' around and lookin' at myself all day.

Darlene: I can tell you, I was afraid of dying. Here I was locked up in a psychiatric unit, locked to a bed. I was tired.

Marginalization from family, friends, children, and work—in short, the loss of traditional life structures—left many of the women vulnerable to chaotic street conditions. For a few, the stresses of street life and the fear of dying on the streets formed sufficient motivation to quit the criminal life.

CONCLUSIONS

Our research suggests that the processes often identified as criminogenic in terms of inner-city males affect women living in these communities as well. For both men and women in a changing economy, filling the market niche for drug products or other illegal goods is a logical entrepreneurial response, particularly when historical avenues to labor-market participation have been truncated by the restructuring of the city and regional economy. The growth in drug use and the rapid expansion of the cocaine and crack markets in the 1980s created a complex drug industry, albeit one that functioned outside formal (legal) systems of regulation and that relied on violence for its maintenance. To the extent that women's roles and prominence have changed in transformed neighborhoods, their involvement in drug selling and other crimes that include street violence reflects the dynamics of the neighborhoods themselves.

REFERENCES

Adler, Patricia. 1985. *Wheeling and Dealing: An Ethnography of an Upper-Level Dealing and Smuggling Community.* New York: Columbia University Press.

Anderson, Elijah. 1990. *Streetwise.* Chicago: University of Chicago Press.

Baskin, Deborah, Ira Sommers, and Jeffrey Fagan. 1993. "The political economy of female violent street crime." *Fordham Urban Law Journal* 20: 401–417.

Belenko, Steven A., Jeffrey Fagan, and Ko-lin Chin. 1991. "Criminal justice responses to crack." *Journal of Research in Crime and Delinquency* 28: 55–74.

Colten, Mary Ellen, and Judith E. Marsh. 1984. "A sex-roles perspective on drug and alcohol use by women." In *Sex Roles and Psychopathology,* ed. Cathy Spatz Widom. New York: Plenum Press.

Erickson, Patricia, and Glenn Murray. 1989. "Sex differences in cocaine use and experiences: A double standard revived?" *American Journal of Drug and Alcohol Abuse* 15: 135–152.

Goldstein, Paul J. 1979. *Prostitution and Drugs.* Cambridge, MA: Lexington Books.

Goldstein, Paul J., Barry Spunt, Patricia Belluci, Thomas Miller. 1991. "Volume of cocaine use and violence: A comparison between men and women." *Journal of Drug Issues* 21: 345–367.

Hser, Yih-Hing, Douglas Anglin, and William H. McGlothlin. 1987. "Sex differences in addict careers: 1. Initiation of use." *American Journal of Drug and Alcohol Abuse* 13: 33–57.

Jencks, Christopher. 1991. "*Is the American underclass growing?*" In *The Urban Underclass,* ed. Christopher Jencks and Paul E. Peterson. Washington, DC: Brookings Institution.

Johnson, Bruce D., Paul J. Goldstein, Edward Preble, James Schmeidler, Douglas Lipton, Barry Spunt, and Thomas Miller. 1985. *Taking Care of Business: The Economics of Crime by Heroin Abusers.* Lexington, MA: Lexington Books.

Kleiman, Mark. 1992. *Against Excess: Drug Policy for Results.* New York: Basic Books.

Mieczkowski, Thomas. 1986. "Geeking up and throwing down: Heroin street life in Detroit." *Criminology* 24: 645–666.

Murphy, Sheila, Dan Waldorf, and Craig Reinarman. 1991. "Drifting into dealing: Becoming a cocaine seller." *Qualitative Sociology* 13: 321–343.

Rosenbaum, Marsha. 1981. *Women and Heroin.* New Brunswick, NJ: Rutgers University Press.

Sassen-Koob, Sassia. 1989. "New York City's informal economy." In *The Informal Economy: Studies in Advanced and Less Developed Countries,* ed. Alejandro Portes, Manuel Castells, and Lauren A. Benton. Baltimore, MD: Johns Hopkins University Press.

Stephens, Richard C. 1991. *The Street Addict Role: A Theory of Heroin Addiction.* Albany: State University of New York Press.

Wacquant, Loic D., and William J. Wilson. 1989. "The costs of racial and class exclusion in the inner city." *Annals of the American Academy of Political and Social Science,* no. 501: 8–25.

Waldorf, Dan, Craig Reinarman, and Sheila Murphy. 1991. *Cocaine Changes: The Experiences of Using and Quitting.* Philadelphia: Temple University Press.

Williams, Terry. 1989. *Cocaine Kids.* Reading, MA: Addison-Wesley.

Zimmer, L. 1987. *Operation Pressure Point: An Occasional Paper of the Center for Crime and Justice.* New York: New York University School of Law.

CHAPTER 4

Negotiating the Streets

WOMEN, POWER, AND RESISTANCE IN STREET-LIFE SOCIAL NETWORKS

Christopher W. Mullins

INTRODUCTION

Drugs and violence are inextricably connected on the streets of U.S. cities. Much work has established the association of drug use with other forms of criminal behavior, including violence. This symbiosis is a product of personal, neighborhood, subcultural, and systemic factors, making it nearly impossible to isolate the individual influences of these factors (Baumer 1994; Baumer et al. 1998; Conklin 2003; Goldstein 1985; Goldstein et al. 1991; Grogger 2000; Ousey and Lee 2002; Wright and Decker 1994). In this chapter, I will follow Wright and Decker's (1994) characterization of criminal embeddedness as inseparable from a culture of desperate partying. Participation in this subculture produces a mutually supporting loop of drug use and other criminal involvements.

Although "life as party" is clearly dominated by men, scholars have found varying levels of female participation in it (Shover and Honaker 1992; Shover and Henderson 1995). Most career criminals are male, but women are not completely absent from criminogenic social networks. Although there are key differences between male and female criminal careers, or between male and female embedded offenders, deep involvement in drug use, drug sale, property offenses, and violence (especially assaultive violence) is characteristic of all heavy offenders regardless of gender. Yet male offense rates, even in embedded and career populations, are higher and composed of more serious offenses. Men are also more likely to become embedded offenders, so much so that it is only recently that criminologists have begun to explore issues of criminal careers among female offenders (DeLisi 2002).

One possible reason for this pattern also strongly shapes the experiences of those women who do enter career offending: male dominance of the streets and street-life social networks. Female criminals, including drug users, face a powerful, institutionalized sexism in the strongly segregated criminal underworld (Maher 1997; Mullins and Wright 2003; Steffensmeier and Terry 1986; Steffensmeier 1983). Such structures limit opportunities for involvement in criminal activities, limiting the roles that women are allowed to take (e.g., look-out in a burglary, corner dealer or runner in a drug sale), which limits the financial return female offenders receive.

The misogyny internalized by male offenders also increases the probability of violent and sexual victimization. The streets are hard for everyone, but they are especially so for women. When presented with social messages of inferiority and rejection, some individuals internalize these messages and conform to expectations, yet others respond through creation of identities of resistance; these self-perceptions frame counternormative social actions and interactions as a way to reject marginalization and reassert a sense of personal power and meaningfulness (Ettore 1992; Friedman and Alicea 1995; Giroux 1983; MacLeod 1995).

This chapter will examine the contours of violence within the lives of criminally embedded women in Saint Louis, Missouri. The chapter examines the general criminal involvement of women embedded in street-life social networks, including their participation in sex work, drug-market activities, and acquisitive violent crimes. It further explores the ways many women respond to the widespread sexism they experience by creating identities resistant to general conditions of disenfranchisement.

The sociology of gender literature has suggested broad (even stereotypical) ascriptions of mainstream masculinities as focused on instrumental behaviors and characteristics, while framing femininities as typically focused on expressive, socioemotive elements. Yet literatures of violence, especially subculturally based violence on the streets, have provided an oppositional characterization. Men's assaultive violence is characterized as expressive; such acts are seen as part and parcel of expressing and maintaining a masculine identity and image on the streets, and women's assaultive violence has been described as instrumental acts growing out of the need for self-protection. This position is consistent with what Anderson calls the "pathology and powerless perspective" that women's violence is a response to their prior victimization (see Anderson's introduction and chapter 1, this volume).

This gendered dichotomy is, clearly, too simplistic. Existing work establishes that male prestige-based violence has instrumental, pragmatic elements (Anderson 1999; Mullins et al. 2004). Also, women's use of violence in these contexts can be expressive as well (Campbell 1999). A long-standing conceptual problem in the study of gender and crime is the attempt to straitjacket men and women into traditionally dichotomous gender roles. Although this tendency has produced a workable explanation for men's violence, such attempts to tie violence directly to gender have done little to help us understand women's violence (Miller 2002; Miller and Mullins 2006).

Some scholars have suggested that women who embody violence are enacting "masculinized" gender identities (Anderson 1999; Baskin and Sommers 1998; Messerschmidt 2004; Messerschmidt 1997). Others point out that women's violence in street-life contexts occurs more often for self-defense and survival, suggesting that these presentations of self lack any true aspect of gender identity (Maher 1997).

As with any polarized academic debate, the truth may lie between the poles. It is possible that women on the streets use violence both as a form of resistance to male dominance and as a form of survival behavior. Social behavior need never be reduced to an either/or situation; a single action can result from multiple social forces simultaneously.

According to Connell (1987), gender is not simply dichotomous, but rather exists as a set of oppositional pluralities. There are dominant and subordinate masculinities, as well as emphasized femininities that vary greatly according to social context. These positions are hierarchically arranged, with hegemonic masculinity being not only the apex of social valuation but also the point of comparison for other constructions. When examining links between gender and violence, we must be cognizant of the variances of gender demands within a given social context. Connell's theorization also opens up analytical space to explore the creation and implementation of resistant gender identities that can form from a mixture of characteristics.

Contemporary feminist work also realizes that gender is dynamic rather than static. Structural gender demands exist, but they have little influence or reality unless put into action. Individual actors create and recreate social structures when they "do gender." Building upon the work of Garfinkel (1967) and Goffman (1955), West and Zimmerman assert that "participants in interaction organize their various and manifold activities to reflect or express gender, and they are disposed to perceive the behavior of others in a similar light" (1987). The process of actualizing normative gender expectations—commonly called "doing gender"—guides the ways that behavioral decisions are made, self-presentations are constructed, and others' actions are predicted and interpreted; social actors engage and reproduce gendered structures in their daily, mundane behavior. In this conceptual approach, gender is "much more than a role or an individual characteristic: it is a mechanism whereby situated social action contributes to the reproduction

of social structure" (Candace and Fenstermaker 1995). Social action is the
scaffolding of social structure; it is through the enactment of gendered behavioral demands that gendered social structure is reproduced within each
social interaction. This approach implies that gender is "potentially omni-
relevant" to all actions and activities.

Much recent feminist work has explored how female offenders respond
to inequity through the establishment of a counterhegemonic gender identity as a form of resistance. For example, Maher (1997) thoroughly explored how street-level sex workers/drug users enacted resistance to both
broader and more immediate inequalities though a multitude of survival
strategies. Friedman and Alicea (1995) examined how primarily middle
class women drug users (of heroin, specifically) established a counterhegemonic identity and resisted gender and class-based social expectations of
their behaviors and identities. Miller (2001) examined how gang-member
identities among younger women often arose out of experiences of social
rejection and marginalization.

Building upon this work, this chapter examines the criminal contexts
of the lives of women drug users in Saint Louis, Missouri. Drawing upon
open-ended interviews with active offenders, it explores how women negotiated participation in street-life social networks. It especially looks at how
some of these women constructed identities of resistance as a broader part of
subcultural embeddedness.

RESEARCH METHODS

The interviews used here were collected in Saint Louis, Missouri, a
moderately sized Midwestern city. This locale is highly racially segregated
(Massey and Denton 1993), has been hit hard by deindustrialization, and
has experienced substantial levels of white flight since the 1960s (Suarez
1999). These forces generate neighborhoods burdened with conditions of
concentrated poverty and disadvantage (Wilson 1987), known to produce
strong street-life social networks (Anderson 1990), often dominated by a
culture of desperate partying (Shover and Honaker 1992; Shover and Henderson 1995; Wright and Decker 1994; Wright 1997).

The sample reported on here was drawn from four separately conducted interview projects in Saint Louis over a five-year period. Drug robbers were interviewed in 1998 and 1999, carjackers in 2000, snitches in
2001, and retaliators in 2002 and 2003 (Jacobs 2000; Rosenfeld 2003;
Mullins et al. 2004). The total sample is twenty-four women. The interviewees were all African American. The drug robbery sample contributed
four cases; the carjacking sample contributed four; the snitching sample
contributed four; the retaliation sample contributed ten; two cases were

combined from multiple interviews of the same respondent in different samples. This represents all of the women interviewed within the projects. Although females were purposefully sought out in all of the projects, more directed measures were taken during the criminal retaliation project to interview women, as there were gender-specific questions within the interview protocol. The mean age for the sample was twenty-eight years, with eighteen the youngest and fifty-nine the oldest. No significant differences in age existed between the samples.

Although secondary analysis of existing data is very common in quantitative studies, it is rarer within qualitative work (Sampson and Laub 1993). The actual merging of data sets for secondary analysis is even rarer, both quantitatively and qualitatively. A scarce few examples of this technique can be found in the health-care literature (Heaton 1998). A rationale for combining these potentially disparate samples is required. The data sets for this project were chosen from data originally collected to study the accomplishment of specific offenses. Although collected at different times, all samples drew on the same social and geographic region: African American neighborhoods in northern Saint Louis that have experienced a significant concentration of disadvantage. They are all essentially drawn from the same population (predominantly working- and lower-class, criminally involved African Americans in Saint Louis).

The interviews in all the data sets followed an open-ended interview protocol that primarily focused on issues surrounding motivation and accomplishment of the crime emphasized by the particular project. The questions were designed to elicit thick descriptions of criminal incidents, with interviewers probing respondents for a fuller depiction of exactly what happened, who else was present (and the role such persons played), how the offense in question was carried out, what precise proximate and distant motivations existed, and, if appropriate, what was done with the proceeds of the crime. Additional demographic questions were asked at the end of the interview (for instance, age, educational attainment, marital status, parental status, work status). The data were collected under the guidelines for human-subjects research outlined by the Institutional Review Board at the University of Missouri–Saint Louis. Accordingly, the participants were promised confidentiality and anonymity. The interviews lasted from one to two hours; they were tape-recorded with the permission of the interviewee, then transcribed verbatim. The tape recordings were then destroyed. I received the data in transcript form, with interviewees only identified by pseudonym.

One of the strongest qualitative checks on the validity of data is the emergence of consensus among interviewees concerning the subject matter of the interviews. As broad themes emerged during analysis, and numerous subjects reported the same things in the same ways, I became more assured that I had tapped into valid categories of knowledge (Weller and Romney 1988). Due to the sampling procedures, this combined sample is not representative of all individuals, or even criminal offenders, within these communities. However, the samples do provide a reasonable cross-section of individuals with regard to age, gender, offenses committed, and depth of criminal involvement. Since only a comparatively small number of individuals was sampled, and this sampling was distinctly nonrandom, it is not possible to determine the representiveness of trends and patterns uncovered.

FINDINGS

All but one of the respondents were drug-involved, most quite heavily. This was not an express aim of the sampling procedures, which, as discussed above, focused on other aspects of criminal involvement. It is, however, a strong reflection of the more systemic intersection of drugs and crime on the streets. Most of the women used crack, many on a daily basis. The few noncrack users smoked marijuana. Two mentioned heroin use. None mentioned other substances. As the women became more embedded in drugs and in street life, their experience with using violence and being violently victimized increased. The women most strongly invested in drug use and sales were those with the greatest experiences with violence. Twenty-two of the women discussed being violently victimized at some point in their lives; most discussed recent (within the last twelve months) victimization experiences. Only two respondents made no mention of victimization.

These women were raised, and currently lived, within violent neighborhoods with strong and active street criminal networks. This situation provided access to multiple criminal networks and experiences, and established a personal habitus of ubiquitous potential for victimization that the women had to negotiate, not only in daily life but, as explored later, in identity construction and presentations of self. The following exchange between an interviewer and Big Mix illustrates wide-spread perceptions and attitudes of women in this sample toward violence and toward their experiences on the streets.

INT.: It sounds like you're doing a lot of hustling and stuff that involves . . . violence. Is it uncomfortable for you to be living like this?
BIG MIX: It don't bother me . . . I don't feel unsafe. I don't feel the safest but I don't . . . feel unsafe either. I feel comfortable . . . that's what I'm used to.

Most of the women here knew that victimization was a constant possibility. Safety was not a commodity easily obtainable. Yet this was the nature of the neighborhoods they had grown up in, a daily experience to which they had reconciled themselves.

CRIMINAL INVOLVEMENT

The intersections of drugs, crime, and street life are manifold. All of the women interviewed admitted to being involved in a variety of criminal acts, which framed the context for their drug involvement and experiences (including uses) of violence.

Several women in the sample admitted to prostitution. This is not surprising, as prostitution is one of the more frequent ways that women involved in street life and drug use acquire needed cash. Marginalization from other underground economic activities, and the subsequent push into sex work, no doubt heightens the antagonistic views and relationships many women here held toward men. Involvement in sex work was not strictly limited to streetwalking, but often involved a multifaceted series of activities designed to gain economic resources whenever possible.

Kimmy's approach is a good illustration. She at first described herself as a stripper and a dancer, but later said that, when she danced, she and her partners would "you know do all kinds of shit females do, whatever." She also described a relationship she had with "a sugar daddy—a older guy that take care of the little females or whatever," who would pay her bills and buy her things, though she insisted throughout the interview she never had sex with the man. When asked why she hadn't had relations with the individual, Kimmy claimed that he was too "Big, fat, I mean I could try to do something . . . it's just some things you just can't bring yourself to do. I don't care how much money he put on the table." Although Kimmy said she used the money from dancing and hooking primarily to pay bills and support her six-year-old daughter, she made frequent references to drug use and being unable and unwilling to hold a steady job.

Asked why she prostituted, Baby Doll explained, "Sometimes when I have a gun, you know, I ain't got use of a gun, so I have to use my body to get what I want." Further queried about why she would commit armed robbery, she replied, "You don't make that much [in prostitution]. You might make about $20 here, $15 there, it be kind of slow. I smoke crack, not just no little crack, I like the crack." Baby Doll made the connections between her drug use and crime clear: the constant pressure to obtain crack drove her to a multitude of criminal activities. Nicole similarly described how her criminal activities flowed from her drug use:

> I was completely dry, I was losing money. I stayed sick [from heroin withdrawal] . . . I had to do something. I wasn't gonna find no job. I didn't like

the hours ... [ended up] snatching purses, reading people's credit cards, opening people's mail. I was doing some wild shit ... breaking into cars ... stealing radios ... I'm open to anything, I'm open for everything.

As mentioned above, a few of the women interviewed had marginal involvement in both street life and drug usage, but the majority described lives strongly bounded by drug use and the criminal activities often associated with life on the streets. These included robbery, burglary, petty theft, prostitution, drug dealing, and, for some, involved an almost constant exposure to the potential for assaultive violence.

DRUG MARKET VIOLENCE

As is the case in any urban area, involvement in drug markets, for both low-level dealers and customers, eventually meant involvement in violence. This systemic violence (Conklin 2003; Goldstein 1985; Goldstein et al. 1991; Grogger 2000; Ousey and Lee 2002) is characteristic of urban drug markets, especially crack markets. Women in this sample were both perpetrators and victims of such events. Those few who engaged in street-level dealing discussed the omnipresent threat of robbery that faced dealers. Sugar, in discussing how she protected herself against such victimization, said,

I ain't gonna let nothing go ... anybody can just walk up and take my shit [drugs]. Come and punch me and take my dope and take my mother'ing weed, they'll be thinking I ain't shit. [They will think] I ain't standing up on mine ... I ain't going for that. I stood out there and worked for that shit, and not them.

Although she did not carry a gun while dealing (as Saint Louis police at the time were heavily enforcing firearms laws [see Jacobs 2000]), if she were robbed there would be, she explained, consequences for the robber. If a woman robbed her, she would seek revenge, she insisted, by hunting her victimizer down and assaulting her, or worse. But, if a man robbed her, her male associates, she felt confident, could exact revenge: "If a nigger [male] step in—I got a whole lot of niggers—I know they can break him down." As Mullins, Wright, and Jacobs (2004) uncovered, women often rely upon male associates to either act as a deterrent for violent victimization on the streets or to carry out vengeance if required.

Other women in the sample worked the other side of this equation. Robbing drug dealers was seen as a lucrative, even if highly risky, endeavor. Men and women alike discussed the issue of potential retaliation for such crime. (For a more extensive discussion of this see Jacobs 2000 and Jacobs et al. 2000.) Yoyo, an admitted drug robber, explained how she avoided payback:

If anybody come tripping ... they [male associates] already know what's up. So I already got them where they can be ... they got my back, trigger-happy ... I just went up and told them I robbed a victim today and she seen my face so therefore if I have any static [trouble], if any mother-fuckers act like they gonna do something to me, just get my back ... as long as I got my partners to back me up, I'm cool.

Like male offenders, Yoyo presented a face of bravado and toughness, appearing unafraid of the consequences of her criminal activities. Yet in opposition to the language and the presentation of self seen in male robbers (Wright and Decker 1994), here is a self-assuredness produced by having violent male peers to call upon.

The discussions provided by both Sugar and Yoyo illustrate the secondary position of women within Saint Louis drug markets. Although some of these women did have involvement in the drug trade, and in systemic drug trade violence, these interactions were predicated on their relationships with men—specifically, the ability of men to provide "back up" in case of violence.

VICCING

Many scholars have established the prevalence of viccing on the streets (Maher 1997; Miller 1998; Mullins and Wright 2003). Setting up robbery targets by appearing sexually available, then taking advantage of the target when, literally, his pants were down, has strong pragmatic elements as well as embodying a form of gender resistance. In a practical sense, it allows women to take advantage of men's ignorance about victimization risk, an ignorance that arises out of broader sexist street norms: as the men typically view women as objects of desire, they do not perceive them as threats. A number of women on the streets are well aware of this fact, and capitalize on it. Further, it serves as a way for women to feel they are getting over on men who oppress and otherwise take advantage of them in other social locales. By turning the tables of exploitation, women not only accomplish their immediate goals of property and drug acquisition, but also manage to assert a level of control over males, something rare within a street-life context.

Many of the female offenders described scenarios in which they set men up for criminal victimization by appearing sexually available. Some did it for their own gain; others were working for male colleagues. Big Mix describes an archetypical viccing incident:

I acted like I was going to take him home, lay him real good.... that gets them every time ... we was talking, trying to talk up on some ass and everything, and I'm acting like I'm falling for it, for real ... they want

some ass and that shouldn't be an issue . . . 'cos if you a big baller [a successful criminal with strong street credibility] then you can get some ass
any time. But you're gonna talk up on this ass and get yourself jacked . . .
We got a back alley in the back of our house . . . they [three male co-
offenders] jacked him or whatever. He just ran. And I screamed like I act
like I didn't know what was going on and I ran.

This excerpt is typical in three respects. First, it shows how Big Mix draws
upon the appearance of sexual availability to place her victim in a situation
where her male co-offenders can catch him by surprise. She maintains the
charade by acting unaware as the men rob the victim. This not only protects her from future retaliation but also allows her to use a similar tactic in
the future. Second, whereas Maher (1997) and Miller (1998) provide discussions of women accomplishing the victimization on their own (often because of a lack of male assistance), the women in this study often discussed
working with (or for) men. Third, the manner in which Big Mix inverts the
power relationship with her victim is noteworthy. A "big baller" could get a
woman anytime he wants, and he thought he was playing his street reputation into a sexual conquest; yet, in an instant, he became a disempowered
victim, with no choice but to comply with the robbery.

Popo also described playing upon men's desires for sexual gratification
when working with men to set up robbery victims.

Before I go to the club we [she and her male accomplices] basically get
the plan together that we're going to do. And we going to play it and
how we gonna get to the point where we gonna get 'em at . . . basically
I go up to the old heads, you know, they flirt, whatever. They like to
suck your pussy and all that old kind of stuff. So, basically I . . . get them
where I want to.

Teaser described drawing upon this technique to exact vengeance on a guy
who had done her wrong. In order to keep the element of surprise, she used
one of her female friends to set him up.

I had my girlfriend . . . got him real drunk or whatever. [He] passed out.
After she left the club with him and went to a hotel . . . she gave me the
keys [to his apartment] . . . took as much as we can, looked for his money
'cos he usually have a safe in there.

Such offenses do not always come off so easily. Popo described an attempt at viccing that went wrong. Discussing the source of a series of visible
bruises to the interviewers, she explained: "This bitch got it on me because
I was on her big daddy. I was trying to get him. I was going to get him,

too . . . but it didn't work out. Her and her little homies jumped me . . . she didn't know what the fuck I was doing. She just didn't want me on her man." Popo had run up against another aspect of female uses of interpersonal violence—status challenges (which I shall discuss).

ATTITUDE AND IMAGE

Maher (1997) described how many of the sex workers she interviewed presented a "crazy" persona to avoid victimization. Many women in this chapter's sample presented images of toughness very similar to those of men (Mullins 2006). Since gender issues are highly salient on the streets, many of these women presented images of strength and toughness especially *in opposition to* male attitudes about appropriate female behavior. For example, Popo explained:

> I just like to fight. It's in me, I just can't help that. I beat up my boyfriend . . . if he say the wrong thing . . . I like to be bad. I don't know why. My grandma say I need to go get the Lord in me but I try to find him and he say 'You too God damn bad. You got to get out of here.' I don't think he wants me. I'm serious. I'm a bad person . . . My own family don't fuck with me. That's why I can't be around them because they think I'm crazy . . . [I had a] so-called . . . man but he didn't fuck with me either. I'm saying he want to be with me when I want to go out and do some dirt. I can come out with some money or some dope he cool. Shit, fuck him, [he comes around] when he want some pussy or something. . . . my attitude too God damn bad for me to take rules from any motherfucking body. That's just how I am.

In this excerpt, Popo defined herself, and her street persona, against normative gender demands for subordinate femininity as embodied in the family, in the church, and in romantic relationships with men. She rejected the typical role demands and embraced an identity that is similar to street masculinity in its insistence upon individuality, agency, and toughness.

Similarly, Lady Bug rejected more subordinate femininities when she described herself as undesirable to men, saying,

> Don't nobody want to marry me, 'cause they say I'm too mean. I act like a man. This one dude I'm dating now, I had to beat his ass. He's scared of me. He said don't bring no gun in my house 'cause I told him my stories and stuff. But when that bitch want some money, he know who to call and there go my dumb ass [to commit a crime for him].

Nicole provided a similar self-description when asked if she was married or involved with anyone. "['I'm] [t]oo violent for boyfriends, they just don't like me . . . I ain't got no man in my life. I'm too thuggish for that . . . we would be ready to kill each other . . . ain't no lie. He can't like what I do and he trying to do it and trying to keep me at home, no."

Not only does she reject the dominant ideal of a passive woman as incompatible with her street-based identity; she also rejects the male-imposed segregation of criminal networks on the streets. This sensibility is vividly embodied in the following exchange:

INT: Why do they call you [Lady Ice]?
LADY ICE: Because they say I'm just too cold! . . . Nobody can handle me . . .
    I'm very tough. I just can't let anybody handle me.

In part, these expressions clearly mirror Maher's (1997) discussions of being "crazy," yet, as many of the women discussed, theirs was much more than mere presentation of self. Actual violence backed up this image construction; it was not merely a victimization-deterrent façade.

STATUS CHALLENGES

This form of attitude and image construction often leads to interpersonal violence. Work on masculinities and violence has strongly shown the enactment of a street persona as a key causative factor in male–male violence episodes (Anderson 1999; Messerschmidt 2000; Messerschmidt 2004; Messerschmidt 1997; Mullins et al. 2004; Oliver 1994). Typically drawing upon the framework of masculinity challenges, this work has framed male–male violence episodes as a way to establish and maintain "juice" (street credibility). In comparison, women were less likely to engage in street violence than men were, and, when they did, were less likely to use weapons or produce fatalities. Similarly, although many women–women assaultive events concerned status and the maintenance of respect on the streets, many of these status challenges had slightly different triggers then those among similarly situated men. Like men, women used violence to protect their reputations, but what would be seen as a slight was different, in some cases, between the sexes.

Romantic entanglements with men were one of the most common subjects of violent encounters among women. In a typical scenario, Hodemont described why another woman had attacked her on the streets:

[It was] over my baby's Daddy . . . he [the man] was messing around with both of us and I had no idea . . . I got pregnant by him. Me and her had a few words . . . she saw me and she and her other friends they had jumped me . . . had me out on the ground and stuff like that . . . she didn't care about me, she didn't care about my baby. I mean, hell, she . . . she could have waited 'til I had had my baby . . . she did it on purpose cause I was pregnant by the guy she wanted . . . but he fucked me last and she wanted to fight me over my man . . . [that's] disrespect.

Lady Ice described a very similar situation.

Me and the girl we had a fight earlier [over a guy] so I beat her up and she came back with eleven girls a couple of days later, hit me in the head with a bat . . . I had to go to the hospital . . . she started it . . . she called me "bitches" and "whores" and "mama kick you ass" and all this . . . [I saw her in the ER and] beat her up real bad and banged her head into the soda machine . . . I didn't say nothing. Just walked up to her and I just sort of beat the crap out of her.

KLOC also described this sort of interpersonal assault.

Recently when this girl was messing around with my baby's daddy . . . and I found out, eventually I seen her again and we got to fighting in the shop. Hard as we could.

As these excerpts show, the women's violence is not only an issue of persona but also a way to avoid victimization in a dangerous world. The personas are often backed up with violence. Like men's in similar social locations, these episodes had the potential to produce a long-running tit-for-tat exchange of assaults between the parties, and between their friends and relatives.

Not all assaults committed by women arose out of problematic romantic relationships with men. As discussed above, women involved in drug markets were ready to retaliate against people who compromised the economic successes of their endeavors. Kimmy, for instance, described a violent outburst after discovering that one of her coworkers robbed her. (Recall that Kimmy supplemented the meager income from unsteady legitimate work with stripping and prostitution.) On one job, while servicing a client in a hotel bathroom, she discovered that one of her stripping partners had run off with the money. After she returned home, an associate informed her that the thief's cousin was down the block at a local convenience store. Kimmy hurried down to the store and severely beat the woman. In justifying her use of violence against this women, she said:

Anybody fuck with my money, I feel you fucking with my daughter. 'Cause that's where my money go. I'm not doing this shit [prostitution and stripping] because I like doing this shit. I'm doing this shit because I have to . . . I live check to check, so when I go out here and shake my ass for somebody, [it does not matter if you are] male or female, don't fuck with me.

Save for the attachment to the actualization of a parent identity, such discourse is a near mirror of male criminals talking about their financial interests and how they respond to others who threaten the monetary returns of illegal enterprises.

DISCUSSION

Drug use, violence, victimization, and other criminality were tightly intertwined in the lives of the women interviewed here. Once a woman was embedded in street-life subculture, these elements were inseparable. Although the sample is neither random nor representative, it does provide a window into the lives of women on the streets of Saint Louis. Using a strategy like that of Baskin and Sommers (1998), these interviews sought out intensely criminal women to capture a female perspective on criminal enactment. Although there is a small variation in the criminality of the women, there is not enough to draw strong comparisons and contrasts among them. It is also not possible to separate the effects of race, gender, and socioeconomic class from the effect of interaction in underworld social networks. (All of these women were African American and lived in an area of Saint Louis plagued with concentrated disadvantage.)

The interlinkages of drugs and violence within this data both parallel and diverge from existing literature. Not surprisingly, economic compulsive relationships abounded. As explored above, much of the crime described here—violent and nonviolent—was a direct product of drug use, with the main motivation for the offense being to obtain money to support substance use. Like other male offenders studied in Saint Louis (e.g., Wright and Decker 1994), these were "smorgasbord" offenders, pursuing whatever criminal opportunities presented themselves. Yet, like Maher's (1997) sex workers, they found opportunities for offending highly limited, and often found themselves either working at the edges of the underground economy (such as doing sex work, taking minor roles in street-level drug sales, helping men set up other men for victimization), or taking extreme risks for minor rewards (for instance, viccing drug dealers and other "old heads"). However, these crimes were not the limit of the intersection of drugs and offending in their lives.

A few of the women were tied into to the broader systemic connections of drugs and violence, especially in relation to drug markets. Although open-air drug markets are not so violent in Saint Louis as in other locales (Jacobs 1999; Jacobs 2000), the risks of violent victimization, especially robbery, were significant.

A less discussed interconnection of drugs and violence, one that goes beyond the market-oriented systemic explanations, is a broader, subcultural fusion of elements. Life as party integrates crime, violence, drug use, and subcultural identify processes into a holistic system of self-presentation and social action. It is here that many of the daily violences that women on the streets of Saint Louis experienced (whether as offender or victim) came together. Once drawn into subcultural networks through a variety of processes, women experienced systematic, nearly continual, misogyny. Such experiences engender attitudes of violence that are both self-protective and resistive to this male dominance.

Identities of resistance developed most immediately out of experiencing intense sexual segregation on the streets. Many of the strongest expressions of counterhegemonic senses of self directly occurred in the context of women talking about their relationships (or more precisely, lack of relationships) with men. The high degree of disdain and disregard that men in street-life subculture have for women is well known. The women interviewed here not only acknowledged those perspectives but were more than willing to return the same level of distrust, disgust, and dislike. Being marginalized from criminal networks and drug-dealing activities, and being treated as little more than objects for the satisfaction of male desire, seemed reason enough to construct personal ideologies of self strongly counter to the general demands of emphasized femininity experienced by the interviewees.

It is possible that the women's current experiences, as highlighted in this chapter, are merely the most recent events in long histories of disadvantage and inequality. Miller (2001) explored how adolescent female gang members used the gang and its constituent structures of street-life subculture to construct and present images of self that flew in the face of the demands of normative female gender roles. By exploring the experiences of rejection that many of her interviewees faced, she grounded their adoption of gang subculture, especially the "one of the guys" gender position, in a rejection of social marginalization. Although the women interviewed here discussed little about their childhood and adolescent experiences, save a few accounts of early physical and sexual victimization experience within their families and neighborhoods, they were all raised with triple race, gender, and class stigmas. It is doubtful that these identity formation processes can be solely attributed to participation in the criminal subculture of the streets of Saint Louis, but street life clearly intensified and assisted these processes.

Although recent work has rejected Pollak's (1950) assertion that women are only criminal as a result of relationships with male co-offenders, the same work has reaffirmed that women are most likely to be criminal, and exhibit the greatest criminality, in association with male co-offenders. This likelihood results from opportunities provided by social network association (Mullins and Wright 2003), potential socialization influences (DeLisi 2002), and a synergy of crime intensification that emerges out of mixed-gender criminal group dynamics (Miller 2001; Peterson et al. 2001; Haynie 2002).

At first glance, there appears a contradiction between, on the one hand, women's rejection of hegemonic femininity and, on the other hand, their association with males and with the more general findings of strong ties between female offending and intergender relationships. However, two other studies from Saint Louis (Miller 1998; Mullins and Wright 2003) both uncovered rare, gender-homogeneous offending networks. In these groups, the women had, earlier in their criminal careers, been part of male-dominated offending networks. Due to various circumstances, they separated, voluntarily or involuntarily, from those networks and created their own crews, while maintaining some level of street-based contacts with male-dominated networks. Women who expressed the strongest resistance to men and to subordinate femininities described similar patterns and social positions.

Women offenders present an interpretive problem for criminologists. The characteristics of female criminality show both convergence and divergence with male offending patterns and experiences. Recent feminist criminology has focused on separating these varying threads. It has attempted to provide a general understanding of the intersection of gender and crime, as well as the specifics unique to women's experiences. Explaining female street violence has proved more theoretically problematic than explaining male street violence, due to mainstream and subcultural gender-role expectations. The idea of aggression and violence as quintessentially male has been framed as a truism within criminology. Conceptualizations that hold to a bifurcated view of gender define female violence either as "unexplainable" or as an example of the "masculinization" of women.

Recent directions in feminist work have pointed out that gender is a nondichotomous social structure, with a plurality of forms in certain social contexts. Variant gendered positions are defined in opposition and relation to one another.

Even in mainstream cultural contexts, scholarship has established that women, on the whole, are more aggressive than stereotypical gender demands would dictate. Although there are gender differences in what is defined as aggression and in the form it is likely to take (verbal, emotional, social, physical), overall levels of aggression are relatively equal between men and women. The women in these Saint Louis interviews are more violent than is typical in other contexts. In other words, they are more violent than many men in mainstream cultural contexts.

The practicalities of self-protection clearly molded the behavior of interviewees, yet the self-presentations uncovered in these accounts exhibit a level of commitment to and identification with violence that goes beyond self-preservation. This is especially highlighted in intragender violence and status challenges. Crystallized in the antimale attitudes uncovered, the identities of resistance developed by criminally embedded women on the streets of Saint Louis drew upon violent presentations of self and action. They did so not only because this form of self-presentation was practical, but also because it was in stark contrast to the essential elements of a subordinated femininity pushed upon them by normative elements of society (e.g., their families), as well as by the crime-embedded men within street-life social networks.

REFERENCES

Anderson, Elijah. 1990. *Streetwise: Race, Class, and Change in an Urban Community*. Chicago: University of Chicago Press.

———. 1999. *Code of the Street: Decency, Violence, and the Moral Life of the Inner City*. New York: W. W. Norton.

Baskin, Deborah R., and Ira B. Sommers. 1998. *Casualties of Community Disorder: Women's Career in Violent Crime*. Boulder, CO: Westview.

Baumer, Eric. 1994. "Poverty, crack and crime: A cross-city analysis." *Journal of Research in Crime and Delinquency* 31: 311–327.

———, Janet Lauritsen, Richard Rosenfeld, and Richard Wright. 1998. "The influence of crack cocaine on robbery, burglary, and homicide rates: A cross-city longitudinal analysis." *Journal of Research in Crime and Delinquency* 35: 316–340.

Campbell, Anne. 1999. "Female gang members' social representations of aggression." In *Female Gangs in America*. Edited by Meda Chesny-Lind and John H. Hagedorn. Chicago: Lakeview Press.

Conklin, John. 2003. *Why Crime Rates Fell*. Boston, MA: Allyn and Bacon.

Connell, R. W. 1987. *Gender and Power: Society, the Person, and Sexual Politics*. Stanford, CA: Stanford University Press.

DeLisi, Matt. 2002. "Not just a boy's club: An empirical assessment of female career criminals." *Women and Criminal Justice* 13: 27–44.

Ettore, Elizabeth. 1992. *Women and Substance Use*. New Brunswick, NJ: Rutgers University Press.

Friedman, Jennifer, and Marisa Alicea. 1995. "Women and heroin: The path of resistance and its consequences." *Gender and Society* 9: 432–449.

Garfinkel, Harold. 1967. *Studies in Ethnomethodology*. Englewood Cliffs, NJ: Prentice Hall.

Giroux, Henry A. 1983. *Theory and Resistance in Education*. London: Heinemann Education Books.

Goffman, Erving. 1955. *Interaction Ritual: Essays on Face-to-Face Behavior*. Garden City, NY: Anchor.

———. 1959. *The Presentation of Self in Everyday Life*. Garden City, NY: Doubleday.

Goldstein, Paul J. 1985. "The drugs/violence nexus: A tripartite conceptual framework." *The Journal of Drug Issues* 15: 493–506.

———, Patricia A. Belluccii, Barry J. Spunt, and Thomans Miller. 1991. "Volume of cocaine use and violence: A comparison between men and women." *The Journal of Drug Issues* 21: 345–367.

Grogger, Jeff. 2000. "An economic model of recent trends in violence." In *The Crime Drop in America,* ed. Alfred Blumstein and Joel Wallman. Cambridge: Cambridge University Press, 2000.

Haynie, Dana. 2002. "Friendship networks and delinquency: The relational nature of peer delinquency." *Journal of Quantitative Criminology* 18: 99–134.

Heaton, Janet. 1998. "Secondary analysis of qualitative data." *Social Research Update* 22. http://www.soc.surrey.ac.uk/sru/SRU22.html.

Heimer, Karen, and Stacy DeCoster. 1997. "The gendering of violent delinquency." *Criminology* 37: 277–312.

Jacobs, Bruce. 1999. *Dealing Crack: The Social World of Drug Selling.* Boston, MA: Northeastern University Press.

———. 2000. *Robbing Drug Dealers: Violence beyond the Law.* New York: Aldine de Gruyter,

———, Volkan Topalli, and Richard T. Wright. 2000. "Managing retaliation: Drug robbery and informal sanction threats." *Criminology* 38, no. 1: 171–198.

MacLeod, Jay. 1995. Ain't *No Makin' It: Aspirations and Attainment in a Low-Income Neighborhood.* Boulder, CO: Westview.

Maher, Lisa. 1997. *Sexed Work: Gender, Race, and Resistance in a Brooklyn Drug Market.* Oxford: Oxford University Press.

Massey, Douglas S., and Nancy Denton. 1993. *American Apartheid: Segregation and the Making of the Underclass.* Cambridge, MA: Harvard University Press.

Messerschmidt, James W. 1997. *Crime as Structured Action: Gender, Race, Class, and Crime in the Making.* Thousand Oaks, CA: Sage.

———. 2000. *Nine Lives : Adolescent Masculinities, the Body, and Violence.* Boulder, CO: Westview Press.

———. 2004. *Flesh and Blood: Adolescent Gender Diversity and Violence.* Lanham, MD: Rowman and Littlefield.

Miller, Jody. 1998. "Up it up: Gender and the accomplishment of street robbery." *Criminology* 36: 37–66.

———. 2001. *One of the Guys: Girls, Gangs, and Gender.* New York, NY: Oxford University Press.

———. 2002. "The strengths and limits of 'doing gender' for understanding street crime." *Theoretical Criminology* 6: 433–460.

———, and Christopher W. Mullins. 2006. "Stuck up, telling lies, and talking too much: The gendered context of young women's violence." In *New Directions in the Study of Gender, Crime, and Victimization,* ed. Karen Heimer and Candace Kruttschmidt, 41–66. New York: Routledge.

Mullins, Christopher W. 2006. *Holding Your Square: Masculinities, Streetlife, and Violence.* Cullampton, Devon: Willa Press.

———, and Richard T. Wright. 2003. "Gender, social networks, and residential burglary." *Criminology* 41: 813–840.

Mullins, Christopher W., Richard T. Wright, and Bruce A. Jacobs. 2004. "Gender, streetlife, and criminal retaliation." *Criminology* 42: 911–940.

Oliver, William. 1994. *The Violent Social World of Black Men.* New York, NY: Lexington Books.

Ousey, Graham C., and Matthew Lee. 2002. "Examining the conditional nature of the illicit drug market–homicide relationship: A partial test of the theory of contingent causation." *Criminology* 40: 73–102.

Petersen, Dana, Jody Miller, and Finn-Aage Espensen. 2001. "Impact of sex Composition on gangs and gang member delinquency." *Criminology* 39: 411–439.

Pollak, Otto. 1950. *The Criminality of Women.* Philadelphia: University of Pennsylvania Press

Rosenfeld, Richard, Bruce A. Jacobs, and Richard T. Wright. 2003. "Snitching and the code of the street." *British Journal of Criminology* 43: 291–309.

Sampson, Robert, and John Laub. 1993. *Crime in the Making: Pathways and Turning Points through Life.* Cambridge, MA: Harvard University Press.

Shover, Neal, and Belinda Henderson. "Repressive crime control and male persistent thieves." 1995. In *Crime and Public Policy: Putting Theory to Work,* ed. H. Barlow. Boulder CO: Westview Press.

Shover, Neal, and David Honaker. 1992. "The socially bounded decision making of persistent property offenders." *Howard Journal of Criminal Justice* 31: 276–293.

Steffensmeier, Darrell. 1983. "Organization properties and sex-segregation in the underworld: Building a sociological theory of sex differences in crime." *Social Forces* 61: 1010–1032.

———, and Robert Terry. 1986. "Institutional sexism in the underworld: A view from the inside." *Sociological Inquiry* 56: 304–23.

Suarez, Ray. 1999. *The Old Neighborhood. What We Lost in the Great Suburban Migration, 1966–1999.* New York: Free Press.

Weller, Susan, and A. Kimball Romney. 1988. *Systematic Data Collection.* Thousand Oaks, CA: Sage.

West, Candace, and Sarah Fenstermaker. 1995. "Doing difference." *Gender and Society* 9: 3–37.

West, Candace, and Don Zimmerman. 1987. "Doing gender." *Gender and Society* 1:125–151.

White, Jacquelyn W., and Robin M. Kowalski. 1994. "Deconstructing the myth of the nonaggressive woman: A feminist analysis." *Psychology of Women Quarterly* 18: 487–508.

Wilson, William J. 1987. *The Truly Disadvantaged: The Inner City, the Underclass, and Public Policy.* Chicago: University of Chicago Press.

Wright, Richard T. 1997. *Armed Robbers in Action: Stick Ups and Street Culture.* Boston, MA: Northeastern University Press.

———, and Scott H. Decker. 1994. *Burglars on the Job: Streetlife and Residential Break-ins.* Boston, MA: Northeastern University Press.

Exercising Agency in Managing Drug Dependencies

Part II addresses the more interpersonal matters related to women's substance abuse. It focuses on the ways women use agency and power in managing or dealing with drug dependencies and with the relationship complications that arise from these.

As we have noted, past research has stereotyped women substance abusers as having been introduced to drugs by men and forced to support their own drug habits through prostitution, which subsequently exposes them to more violent victimization. This stereotype is based on presumptions of women's subordination and of an inability to control their own actions or destinies. In short, women have been viewed as codependent, sexualized objects.

In this section, Katsulis and Blankenship, Saum and Grey, and Kelly challenge this stereotype with four consistent themes about empowerment and agency—themes that yield mostly relational types of power but, in some instances, structural forms. First, the authors reveal that women are sexual subjects who act autonomously, not simply passive objects of male manipulation. Second, Katsulis and Blankenship reveal that women are advocates for their own well-being, within sexual and intimate relationships; they carefully manage their exposure to various risks while preserving their families. Third, even when women substance abusers are mired in codependent relationships, Kelley shows, they are not fully crippled by these; instead, they work within the framework of codependency to improve their own well-being and that of their relationships. Fourth, Saum and Gray find that women utilize intervention resources and experiences more positively than do their male counterparts, to improve intimate and family relationships as well as their own desistence from drugs and to reach prosocial outcomes.

In general, all three chapters provide evidence of more equitable relationships between women and men than previous research has documented. For example, Katsulis and Blankenship show more collaborative relationships between women and men in economic matters pertaining to sex work. Like Anderson and Mullins in their chapters in Part I, Katsulis and Blankenship elaborate on women's use of survival, expressive, and symbolic-resistance forms of agency in illegal activities. Women sex workers, they show, are not exclusively pimped by men, nor do they simply perform men's dirty work. On the contrary, most call their own shots. Women's sex work is an autonomous enterprise and these women reject traditional feminine identities while engaging in it and negotiating the drug world.

This is a more sexual-subject viewpoint of women; it is further supported by Coontz and Griebel's work in Part III, as we shall see, and by certain studies outside the field of criminology.

One recent example is Bernadette Barton's (2006) study of strippers. She found women's dancing at sex clubs a more autonomous activity than many, selected for economic, lifestyle, and symbolic-resistance reasons. Like the chapters in this volume, Barton shows that women "perform" sexuality for their own interests and manipulate the value that men give those performances for their own economic advantage.

Within sexual and/or intimate relationships, women manage risk and consequence, demonstrating survival agency and an advocacy for their own well-being. For example, Katsulis and Blankenship describe how women sex workers attempt to control their exposure to HIV through risk management strategies, including getting males to wear condoms. This is a form of instrumental or survival agency, and it is constantly promoted in both HIV reduction and pregnancy prevention policies. When such women share knowledge about these efforts with others like them, they are engaging in advocacy at an interpersonal level. Advocacy is yet another type of agency neglected in past research. Professionals working toward feminist ends must find ways, therefore, to empower women in their advocacy efforts.

In Part I, Mullins and Anderson wrote about the codependency between female and male substance abusers in funding a drug habit. Kelly's chapter on couples in drug treatment elaborates on the more emotional aspects of male–female codependency. She challenges the charge, for past research, of a single path to women's successful exit out of the drug world: severing of ties to drug-using men. Just as Anderson and Mullins noted more equity between men's and women's active drug use, Kelley finds there is partnership between them in negotiating abstinence.

Although the "pathology and powerlessness" approach in the past has defined women drug users' codependency with male drug users as detrimental to their success in abstinence, Kelley shows how men and women work together to achieve it, precisely because of codependency. Couples can be a source of support in treatment. The system needs to adjust to allow for this, by moving toward intervention models that restore healthy families. Kelley contends that wrap-around models would achieve this.

The final theme to appear in Part II is discussed eloquently by Saum and Gray: women may utilize drug and criminal justice interventions more positively than men to improve simultaneously their own lives and those to which they are intimately connected.

In their chapter about drug courts, a type of therapeutic jurisprudence, Saum and Grey find that women are more likely than men to believe that they are being treated fairly and with respect by all drug treatment professionals. They are satisfied with their treatment and they take seriously what they learn, using the skills and knowledge to empower themselves in conventional activities. Thus they don't simply sign up for drug treatment to take the easy way out of punishment. This fact underscores a need to adopt reintegration interventions and policies outside the punitive "war on drugs and crime" approach that has characterized justice policy for the past few decades. This policy shift toward reintegration will be further elaborated in Part III.

REFERENCES

Barton, Bernadette. 2006. *Stripped: Inside the Lives of Exotic Dancers*. New York: New York University Press.

Chapter 5

Women's Agency in
the Context of Drug Use

Yasmina Katsulis and Kim M. Blankenship

INTRODUCTION

This essay derives from our ethnographic case studies and life-history interviews with thirty-seven female sex workers living in New Haven, CT, who were addicted to crack cocaine, heroine, or both.[1] Framing the interviewees' stories as performance narratives, we use the content derived from these interviews to illustrate how women process their sense of agency over time, and how it is expressed and shared through narratives about their everyday lives. This agency occurs within the context of multiple social constraints, including their experiences as women coping with issues leading to their substance abuse, their current addictions, and the consequences of their addictions in their lives. In spite of these constraints, our participants have been able to exert some amount of control over their lives as well as express some agency in their relationships with others. Through this empirical lens, we explore the idea of women as victims of drug addiction and/or of men generally, we discuss how such stereotypes may be perpetuated by female drug users within the drug treatment setting and the courts, and we speculate as to the functionality (and the consequences) of these gendered performances from an experiential perspective. Our work was made possible, in part, by a pilot project grant (to Kim M. Blankenship) from the Center for Interdisciplinary Research on AIDS. We begin with a story about Mary, a thirty-nine-year-old white woman.

Mary has been using drugs since she was thirteen. She has been in and out of jail five times for drug possession and soliciting, and she has participated in eight different substance abuse treatment programs. Although she has been enrolled in a variety of methadone maintenance programs since 1991, at the time of her interview (summer 2003), she still used crack and powdered cocaine, pills, and alcohol to get high. Mary has a fifteen-year-old son, whom she lost custody of several years ago, and she has continued to suffer emotional anxiety from the loss. Because of her drug use, she has contracted Hepatitis B and C. To support her addiction, she: ran a successful call service out of her home for awhile, but had to shut down after she discovered she was under surveillance by the police; has relied on state and city welfare services; has borrowed money from relatives, friends, and roommates, as well as from former clients with whom she has had a series of long-term relationships; worked as a dancer in strip clubs; and worked in a massage parlor. Currently, she exchanges sex for money with, primarily, clients on the streets and at truck stops. Although Mary found out she was HIV-positive in 1988, she continues to use street-based sex work as a strategy to support her addiction.

Mary is like many of the more than forty women we interviewed between 1992 and 2003, addicted to drugs and working, at least for a time, by exchanging sex for money or drugs. Focusing primarily on analysis of her life history, we allow it to speak for the ways that the lives of substance-using women more generally are both constrained by factors over which they have relatively little control, and shaped by their ongoing actions to challenge these constraints. We focus in particular on several key moments in Mary's life story that are typical of virtually every woman we interviewed: introduction into drug use, negotiation of sexual activity, victimization by violence, and dependence on drugs. More generally, we discuss how the telling of Mary's story, not only the *content* of this story, reveals the dimensions of both her power and her vulnerability.

INTRODUCTION TO DRUG USE

The stereotype of a female drug addict might include her introduction to drug use by a male partner, and her addiction as an aspect of her continuing dependency on that male partner. Although the majority of women we interviewed were introduced to drugs, heroine and crack cocaine in particular, by a male partner, their drug use did not necessarily make them more dependent upon those partners. Many times, as their involvement with drugs increased, their drug use became a point of contention that indicated a greater sense of independence from the relationship, as well as a shift in priorities. Mary, for example, had a series of male partners after having become addicted to drugs. Some of the relationships included drug sharing as a feature; others did not. In those that did include drug sharing, conflicts often arose as Mary scored her own drugs or shared them with people other than her partner. Although the gendered expectation was that the male partner would be "in charge" if drug sharing was present, reality did not often support this expectation.

In relationships that did not include sharing, Mary would attempt to hide her own drug use, because conflict around her going out to score drugs or do drugs with others would inevitably arise, causing jealousy and hostility, things she would try to avoid. In these relationships, Mary was careful and strategic about how much to disclose about her drug-use behavior. She did not, she told us, want her partners to interfere with or try to control her behavior. Too much interference or conflict often meant the end of the relationship, or at least the end of cohabitation with that partner.

NEGOTIATING SEXUAL ACTIVITIES

Mary was, and still is, aware of the potential for HIV transmission between sexual partners. Although she attempts to exert control over the terms of sexual activity, as a precaution, she is not always successful. Still, her continued lack of complete success does not demonstrate her lack of agency; it illustrates instead not only the resistant nature of gendered social constraints that women must navigate, but also the tenacity with which women continue to take some amount of control over sexual activities. For example, consider her discussion with us of her sexual relationship with the man she believes infected her with HIV:

MARY: [He] did not like using those condoms.
INTERVIEWER: Okay. So he wouldn't wear one?
MARY: No, I—I asked him and then a couple times he put it on, and then he took it off. But it was too late. You know . . . Yeah, so then when he started doing that, that's when I, I didn't really break up with him because he was going to jail, I broke up with him because of that too . . . Because I'd be like, you sure don't feel like you got a condom on. And then I knew, 'cause he did it about two, three times.
INTERVIEWER: Yeah, it's kind of hard to tell, because you can't see.
MARY: Yeah, yeah, in the dark. He always wanted to be in the dark.
INTERVIEWER: So he would take it off, without your permission?
MARY: Yeah, he would take it off. Without my permission.

In her current relationship, Mary lives with someone who is not infected with HIV. She is able to exert greater control over condom use, but does not always choose to use them:

MARY: He uses a condom now. I make him use a condom . . . 'Cause I mean, we don't plan to have any more kids right now.
INTERVIEWER: So you only decided to do that [not use a condom] when you decided to have kids?
MARY: Uh-huh.

INTERVIEWER: So, the first time that you guys have sex again after you recon-
nected, did you use a condom?

MARY: The first time . . . The first time, he didn't, I told him he should use a
condom, he said, he don't care.

INTERVIEWER: Right, and he didn't want to use one?

MARY: He didn't want to use one. He said, "I'll just get sick with you." I said,
"Oh, my God, no," I said, "you don't realize what you are messing with
here" . . . Okay, but he goes and gets a check-up every six months . . . He's
blessed. But now, like I said, for the past three years, we've been using
condoms. So he's blessed.

INTERVIEWER: And what, what made him finally decide to protect himself in
that way?

MARY: I, well, I was going through the [HIV-positive support group], I guess,
and by um, 'cause he always goes with me when I go to the doctor . . .
And I just brought him to the clinic and stuff, and then I used to go to
the community health van. I just, and then me just talking to him, I told
him, I said, "One of us got to be there, you know, at least for the kids,
you know."

Although it took her some time to persuade her partner, Mary was finally
able to control the use of condoms within her relationship.

The transition from sexual object to sexual subject is highly contextual.
It can take place over a period of years within one relationship, or even
more gradually over a period of many relationships. It is contingent upon
one's self-perception and sense of rights or entitlement, and is influenced
by one's sense of responsibility toward others. Mary's story makes clear that
the notion of the sexual subject is more than something specifically related
to personal sexual pleasure. It includes issues of agency and empowerment.
Mary's realization of herself as a sexual subject began with her struggle to
protect herself in a situation she felt little control over. Her continued failure to do so encouraged her to leave the relationship to allow room for a
healthier relationship with a different partner. Later, after having already
been infected with HIV, she finds that she is more successful in negotiating
condom use by referring to the protection and well-being of others (the
children). She is able to take the action that she wants (sex with condoms)
by utilizing a different narrative strategy built upon her and her partner's
shared investment in their children's well-being. This latter strategy is perhaps more successful because it is in keeping with gender norms and expectations (woman as protector of the health and well-being of the family) than
is the first strategy in its implicit norms (woman as someone with a right to
set the terms of sexual activity to protect her own health). In an ideal world,

either strategy would work. However, within the context of gendered social constraints in which Mary (and each of us) lives, she does her best to navigate these constraints—not by upsetting or speaking out against them, but by working within them. It is this very dynamic of trying to exert agency within preset constraints that shapes many facets of Mary's life and the lives of those like her.

VIOLENT VICTIMIZATION

After talking with Mary even for a short time about her life, it is clear both that she has been victimized repeatedly, and that there is a connection between her drug addiction and her victimization. In this, she is like many women with a history of drug addiction (McElrath et al. 1997; Sung-Yeon et al. 2002; Brems et al. 2004; Becker and Grilo 2006; Hyman et al. 2006). Her father's alcoholism, his violence toward her and her mother, her mother's acceptance of this violence, the sexual abuse that Mary endured at the hand of a family friend, the date rape that she experienced as a teenager, the lack of residential substance abuse treatment programs truly responsive to her needs (i.e., the lack of counseling and mental health services within such programs to address the connections between her mental health and substance addiction), were all out of her control.

And, depending on the setting, these may be the only stories Mary tells about herself, leaving the sense that being victimized is the only experience she has ever had (or possibly will ever have). .

She may tell these stories because of the kinds of questions she is asked, or as a strategy for eliciting sympathy for her situation. Accommodation to the victim role can protect women from attacks on their moral character in a social setting. It can also be used to gain access to scarce resources in social service settings, and it can help persuade a judge to offer a lighter sentence. There is no question that the idea of women as victims resonates quite loudly within our culture, and that women are both more easily victimized than men and more readily framed as victims than men sharing similar histories. This is the idea behind what Anderson (see this volume) has called the "pathology and powerlessness" perspective. Accommodating to this viewpoint might have individual benefits, but it can also be dangerous insofar as it reinforces idea of women as passive victims in all areas of life, thereby shutting the door on agency, accountability, and the potential for significant purposeful change.

An alternative is to reframe at least the sharing of these stories as an expression of agency, as a performed role selected from a repertoire for a certain purpose. This is not to suggest inauthenticity of the stories, but to view them as a way to build social capital for a particular purpose (see, for comparison, the extensive literature on the performance of the "sick role" by medical anthropologists). As an example, note this experience shared by Mary, describing events leading up to her entry into a homeless shelter and a drug treatment program:

MARY: [T]hat one night I had, I had, like, eight dollars on me or whatever, and I went to crack out without her. And um, one of the guys that we had ripped off, I went to go cop from him, and I didn't realize who it was . . . Because we had ripped off so many different people. But, um, yeah, he knew it was us, he knew it was me. He got in the car with me, and basically he took over. And he wouldn't let me out of the car. He would not let me leave him at all. And he was holding on to me for the whole night. And every time I tried to move away from him, he would pull me back. He kept holding me . . . staying with me physically. I mean, he even hit me in the face. So it was definitely against my will . . . And he was like *I remember you. You know, you're going to do something, you're going to give me something back* . . . He, um, kept me with him all night long, driving the car . . . Being his little, um, chauffeur . . . And ripping off other people.

INTERVIEWER: Okay. So he had you helping him rip off other people? As a way of sort of paying him back?

MARY: Right . . . This is, this guy is a gangster. K, he's going to fuck with me . . . And, um, I felt that if I had told, I would be killed.

INTERVIEWER: Have you still seen him around? I mean, how did, did he just drop you off?

MARY: Well what happened was, um, we had ripped off some girl, and she had a car too of like seven guys. And um, he made it seem like, you know, he was trying to rob me. While I was driving the car.

INTERVIEWER: That was the, the con, or whatever?

MARY: Yeah, so like he smacked me around quite a bit. And, um, I was screaming at him and we were riding around trying to lose this girl, and I lost her eventually. Then we went and smoked it [the crack] and then later on—

INTERVIEWER: After being smacked around and all that?

MARY: Yeah.

INTERVIEWER: Okay. So he shared with you?

MARY: Yeah . . . Anyway, later on, we rolled around back into the streets. We were smoking, we went into the streets, and that's when we ran into that girl in the car. And she tried to open up our door and come at me for the money. And that's when I took off, 'cause he had jumped out of the car to go talk to her. And then she was coming right to my door. And then he was out, the moment I hit the gas, I was out there.

INTERVIEWER: Okay. And you haven't seen him since then?
MARY: No.

For Mary, these events represent being at rock bottom. Her control is stripped from her as a result of her taking advantage of others to support her drug use. Still, there is a striking degree of pride in Mary's descriptions of her ability to handle herself on the street in dangerous and difficult circumstances. In spite of having been victimized repeatedly by others, Mary says many of her friends look up to her as a protector, as someone who is not easily taken advantage of, and as someone who can easily take advantage of others when necessary. But this is not the image that Mary presents to others, such as her probation officer, the police, or her drug-treatment counselor. Indeed, she repeatedly asked for reassurance that her stories not be shared with her drug-treatment counselor, out of fear that she would be judged by that counselor for her activities, that she might be denied services, and that she would certainly be denied the counselor's respect. Her ability to see herself as a savvy street-wise operator who can escape a difficult situation, at least in the eyes of her peers, is something that needs to be acknowledged and worked with to help her reach her current goal of leading a drug-free life; unfortunately, this skill set tends to be made invisible by the social dynamics created in the treatment setting.

DRUG DEPENDENCE: GOING ON A BINGE

Mary has a lot of stories about what she does when she goes on a drug binge—or has a relapse, as she calls it. Often, the binge takes place within the context of her friendship with other female addicts. In these stories, Mary and her friend both vie for control over themselves, their addictions, one another, and people and things on the street. Her framing of herself in these stories is absent, except as someone who reluctantly gives in to a friend who can be overbearing:

MARY: When I relapsed this past time, um, not the one before that, I was relapsing with her. We were living out of a car. We went around, and we didn't have money. We were either boosting or stealing, wheeling and dealing, and beating drug dealers for their drugs. We got the car smashed up. We did a lot of bad stuff . . . [W]hen she wanted to relapse, we would be together already for the day. And one of use would have money, and we're doing our thing. Basically, I would never entice her to go with me, basically she would mention that she wanted to go, and I would give her a hard time about it. And eventually, I just say, screw it, because she's very overbearing, and she's very strong-willed, and she was going to go get it anyway. And when she brings it to that level, when she's just going to get out of the car and go . . . I feel like I can't let her go alone . . . because I'm worried about her, but also because I have a desire to use too. But I'm trying not to. Basically, that's how it went down with her.

Mary laughs when she speaks of how easy it can be for a bold woman to take advantage of drug dealers on the street. She says she has the surprise factor, because they don't expect her to run away with both the money and the drugs, or to knock them down and take off. Clearly, as was the case with the narrative in the previous section, this success can result in violent retaliation after the fact. But Mary says that, when she is on a binge, anything is fair game. Although she acknowledges the risks involved, she does not talk about these stories with shame or guilt but with a certain amount of pride—at least when she is talking to her peers or within the interview setting.

In some other stories, Mary takes pride in being able to gain access to scarce resources. She is particularly skilled with what she calls "making something out of nothing," wherein she offers to cop drugs for a number of fellow drug users, pools their investment money over a period of a few hours, and can then take some of the profits for herself without investing her own money. This is a high yield, short-term investment of Mary's time. She uses this strategy when she goes on a binge but has no cash. The strategy requires experience with establishing, maintaining, and growing a network of fellow addicts, as well as skill to cop drugs even when others can't. In a way, her fellow addicts act as a clientele base, whereas she acts as the middleman. She needs the social skills to deal with her clientele, to quickly establish rapport with others, to negotiate a good enough trade with one of her dealers to maintain a good profit margin. Subsequently, she can use the profits either to buy drugs for herself or to sell so that she can use the cash for something else. This is a day-to-day strategy that she can rely on that exposes her to far less risk than beating drug dealers for drugs, boosting, or hustling tricks. She claims to enjoy the process, for the most part, calling it exciting to be able to make something from nothing; as long as everything goes well, she feels good to be able to support herself in this way.

AGENCY AS GENDERED PERFORMANCE

In this essay, we look for agency through the narratives that Mary has shared with us. To talk about Mary's narratives as story, however, is not meant to indicate that they are in any way inauthentic; rather, it is to emphasize the importance of analyzing not only what she says, but also how she frames the events in her life, and especially her relationship to those events. That she takes pride in her skills means there may be a way to help her translate those skills into a lifestyle free from drugs. In a treatment setting, for example, she can be reminded of the many ways that she is *not* a victim, in order to mobilize the sense of empowerment she feels among her peers or on the street. In many ways, Mary is a highly capable person who has survived a tremendous amount of hardship. We think this is something often lost in a treatment setting, precisely because these kinds of stories are exactly *not* the kind of stories that are usually shared.

Our use of this framework is very much informed by Judith Butler's (1997) understanding of the politics of the performative. As Butler notes, a narrator's identity is tightly intermeshed with her sense of self; she constructs herself as a social being through her stories and has the opportunity at any turn to reinforce or disrupt our shared stereotypes. However, in the treatment or criminal justice setting, the use of victim role narratives suggests that female addicts are quite careful not to disrupt our expectations of the repentant woman (namely, subordination and passivity). These women's use of these narratives is more likely to reinforce our assumptions than to disrupt them. The amount of stigma that they must deal with as a result of their addiction is likely hard enough to cope with without portraying themselves as unfeminine. Female drug addicts may portray themselves and talk about themselves as if they are victims, they may even see themselves as a victim (at least in part), but their use of this repertoire indicates, on at least some level, the functionality of this very strategy as a way to navigate the particular setting or situation in which they find themselves.

We expect that this strategy is more likely to be useful, and therefore more likely to be utilized, when negotiating social, financial, or drug treatment services, as well as within the judicial setting. It is less likely to be useful, and therefore less likely to be used, among peers, especially among peers with whom a woman wants to build a solid social foundation based on mutual confidence and respect (which, in street drug settings, may require reference to successful hustling activities, self-control, or control over others).

Just as narratives based in a victim repertoire are not likely to be helpful among peers, narratives that demonstrate a cunning control over others are not likely to be received well in settings that downplay any recognition of culpability or agency among female addicts. In treatment settings, for example, respondents are socialized to think about the negative consequences of their drug use, about the kinds of things they do because they have given control over to their addiction. They are not taught to think about how they might have used drugs to self-medicate or to control others. In fact, the recovery process might even reinforce this sense of powerlessness by asking addicts to give control over to a higher power (as in a twelve-step program). Even if such a process is effective in maintaining a drug-free life-style, it does not necessarily socialize women to recognize the power that already resides within themselves.

The importance of narratives in the social construction of an addict's identity is seen clearly in the work of Baker (2000) and McIntosh and McKeganey (2000). McIntosh and McKeganey illustrate that the formation of a non-addict identity is perhaps the most essential part of the recovery process—and that recovery narratives are key in constructing this new-found identity. Going a step further, Baker illustrates particular features of these shared narratives, as they are found in her work with addicts. For example, she finds that in their compliance with the institutional socialization process of the treatment setting, women addicts learn to self-define as addicts. This includes accepting that they have a problem with addiction, and learning to discuss the consequences of, and the factors leading to, that addiction. However, this self-definition also includes its own narrative twist. Using the rhetoric of emotional health, women addicts discuss the process of acknowledging their addiction as one of self-discovery. In other words, they tend to argue that they were previously unaware that they were truly addicted and that they were not emotionally healthy. In this way, they are able to both acknowledge and disregard their addict self, replacing it in their narrative with a more aware and emotionally healthy non-addict self. This transformation then becomes a key focal point in the healing process, both psychologically and socially.

Both the addict and those around her learn to distinguish between her past (as an addicted, emotionally unhealthy person) and her current or future potential. This becomes her source of redemption, on a personal level. As those around her rebuild their sense of trust and respect toward her, she is also redeemed in their eyes as a person of worth rather than stigma. In this context, relapse can be particularly troubling, as it signifies a fall from grace and the inability to cut ties to the past self.

In thinking analytically about narratives of transformation or any other socially situated discourse, it is important to remember not to take these narratives at face value. Although the addict and those around her may completely believe that the narrative is an accurate representation of experience, it may just as easily represent a learned social response, with the addict having learned how to craft such a narrative, in the right place, at the right time, for the right audience. Whether the addict or the audience sees the narrative as authentic (and we can imagine it may some time before the addict or former addict builds this trust), the narrative itself can still be understood as a socially constructed story of transformation that may, or may not, shape the experience of the recovery process.

There are at least three additional features of women addicts' narratives to be noted. First, the use of the victim role by female drug addicts is a form of gendered performance. Again, to say this is not to suggest that the women have not been victimized by others, by their addiction, or by the system more generally, or that they are not entitled to services. Rather, the use of this framework acknowledges that image management by all actors must incorporate familiar signs, symbols, and stereotypes to become meaningful and functional in a particular setting. Thus, the use of the victim role incorporates particular gendered stereotypes in a way that can potentially facilitate a desired outcome in a particular setting; it does not disrupt our social expectations about women as passive, and, in this sense, the sharing of a victim narrative by women is some sense preset, or scripted, by social and cultural expectations, norms, and constraints. However, a woman's choice to share this narrative, and her choice about where and how to tell it, does demonstrate her ability to draw from a specific set of narrative repertoires so as to exercise power within, or navigate, her social setting.

Second, the use of this repertoire may be more effective for some actors than for others, and may be more effective in some settings than in others. Not all actors have equal social access to these repertoires. Any actor can try to use the repertoire, and may learn from others how and where to best use it. But not all actors can use the repertoire with equal success. The successful use of the victim role as a strategy depends not only on ability to successfully negotiate a particular image, but also on one's known history, or background, and the way that this has been framed by others (particularly those in a position of power or authority). There is an aura of stigma cast on the woman's present activities that can be difficult to reframe. Has she already been framed as a perpetrator of violence? As a drug dealer? As a thief? Success can also be determined by race and class. That is, white women from a middle- to upper-class background are probably more successful in employing this role—that of a victim of their addiction, or the unwilling participant in a relationship over which they had little control. Poor women of color are likely to have a more difficult time; they are more likely to be seen as culpable for their behavior, both in the courts and in the court of public opinion.

Third, the skill with which one may utilize repertoires may increase and deepen over time. The practice, or use, of the repertoire over time represents a form of what Bourdieu (1992) calls *habitus,* or an orientation practiced over and over until it becomes ingrained. The repeated use of this repertoire inscribes itself upon the body or persona of the actor—it becomes, both literally and figuratively, difficult to separate the repeated successful performance of these repertoires from an inner self not socially constructed. For what is the self, outside of the social self, but a reflection, or a memory, of its engagements with the outside world? Does it really make sense to talk about the self as apart from the social construction of the self?

We would argue: Yes.

It is important to disentangle these issues because it is important to understand the *process* of becoming a constructed social self, so that one can have an element of purposeful control over it. That is, if we can engage with female drug addicts on this level, we may help them develop other repertoires and skill sets, as well as modify their existing ones, in a way that can facilitate their reintegration into a non-illicit lifestyle free from drugs.

CONCLUSIONS

Mary is a composite case study based on a number of interviewees from our project. The use of a composite character allows us to protect the identity of individual participants, while at the same time sharing with our readers some explicit and intimate details of those who participated in our study. Mary's story mirrors that of almost every woman we have met who is struggling with addiction. The first and maybe most important lesson from her story is that substance abuse treatment programs, though widely under-funded and problematic in many ways, can provide a crucial component to the path of healing and recovery for many women—yet, even were they 100 percent effective, free, and widely available on demand, they would still not be nearly enough to address the problems Mary has faced that led to her addiction in the first place. Substance abuse treatment can only be that—a *treatment* much like the chemotherapy used to treat cancer; it arrives when it is nearly too late. It does not prevent that cancer from taking hold, unseen and untreated by the medical establishment, in the first place. To truly have made a difference in Mary's life, it would have had to have addressed a host of other problems.

The second lesson learned from Mary's story is that, regardless of the tragedy and trauma she has faced in her life, she is still alive and she remains capable of making changes to improve her quality of life and that of those around her. One way is by taking control of her future as best she can, by using the skills she has relied on to survive up to this point and by developing new skills. She indicates that she is ready to work for change, but she really isn't sure how to get started. Helping her get started may be as simple as encouraging her to see her life and skills through new eyes. Recognition of her ability to exert agency is an important step in helping her reach the goal she has set for herself—namely, to have a place of her own where she does not have to have sex to have a place to sleep, where she can feel safe, warm, and wanted, and where she can visit with her children when they come into town. This goal, while seemingly modest to others, is still a distant impossibility from Mary's current perspective.

NOTE

1. Life-history interviews were collected between 1992 and 2003. Most interviews occurred in multiple sessions totaling anywhere from four to six hours for each interviewee, and were tape-recorded and transcribed with permission from participants.

REFERENCES

Baker, Phyllis. 2000. "I didn't know: Discoveries and identity transformation of women addicts in treatment." *Journal of Drug Issues* 30, no. 40: 863–880.

Becker, Daniel F., and Carlos M. Grilo. 2006. "Prediction of drug and alcohol abuse in hospitalized adolescents: Comparisons by gender and substance type." *Behaviour Research and Therapy* 44, no.10: 1431–1440.

Bourdieu, Pierre. 1992. *The Logic of Practice*. Palo Alto: Stanford University Press. Reprint ed.

Brems, Christiane, Mark Johnson, David Neal, and Melinda Freemon. 2004. "Childhood abuse history and substance use among men and women receiving detoxification services." *American Journal of Drug and Alcohol Abuse* 30, no. 4: 799–821.

Butler, Judith. 1997. *Excitable Speech: The Politics of the Performative*. New York: Routledge.

Hyman, Scott M., Miguel Garcia, and Rajita Sinha. 2006. "Gender-specific associations between types of childhood maltreatment and the onset, escalation, and severity of substance use in cocaine-dependent adults." *American Journal of Drug and Alcohol Abuse* 32, no. 4: 655–664.

McElrath, Karen, Dale D. Chitwood, and Mary Comerford. 1997. "Crime victimization among injection drug users." *Journal of Drug Issues* 27, no. 4: 771–783.

McIntosh, James, and Neil McKeganey. 2000. "Addicts' narratives of recovery from drug use: Constructing a non-addict identity." *Social Science and Medicine* 50: 1501–1510.

Sung-Yeon, Kang, Sherry Deren, and Marjoria F. Goldstein. 2002. "Relationships between childhood abuse and neglect experience and HIV risk behaviors among methadone treatment drop-outs." *Child Abuse and Neglect* 26, no. 12: 1275–1289.

CHAPTER 6

Facilitating Change for Women?

EXPLORING THE ROLE OF THERAPEUTIC JURISPRUDENCE IN DRUG COURT

Christine A. Saum and Alison R. Gray

INTRODUCTION

Drug courts are the result of innovative case management and treatment strategies designed to break the drugs–crime cycle for offenders and alleviate problems characteristic of overburdened judiciary systems. Branded a judicial experiment, drug courts were conceived by criminal justice practitioners and treatment providers as promising alternatives to incarceration and probation for drug offenders (Drug Strategies 1999). Because the traditional adversarial methods of the criminal justice system failed to meet the challenge of curtailing drug abuse and drug-related criminal activity, a different approach to dealing with substance-using offenders was imperative. As a result, the drug court model has sought to employ *therapeutic jurisprudence,* an approach that underscores the helping relationship between treatment, courts, and corrections and emphasizes rehabilitation over punishment in effecting positive change in offenders. Thus, although the drug court is a legal institution, the goals of the court in this model have become primarily therapeutic (Hora et al. 1999).

A more therapeutic approach to the law and legal decision making would appear to offer promise for improving outcomes for defendants in the legal system. Yet it is possible that the good intentions of legal actors actually can have antitherapeutic consequences. For example, applying rules to the facts of a case without parallel inquiry into a person's needs and reasons for criminal behavior may lead to legally relevant but ineffective outcomes (Casey and Rottman 2000). Moreover, it is difficult to measure therapeutic jurisprudence in practice, and thus little is known about how specific applications of therapeutic jurisprudence affect individuals and what characteristics of those individuals modify the process. It is also possible that the use of therapeutic jurisprudence techniques affect women and men differently.

That little is known about the practical application of therapeutic jurisprudence is of major importance, given the rapid expansion of drug courts in the United States and internationally. Although results are mixed, many drug courts appear to be "working": that is, many offenders have less drug use and crime and improved social functioning after participating in drug court programs (Belenko 2001: Butzin et al. 2002). The drug court movement is relatively young; thus researchers are trying to identify what about drug courts, or perhaps what about the process of therapeutic jurisprudence, may lead to positive outcomes for some participants but lead to poor outcomes for others. Thus, exploring areas such as client–counselor rapport and client–judge interaction is critical for better understanding the complex process of change that occurs in drug court programs. Going further, how drug court participants' gender may influence drug court experiences may lead to some critical insight on these processes.

The research presented here operationalizes and measures specific components of therapeutic jurisprudence through an examination of how this approach has been applied in a drug court program. The ideas of therapeutic jurisprudence suggest that researchers should examine how legal actors and legal actions affect people. Thus, our objective is to explore how the legal actors (treatment staff and drug court judges) and their legal actions (e.g., praise from a judge) are perceived by drug court participants. Within this context, differences in perceptions of drug court experiences according to participants' gender, and according to women participants' completion status, are examined. Exploring the data in this way allows a better understanding of how therapeutic jurisprudence is applied in drug court and how the application of this approach may differentially affect women.

LITERATURE REVIEW
Therapeutic Jurisprudence and the Drug Court Model

In the past, the concept of therapeutic jurisprudence has been applied in psychology and mental health law, where for example, a nonadversarial approach to the rehabilitation and sentencing practices of mentally ill offenders has been utilized by courtroom actors. The application of the concepts of therapeutic jurisprudence to the study of drug courts is a more recent phenomenon. It is believed that treatment drug courts unknowingly apply therapeutic jurisprudence principles to the problems of drug- and alcohol-addicted defendants to encourage treatment-seeking behavior and reduce crime (Hora et al. 1999). Indeed, this approach has been discussed primarily as the theoretical underpinnings of the drug court movement, and only to a lesser extent have discussions centered on its practical applications.

In their essay on therapeutic jurisprudence in the courts, Casey and Rottman (2000) discuss the *rights* and *care* perspectives in the balanced approach to the administration and provision of justice in our court systems. They believe that the *rights* perspective, which focuses on justice and equality issues, is dominant in traditional courtrooms, citing how legal decision making represents a masculine ideal of rationality. Conversely, they believe that the *care* perspective, which encompasses more of a feminine model of compassion and responsiveness to needs, is less prominent in the legal system. Casey and Rottman (2000) argue that therapeutic jurisprudence has the potential for enhancing court performance by bridging the *rights* and *care* perspectives.

One way to understand how therapeutic jurisprudence has been utilized in drug courts is to compare the purposes of drug courts and traditional courts. In a traditional courtroom, the goal may be to dispose of cases efficiently; often this means that the defendant's best interests are not considered. In a drug court, all of the legal actors work together to problem-solve and, in doing so, aim to facilitate positive changes for the client. Drug courts have a more individualized and public health focus, basing case dispositions on broader assessments of whether clients are committed to change (Burns and Peyrot 2003), whereas traditional courts are more focused on adversarial processes ruled by the justice system.

The collaborative environment of a drug court necessitates new roles for the judge, attorneys, probation officer, and treatment provider, referred to appropriately as the "drug court team." The judge performs standard functions such as sanctioning offenders, but also serves in a quasi–social service role, providing guidance and support to clients (Senjo and Leip 2001). Drug court judges usually have received special training in substance use and addiction so they can employ this knowledge to better understand relapse and special needs of drug-involved offenders. Indeed, drug court judges have been described as proactive therapists (Nolan 2001). Operating from more of a social worker perspective allows drug court judges to develop relatively close relationships with their clients over time as they meet regularly in "status hearings" to discuss clients' accomplishments and tribulations in the program. The innovative role of the judge also allows members of the drug court team to communicate effectively—for example, facilitating dialogue between treatment counselors and case managers regarding clients' progress.

The exchange of information about the client between the judge and counselor provides an innovative role for the treatment provider. Working with offenders mandated to treatment is not new, but attending status hearings where treatment updates and recommendations are shared with a judge on a regular basis is new. A progress report is compiled by the treatment provider with regard to the participant's drug test results, attendance, and participation. If program violations have been committed, as seen in positive drug tests or failure to attend treatment sessions, the judge will impose intermediate sanctions that can include increasing drug testing frequency, counseling, and/or court appearances. Although the judge is the final authority in determining whether to terminate a participant from the program, the judge's decision as to what sanctions to impose is often based on the recommendations of the treatment providers (Butzin et al. 2002).

Little research has focused on how these new judicial and counselor roles, the more individualized practices, and the potentially more effective communication/interaction styles operating within a treatment-oriented drug court impacts the drug court clients themselves. Moreover, it must be underscored that clients also take on a new role in drug court—they are active participants in both their treatment and the courtroom proceedings. For example, Nolan (2001) explains that in drug courts, the client's life experiences along with the ability to convince a judge of a willingness to change becomes important.

Along these lines, a study found that the manner of interactions between the judge and offenders can lead to an increased likelihood of participants' remaining engaged in treatment, and a decrease in the likelihood of relapse (Senjo and Leip 2001). The researchers explain that, because supportive comments offered during status hearings have a significant impact on program completion, drug court team members should pay close attention to their verbal interactions with offenders. In particular, they suggest that drug court clients are particularly responsive to the use of positive reinforcement, as opposed to the more traditional use of punishment. Thus it is essential that we learn more precisely how participants employ the therapeutic jurisprudence model along with how participants react to its application.

PARTICIPANT EXPERIENCES IN DRUG COURT

There is a dearth of information in the literature on the actual experiences of the participants in drug court. Most drug court studies examine clients' characteristics (demographics, drug of choice, etc.) and assess relationships between these variables and outcomes (graduation, recidivism). Although this knowledge is certainly important to assess whether and for whom drug courts are effective, it is critical that we ask the participants themselves what it is about the drug court that has contributed to their success or failure in the program. If the specific program components that clients believe effective and the components that the participants believe require change are more completely understood, then programming in drug courts can be improved to meet participants' needs (Cresswell and Deschenes 2001).

If we tap the perceptions of drug court participants, assumptions underlying the drug court model can be tested. Exploring how experiences, attitudes, and opinions of clients correspond to the goals intended by those who operate drug courts is vital (Goldkamp 2001). Moreover, if we better understand offender perceptions of drug court, we may determine whether program models meet participants' expectations and thus whether theoretical concepts are being implemented correctly (Turner et al. 1999). For example, levels of participant satisfaction with drug court have been shown to influence motivation to change, program participation, and treatment retention rates (Johnson et al. 2000; Saum et al. 2002). Thus by examining drug court client perceptions more comprehensively, the legitimacy of the drug court as a model of therapeutic jurisprudence can be assessed.

A few studies have asked drug court participants to indicate what they believe are the essential components of drug courts. Information gathered from a large-scale evaluation of drug court programs across the country found that program graduates describe the most important elements to be the judicial interaction and monitoring, treatment staff support, urine testing, sanctions, and the opportunity to have charges dismissed (Belenko 2001). Similarly, participants who were part of a national sample of drug court offenders indicated that the close supervision and encouragement provided by the judge and treatment providers were the critical factors that promoted their success (Cooper et al. 1997). Finally, the importance of the judge emerged as the most critical factor for drug court clients who participated in focus groups in six U.S. cities. Participants also indicated that drug testing and accountability were key elements of the treatment process, and that they were strongly motivated by incentives and penalties employed by the court (Goldkamp 2002).

Research on gender differences (regarding client characteristics, drug use, and participant perceptions) was conducted in an Ohio drug court. With regard to participant perception, the researchers report that both women and men reported a high rate of satisfaction with the drug court process (Johnson et al. 2000). There were also similar responses from women and men in the study when asked about probation visits, treatment attendance, and future drug use. However, women (91 percent) were more likely than men (73 percent) to report that regular court hearings were helpful in staying clean.

Finally, a study of Delaware drug court participants' perceptions compared the experiences of program completers and program noncompleters. Those who successfully completed drug court were significantly more likely to believe that their counselors were supportive and that the judges had treated them fairly, compared with those who failed to complete the program (Saum et al. 2002). However, the fact that the majority of the participants, including the noncompleters, agreed that praise and warnings about their progress was helpful indicates that client–judicial interaction is a significant part of the drug court process.

A few common themes emerge from the extant literature, including the importance of the judge and the treatment staff and the importance of the court hearings. But, we don't know what specific aspects of the judge/treatment staff, and of the clients' interactions with these key players while in treatment and in the courtroom, the participants believe to be the critical components of their drug court experience. We know even less about how or why experiences with the judge or experiences while in treatment may differ for women and men. The goal of the research presented here is to address these gaps in the literature.

RESEARCH METHODS

Drug Court Program Description

Delaware's Superior Court drug court program is located in New Castle County and has two tracks: a pre-plea diversion track for first-time drug offenders and a post-plea track for probation violators arrested for any new crimes. Clients in each program attend treatment at one of several state-contracted providers. Treatment for most clients includes psychoeducational programming, urine monitoring, group therapy, and individual counseling if required. All participants attend biweekly or monthly status hearings with their regular drug court judge. Clients are required to remain in the program for a minimum of six to nine months. Graduation is contingent upon successful completion of treatment and the approval of the drug court judge. For a more complete description of the Delaware Superior Court drug court programs, see Butzin, Saum, and Scarpitti (2002).

The Sample

This study is part of a larger project designed to measure the influence of drug courts on treatment retention, and post–drug court outcomes. This paper presents findings from 464 drug court study participants who entered the drug court program beginning in January 2000 and were discharged as of July 2004. The focus of this paper is on the women in the sample (n=116), but men are included for important comparative purposes.

Table 6.1.

Drug Court Study Participant Characteristics (n=464) and Participant Characteristics by Gender

	Total	Women (n=120)	Men (n=344)
Age (mean)	29	31	28
Race (% nonwhite)	55	53	56
Employment (% employed)	60	47	67
Education			
High school/GED	45	43	46
Marital status			
Married	11	13	11
Single	77	61	80
Primary drug of choice			
Marijuana	44	33	48
Alcohol	19	22	18
Cocaine/crack	18	18	18
Heroin	10	11	10
Other	9	16	6
Drug court completion graduates	65	66	65

Table 6.1 displays the demographic characteristics of the total sample, and by gender. The average age of the drug court participants was twenty-nine, and 55 percent were nonwhite. About 60 percent of the sample reported they were working full or part-time, and 45 percent had either a high school diploma or GED. With regard to marital status, 11 percent were married, 12 percent were divorced or separated, and 77 percent were single. Marijuana (44 percent) was most often reported as the primary drug of choice, followed by alcohol (19 percent), cocaine/crack (18 percent), heroin (10 percent), and other (9 percent). Nearly two-thirds (65 percent) of the drug court clients completed the program.

Women on average were older than male participants and were slightly more likely to be white. Men were more likely to be employed, but education levels were similar for both genders. Men were more likely to be single and not married. Women were less likely to report marijuana use, but more likely to report alcohol use and use of other drugs (often illegal use of prescription drugs). Finally, completion rates were generally equivalent for both women and men.

Procedures

Clients were recruited into the study by treatment program staff upon entry into the drug court program. At that time, those interested in participating signed a consent form so that data could be collected from their program files. At the end of their program participation, treatment records were collected, clients were contacted, and CDAS researchers conducted the Client Satisfaction Survey (CSS) interview with the respondents. All interviews were voluntary and were conducted by trained CDAS interviewers. Client responses were protected by a grant of confidentiality from NIDA. Participants were paid twenty dollars each for participating in the CSS interview.

Measures

The Client Satisfaction Survey (CSS) is a forty-nine-question instrument developed by CDAS researchers and designed to elicit the opinions of drug court treatment program clients' experiences. Most questions were formatted using a five-item scale ranging from "strongly disagree" to "strongly agree." The survey is divided into two sections: the first section contains questions related to the counselors and treatment program components; the second section contains questions related to the judge and courtroom experiences. Two open-ended questions were included so that respondents could provide comments about their experiences in the program and suggestions on how to improve the program.

Questions were designed to examine reasons for drug court entry, to explore satisfaction with treatment and drug court, and to elicit participants' opinions of logistical issues, treatment staff and service delivery, judicial interactions, and a variety of program components. Given the focus of this paper, only questions relating to the treatment staff and judges (legal actors) and specific judicial actions (legal actions) were utilized for the analyses discussed on these pages. Examples of questions relating to counselors and judges ask respondents if the staff were supportive, or if the judge was fair. Examples of questions relating to legal actions ask respondents if praise/warnings from the judge were helpful. Several responses to the open-ended questions are included in the results section to add a qualitative component to this study. All of the five-point questions utilized for the study are listed in table 6.2.

Analyses

Two types of analysis were conducted with the data. The first was an evaluation of women's and men's drug court experiences according to responses for each CSS question; Chi-square statistics were utilized to determine any statistically significant differences between responses. The second compared the drug court experiences of women who completed drug court and women who did not complete drug court, and chi-square statistics were utilized to determine any statistically significant differences between responses. It should be noted that the subgroups selected for the second set of analyses (women completers and women noncompleters) contain relatively small numbers. Thus, findings based on these results serve primarily as descriptive indicators of differences between groups.

"Strongly agree" responses were chosen as the response measure to report, rather than "agree" or a combination of these measures, due to the greater variation in the full range of responses. Due to the exploratory nature of this study, we believed that more meaningful information could be ascertained from responses representing stronger opinions about the participants' drug court experiences.

RESULTS

CSS Questions by Gender

Relationships between drug court participants' gender and perceptions of drug court program experiences were examined and the results are presented in table 6.2. Overall, women drug court participants had more positive feelings toward the treatment program staff (counselors) than did men participants. There were statistically significant differences in responses to the statement "Staff believed that I could grow, change and recover" (p=.007); though only 36 percent of the men strongly agreed with the statement, 53 percent of women reported that they strongly agreed. Female drug court clients (46 percent) were also more likely than their male counterparts (33 percent) to strongly agree that staff knew a lot and knew how to do their jobs well (p=.019).

Over half of the women strongly agreed that the staff was very supportive, while about 37 percent of the males felt the same (p=.012). A female client explained, "The people at the treatment center were there for me. They helped me with all my problems. They made me feel like I was part of the family; they gave me hope and made me feel I belonged to something." Another female client had a similar comment, "The counselors are there with you every step of the way." Women in the program were also more likely to believe in the fairness of the counselors: nearly 56 percent of women compared to 43 percent (p=.037) of men clients strongly agreed that staff treated them fairly. Finally, a smaller percentage of the men (40.4 percent), compared to 58 percent of the women, strongly agreed with the statement "Staff treated men and women with the same respect" (p=.011).

TABLE 6.2.

Drug Court Participants' Opinions of Treatment Staff and Drug Court Judge by Gender and by Completion (women only) (percent strongly agreeing)

	Women (N=120)	Men (N=344)	Women Completers (N=41)	Women Noncompleters (N=79)
Treatment Staff				
Staff believed that I could grow, change, and recover	52.5%	36.3%★★	62.8%	30.0%★★
Staff knew a lot and did their jobs well	45.8%	32.6%★	53.8%	30.0%★★★
The staff was very supportive	53.3%	36.8%★	64.1%	30.0%★★★
Staff treated women and men with the same respect	57.5%	40.4%★	69.2%	32.5%★★★
Staff treated people of different races/ethnicities with the same respect	52.9%	41.6%	64.9%	27.5%★★★
Staff treated me fairly	55.8%	43.4%★	65.4%	35.0%★★
Drug Court Judge				
I would have preferred more time with the judge	9.3%	5.7%	5.2%	17.9%
The judge was biased against me	2.5%	3.9%	1.3%	5.1%★★
Praise from the judge for my progress was very helpful	46.6%	27.3%★★	52.6%	31.6%★★★
A warning from the judge about my progress was very helpful	33.1%	26.1%	37.7%	20.5%★★★
The judge gave me a chance to tell my side of the story	35.3%	17.4%★★	42.3%	20.5%
The judge was too hard on me	3.4%	5.4%	0%	10.3%★★★
The judge tried hard to be fair to me	38.7%	25.4%★	43.6%	28.2%★
The judge treated me with respect	51.3%	33.0%★★	62.8%	25.6%★★
I trusted the judge	43.7%	25.4%★★	55.1%	17.9%★★★
Overall, the judge treated me fairly	52.5%	34.9%★	64.1%	26.3%★★★
The judge was a very important influence on how well I did in the program	40.0%	28.3%	54.7%	10.5%★★★

*p<.05
**p<.01
***p<.001

Gender differences in perceptions of judicial interaction were examined. These analyses revealed that, as in the findings regarding treatment staff, women were more likely to be satisfied with their interactions with the judge. Nearly half the women, compared to only a quarter of the men, strongly agreed that praise from the judge was helpful in their progress (p=.004). Two times as many women as men also reported feeling that the judge gave them a chance to tell their side of the story before making any decisions (p=.001). Women drug court clients were also more likely to report that the judge tried hard to be fair to them (p=.042), that the judge treated them with respect (p=.004), that they trusted the judge (p=.001), and that overall the judge treated them fairly (p=.013). A female client made the following observation: "He is a fair and honest judge that listens to your side of the story. He always gave me an opportunity to speak on my behalf after the counselor spoke."

CSS Questions by Completion Status (Women Only)

Data were used to examine any differences in perceptions of drug court experiences between women who completed drug court and women who did not (table 6.2). When asked if program staff believed that they could grow, change, and recover, those who completed the program were more likely to strongly agree than those who did not complete it (p=.006). Over 50 percent of the completers strongly agreed that staff knew a lot and knew how to do their jobs well, but only 30 percent of the noncompleters reported the same (p=.0001). A female participant illustrates this point: "They are the most important part. If the counselors are trained well and have had to deal with some type of addiction, what they say is taken to heart." In addition, over two times as many female completers as noncompleters felt that staff was very supportive (p=.0001), that the staff treated men and women with the same respect (p=.0001), and that staff treated people of different races and ethnicities with the same respect (p=.0001). Finally, when clients were asked if staff treated them fairly overall, 65 percent of the female completers and 35 percent of the female noncompleters strongly agreed (p=.001).

Women who completed the program also had more favorable perceptions of their interactions with the drug court judge. One female client explained, "I feel that the judge making the decision to send me to the program was good for me. I am very confident in my recovery because of this." Over 50 percent of the women completers strongly agreed that praise from the judge regarding their progress was helpful, but only about 32 percent of the noncompleters felt the same (p=.0001). Female completers also more often strongly agreed that warnings from the judge were helpful to their progress (p=.0001). Two times as many female completers strongly agreed that they were given a chance to tell their side of the story before the judge made any decisions in their case (p=.063). Successful completion was also significantly related to strongly agreeing that the judge tried hard to be fair (p=.027), the judge treated them with respect (p=.001), they trusted the judge (p=.0001), and the judge was an important influence on how well they did in the program (p=.0001). A female graduate discussed how the judge influenced her success: "Being in front of the judge really put my goals in perspective. He is a man of honor and made me feel as though he cared about my recovery."

Women who failed to complete the drug court program were more likely to strongly agree that they would have preferred more time with the judge (p=.056). A female participant commented that it was important to "see the judge more often to allow the judge to get to know you and get your side of the story across." At the same time many women who did not complete the program were also more likely to strongly agree that the judge was biased against them (p=.004) and that the judge was too hard on them (p=.0001).

DISCUSSION AND CONCLUSIONS

The objective of this study was to explore therapeutic jurisprudence in drug court through an examination of how the legal actors (treatment staff and drug court judges) and their legal actions (e.g., praise from the judge) were perceived by the drug court participants. Within this context, differences in perceptions of drug court experiences according to gender and completion status were examined. Overall, findings indicate that women drug court participants experienced more positive interactions with treatment staff and with drug court judges than did their male counterparts. In addition, the drug court experience appears to have been most favorably experienced, for the subgroup of women who successfully completed the program.

With regard to treatment staff, it was apparent that women drug court participants were more confident in the staff's ability to treat their substance abuse problems than were the men participants. Moreover, feeling supported by their counselors and being able to develop trusting and meaningful relationships with their counselors related to positive outcomes for these women. Indeed, women who completed the drug court program most often expressed satisfaction with those characteristics and qualities of the treatment staff about which they were questioned. This finding supports research on substance abuse treatment that points to clients' relationships with their counselors as a key predictor of successful treatment outcomes (Broome et al. 1996; Goodrum 2003). The research presented here moves this literature forward by suggesting that developing good relations with their counselors may be of particular importance for women drug court clients.

The finding that women participants are more satisfied with, and more influenced by, the drug court judge than are men is of related significance. Indeed, whereas previous research has found the judge to be a key element of drug court success (Goldkamp 2002), this research indicates that the drug court judge may have a stronger impact on women clients. In almost all questions that focused on the character of the judge (trust, fairness, respect), women were overwhelmingly more likely to respond positively than were men. These relationships were even stronger for women who completed the drug court program. That the women could trust the judge, felt he was fair, and believed he respected them, were all qualities necessary to form and maintain a strong, positive relationship.

Questions that focused on the actions of the judge provide even greater insight into the client–judge relationship. Women placed more significance on their interactions with the judge; the judges' praise and the judges' ability to listen were perceived as very important. Findings regarding judicial praise support Sanjo and Leip's (2001) research indicating that clients respond well to encouragement from the bench. Moreover, feeling satisfied with the relationship one has with a judge (who in the past may have been experienced as an adversary figure) may increase women's psychological well-being and may empower women to feel capable of success.

Women participants also found that being able to talk with the judge during their regular status hearings and tell the judge their story was a critical part of the drug court process. "Telling their story" had different meaning for different people, and encompassed discussions about reasons for using drugs and engaging in crime. But these discussions could be expanded to include problem-solving about family and childrearing concerns and other life issues. Thus, being able to be heard and being included in the problem-solving process may be especially beneficial to women drug court participants.

Many findings of this research are supportive of procedural justice research that indicates that clients who believe they play an important role in their own courtroom proceedings, and believe that the processes are fair, are often content with the outcomes (Lind and Tyler 1988). Moreover, the potential impact of perceptions of fairness among clients was discussed by an experienced judge who was part of a symposium on judicial perceptions of drug courts and other problem-solving courts (courts that use therapeutic jurisprudence principals, such as mental health courts). The judge explained that over time he had learned that ineffective treatment often follows when subjects feel that they are not being related to fairly (*Fordham*

Urban Law Journal 2002). The judge's comment validates drug court clients' experiences regarding the importance of fairness. In our study, it was apparent that women participants, and particularly women who were successful in the drug court program, were most likely to believe that both their counselors and their judges treated them fairly.

Overall, our research findings indicate that women, more than men, are able to utilize the components of the therapeutic jurisprudence model to their advantage. Many female participants appeared to develop meaningful connections with their counselors and judges, the two key players in the drug court model. Women utilized the opportunity provided by this therapeutic approach to communicate their needs and to respond to the requests of legal actors in treatment sessions and in status hearings, thereby working to form important, supportive relationships with members of the drug court team. Indeed, the fact that women who were not successful in the program wanted more time with the judge may indicate that they wanted more chances to improve their communications and their relationship with the judge. Thus, the ability to effectively express themselves appears to serve a dual function for women drug court participants—it is personally fulfilling and it serves to facilitate the drug court process. Finally, it is apparent that a "care perspective" is operating in this drug court, and, as such, this more feminine model of justice appears particularly beneficial to the women who encompass it.

A therapeutic jurisprudence orientation would maintain that responding to the needs of drug court clients is critical. Thus the findings presented here, which are based on perceptions and experiences of drug court clients, should be considered by drug court planners, judges, and treatment providers as they implement and improve drug courts around the nation. Although these findings from a single drug court program cannot be generalized across all drug courts, they can serve as a basis for future investigations into how the drug court model is implemented (for instance, how legal actors and legal actions may differentially affect clients). More specifically, the potential for positive or negative change resulting from the interactions that drug court clients have with their judge and counselor warrants further study.

References

Belenko, S. 2001. *Research on Drug Courts: A Critical Review.* New York: Columbia University Press.

Broome, K. M., K. Knight, M. L. Hiller, and D. D. Simpson. 1996. "Drug treatment process indicators for probationers and prediction of recidivism." *Journal of Substance Abuse Treatment* 13, no. 6: 487–492.

Burns, S. L., and M. Peyrot. 2003. "Tough love: Nurturing and coercing responsibility and recovery in California drug courts." *Social Problems* 50: 416–438.

Butzin, C. A., C. A. Saum, and F. R. Scarpitti. 2002. "Factors associated with completion of a drug court diversion program." *Substance Use and Misuse* 37: 1615–1633.

Casey, P., and D. B. Rottman. 2000. "Therapeutic Jurisprudence in the Courts." *Behavioral Sciences and the Law* 18: 445–457.

Cooper, C. S., S. R. Bartlett, M. A. Shaw, and K. K. Yang. 1997. *1997 Drug Court Survey Report: Participant Perspectives.* Washington, DC: United States Department of Justice.

Cresswell, L. S., and E. P. Deschenes. 2001. "Minority and nonminority perceptions of drug court program severity and effectiveness." *Journal of Drug Issues* 31, no. 1. 259–292.

Drug Strategies 1999. *Drug Courts: A Revolution in Criminal Justice.* Washington, DC: Drug Strategies.

Goldkamp, J. S., M. D. White, and J. B. Robinson. 2001. *An Honest Chance: Perspectives on Drug Courts: Findings from Participant Focus Groups in Brooklyn, Las Vegas, Miami, Portland, San Bernardino, and Seattle.* Philadelphia: Crime and Justice Research Institute.

Goodrum, S., M. Staton, C. Leukefeld, J. M. Webster, and R. T. Purvis. 2003. "Perceptions of a prison-based substance abuse treatment program among some staff and participants." *Journal of Offender Rehabilitation* 37, nos. 3/4. 27–47.

Hora, P. F., W. G. Schma, and J. T. A. Rosenthal. 1999. "Therapeutic jurisprudence and the drug treatment court movement: Revolutionizing the criminal justice system's response to drug abuse and crime in America." *Notre Dame Law Review* 74, no. 2: 439–537.

Johnson, S., D. K. Shaffer, and E. J. Latessa. 2000. "A comparison of male and female drug court participants." *Corrections Compendium* 25, no. 6: 1–9.

Lind, E. A., and T. R. Tyler. 1988. *The Social Psychology of Procedural Justice.* New York: Plenum Press.

Nolan, James L. 2001. *Reinventing Justice: The American Drug Court Movement.* Princeton, NJ: Princeton University Press.

Problem Solving Courts Panel Discussion. 2002. "The judicial perspective." *Fordham Urban Law Journal* 29, no. 5: 2041–2062.

Saum, C. A., F. R. Scarpitti, C. A. Butzin, V. W. Perez, D. Jennings, and A. R. Gray. 2002. "Drug court participants' satisfaction with treatment and the court experience." *Drug Court Review* 4, no. 1: 39–82.

Senjo, S., and L. A. Leip. 2001. "Testing therapeutic jurisprudence theory: An empirical assessment of the drug court process." *Western Criminology Review* 3, no.1: 66–87.

Turner, S., P. Greenwood, T. Fain, and E. P. Deschenes. 1999. "Perceptions of drug court: How offenders view ease of program completion, strengths and weaknesses, and the impact on their lives." *National Drug Court Institute Review* 2, no. 1: 61–85.

CHAPTER 7

Negotiating Gender for Couples in Methadone Maintenance Treatment

Margaret Kelley

INTRODUCTION

Women and men have been shown to experience drug treatment differently. My primary research goal here is to examine the experiences of seventeen drug-using couples in methadone maintenance treatment. The data provide a unique opportunity to follow the progress of couples over time as they struggle with drug addiction and gender differences in treatment. In this analysis, I seek to answer the following two questions:

- How do injection drug using couples manage their drug use and treatment?
- How are issues of gender and power negotiated by couples as they move in and out of treatment?

There is substantial evidence that alcohol and drug treatment that includes family members is more likely to be successful than is treatment of individuals (Fals-Stewart, O'Farrell, and Birchler 2004). There is also a growing body of clinical research, primarily in relation to alcohol use and marital adjustment, emphasizing the importance of treating both members of a couple when one or both are addicted (Ferrari et al. 1999; Kelley and Meersman 2000; Leonard and Roberts 1996; Leonard and Rothbard 1999; Osterman and Grubic 2000; Prest, Benson, and Protinsky 1998). However, there is no published qualitative sociological research dealing exclusively with dually addicted *couples* in methadone treatment and presented from *their* perspectives.

Research suggests that women injection-drug users face unique barriers to treatment and inequality while in drug treatment programs (Allen 1994; Bahna and Gordon 1978; Copeland and Wall 1992; Fraser 1997; Kelley et al. 1996; Reed 1985; Root 1989; Rosenbaum 1982; Vannicelli

1984; Wilsnack 1991; Woodhouse 1990). Although much of this research has focused on pregnancy and the effects of drug use and treatment on newborns, other themes do emerge, including differences in structural programming at clinics and in experiences with intimate violence.

Some drug treatment programs operate on the assumption that women's primary needs are to focus on responsibilities to their families and their partners. For couples in treatment, this can result in women assuming responsibility for their partners' behaviors while at the clinics, making sure they follow the rules and stay in the program. However, when the male partner feels ready to leave any treatment program, the woman usually follows, regardless of her own advancement in the program (Woodhouse 1990). For men, however, it is usually assumed the primary need is for vocational training, and men do get more vocational help while in treatment. Extensive research has also documented that women drug users, in and out of treatment, report higher rates of past and current violence than do men. Insensitivity to women's life experiences, including sexual and domestic assault, during treatment and counseling in methadone clinics may also prevent women from seeking treatment (Lowrance 1990; Russell and Wilsnack 1991), and it may keep women from fully engaging in treatment and reaching successful treatment outcomes (Kelley et al. 1996).

Another common theme in the literature is the all-consuming nature of addiction, for the "dually addicted" couple. Most relationships require high levels of similarity in needs and values, for good marital adjustment; for heroin-using couples, interactions are based on the drug itself (Gasta et al. 1978). However, codependency is often a controversial topic, and researchers do not agree on its clinical nature and definition (Asher and Brissett 1988; Cowan and Warren 1994; Gemin 1997; Irwin 1995; Kirby-Green and Moore 2001; Lindley, Giordano, and Hammer 1999; Loughead, Spurlock and Yuan-yu 1998; Rotunda and Doman 2001; Wright and Wright 1991). For example, many diverse problem behaviors have been included under the umbrella of codependency; most definitions directly relate current adjustment problems to familial relationships, with problems beginning in the family of origin (Harkness 2003; Roehling, Koelbel and Rutgers 1996; Wells, Clickauf-Hughes and Jones 1999) and including "learned helplessness" (O'Gorman 1993) that results in problems with self-esteem. Of importance, codependency has often been linked to living with someone with a substance abuse disorder, but may exist independently (O'Brien and Gaborit 1992). Codependent individuals tend to seek out relationships with codependent partners (O'Brien and Gaborit 1992). Sociologically this tendency has the effect of funneling individuals into deviant relationships and away from ties to conventionality (Rosenbaum 1981).

There is very little research on drug-using couples and their joint experiences of codependency. Most codependency research has been done with alcohol and alcoholism. For example, Zetterlind and colleagues used a series of codependence scales and concluded that it is possible to measure codependency with alcohol users and relate it to coping styles and difficulty in the relationship (Zetterlind and Berglund 1999). In addition, research shows that less consumption of alcohol and drugs leads to greater reported marital quality and less reported marital violence and marital disruptions (Fals-Stewart, Birchler, and O'Farrell 1999; Leonard and Roberts 1996; Leonard and Rothbard 1999). Further, the nature of a couple's drinking partnership—that is, the interplay of each spouse's drinking and the context of the drinking patterns—was found important in determining marital quality (Leonard and Roberts 1996). Finally, in a study of men and women in a residential alcohol treatment facility, it was found that the greater the codependency, the less accepting of children and more depressed about parenting abilities the person was (Ferrari et al. 1999); the researchers concluded that women with children have greater stressors, which need to be taken into account in treatment.

Men and women are likely to report both similarities and differences in treatment experiences. After describing my study methodology and sample demographics in detail, I report on these similarities and differences from the perspectives of the respondents. Codependency, in particular, served a unique role in defining their life experiences. I explore how this codependency played out differently for men and women in their reports on the treatment experience.

METHODOLOGY

The data to be analyzed come from a longitudinal study of 233 injection drug users, both in and out of methadone maintenance programs in the San Francisco Bay Area.[1] Study participants were recruited from five local methadone maintenance treatment clinics in three counties, from treatment waiting lists, and from several needle exchange sites. Each individual was initially interviewed using a qualitative life-history guide and an extensive close-ended instrument covering demographics, drug use, treatment status, needle sharing, risky sexual behaviors, family history, and criminal activity. Each was then contacted every six months and reinterviewed over the phone, using a shorter qualitative schedule and an abbreviated quantitative close-ended component. A total of five interviews were completed over a period of three years (1990–1993), with an attrition rate of only 10.7 percent.

The in-depth interviews were qualitatively coded using Ethnograph, a computer program designed to assist with qualitative data analysis (Seidel, Friese, and Leonard 1995). After expanding the original coding to reflect our research questions, for this paper I used Ethnograph to connect the codes to these questions. Ethnograph puts the vast amounts of data gleaned through the interviews into a search-and-retrieve database. The user can link files, attach memos to files, and organize files in many ways. For example, after coding chunks of text on a number of clinic and methadone treatment characteristics, I was able to have Ethnograph group these chunks and produce the context of the groupings, connecting clinics to drug use patterns. This analysis focuses on the qualitative findings from a subset of seventeen heterosexual couples. These individuals were self-identified as couples in the course of the interviews (some had referred their partners to the study), and total 11.6 percent of the study population.

DEMOGRAPHIC DESCRIPTION OF THE COUPLES

The majority, 67.7 percent, of the couples respondents were white, with 17.6 percent reporting as Latino and 14.7 percent as African American. The average age in years was forty-one for men and thirty-five for women. Women reported slightly more years of education, although almost a third of the couples sampled had not graduated from high school. Women also reported slightly higher levels of income over the past six months. Research has shown that men and women often report different pathways to drug use and treatment. The men and women in this sample reported similar backgrounds in terms of family structure. Half grew up in nuclear families, and the vast majority (70.6 percent) were born in California. The men and the women also reported comparable experiences with parental drug use. Almost 70 percent of the sample had at least one parent an alcoholic; marijuana use was also common. A significant number (44 percent) did not have a stable living arrangement at the time of the first interview. Ten of the couples were married, and most had children.

For categorical analysis, I collapsed level of heroin and other drug use into: "none"; "occasional" (less than four days per month); "moderate" (one to four days per week); and "heavy" (five to seven days per week). As shown in table 7.1, the most popular drug of choice for all respondents throughout the study was heroin, followed by marijuana and cocaine. Speed and crack use were very low for this subset of respondents. The men had been injecting significantly longer than the women. At the initial interview, two-thirds of the couples were in methadone treatment. Slightly more of the women were still in treatment at the final interview.

I present the qualitative results in two main areas. First I focus on codependency and gender roles. I then describe how codependency impacts the treatment experience for the seventeen couples by considering their pathways to and from drug use and treatment and the effect of treatment on

TABLE 7.1

Drug Use Patterns, Time 1 and Time 5 (number and percent)

	Time 1 Men		(n=34) Women		Time 5 Men		(n=33)* Women	
Mean years injecting	22.4		16.1		NA		NA	
No./% subjects in treatment	12	77.6	12	77.6	9	43.8	11	61.7
Weekly heroin use								
None	1	5.9	2	11.8	6	37.5	4	25.0
Occasional	7	41.2	3	17.6	3	18.8	6	37.5
Moderate	5	29.4	9	52.9	4	25.0	3	18.8
Heavy	4	23.5	3	17.6	3	18.8	3	18.8
Weekly cocaine use								
None	9	52.9	11	64.7	13	81.3	13	76.5
Occasional	5	29.4	3	17.6	3	18.8	4	23.5
Moderate	1	5.9	2	11.8	0	0.0	0	0.0
Heavy	2	11.8	1	5.5	0	0.0	0	0.0
Weekly marijuana use								
None	12	70.6	9	52.9	12	75.0	7	41.2
Occasional	4	23.5	1	5.9	3	18.8	6	35.3
Moderate	0	0.0	1	5.9	1	6.3	1	5.9
Heavy	1	5.9	6	35.3	0	0.0	3	17.6

*One male respondent committed suicide before the end of study.

relationship stability. Throughout, I examine the experiences of couples as units and also as individuals in gender-bound roles. I found a surprising pattern of gender agreement in many areas of drug use and treatment. That is, both members tended to agree on many of the important issues and to provide similar accounts of their experiences.

CODEPENDENCY AND GENDER ROLES

Since I do not have access to clinical diagnoses for the individuals in the study, I discuss codependency here from the perspectives of the respondents, because it emerged as a major theme in the negotiation of gender roles. Although the self-help literature usually uses *codependent* to describe someone living with a person with a drug addiction, here both members of the couple are drug dependent. The respondents regularly described their relationships with their partners as codependent. They felt comfortable with the term and seemingly knowledgeable about what it meant and how it defined their partnerships. In fact, codependency was a convenient explanation for many of their problems and was tossed around easily. As Amy explained:

> Codependency is when two people are addicted, but they're also in love. So, I don't run around and go get high by myself behind his back. We do it together. If I'm feeling really great one day like, "Oh yeah, I don't need any drugs. Nothing, you know." I'm feeling really strong mentally, physically, blah blah. All that Gerard has to do is call me from the city, and suggest we get high. You know, it's like you have some weird control over each other.

Katy also described what it meant to be part of drug codependency as the following:

> One of the problems is, as I'm sure you know, is couples playing off each other. One will be this way and one will be the other and we all pull each other to do drugs. And the "yes, let's do it" always wins out. It will be one day I'll be saying "No, no, no" and he'll talk to me and talk to me. And the next day he'll be saying "No, no, no" and I know how to get him to do it and he knows how to get me to do it. So we sort of play off each other.

Because of this collaborative drug use, the respondents repeatedly discussed the importance of being in treatment at the same time. Many although not all of the couples were able to manage concurrent stays in treatment programs during the course of the study. Ernesto and Gabrielle tried for some time to secure treatment slots together. He explained:

> When you get two ex–drug addicts together it's hard to quit. We tried because of the kids. We love our kids. But it's just hard. If I didn't do the drugs and Gabrielle did, it would probably be easier for her to quit. Or if she didn't do the drugs at all I know damn well she wouldn't give me the money to get me high. But while we're both using it and sitting here feeling real blah because something happened, we get high.

Gabrielle believed that her treatment became much more successful after Ernesto was able to join her. She said:

> Ernesto got on maintenance and we did really good. I mean, it was a shock. And we didn't spend any money, because we weren't doing drugs any more. We used to go out to breakfast every day. It was a radical change, getting on methadone. I mean it didn't do much good for him to be off and me to be

on, because with one person, like he was still going to use. So every time he got off, we went through the same thing.

Another couple struggled with the decision about whether or not one could remain in treatment when the other was facing a forced detoxification because of lack of funds. Rita described her concerns about losing her funded treatment slot:

> My husband is going to try to detox along with me, but then it's affecting him too. And I explain to him "Just because I'm getting off, doesn't mean you have to get off." And so he says "Well you know, it's affecting you, it's affecting me. We'll try to do it together. We'll just try to detox together and we'll try to pursue whatever changes come about together."

Rita and her husband, Marshall, were able to remain free of heroin for the rest of the study. When asked why their detoxification was successful, Rita said, "We made a change. We changed residences. We changed cities. We don't go around in the same circles." Marshall also reported difficulties when he and his wife on different treatment schedules. He said, "I not only have to deal with my addiction, but hers also. So it makes it really kind of difficult."

Of course, the couples in this study did not always agree about treatment schedules and who should be in treatment at any one time. Jorge's wife, Flora, was in treatment at the first interview. According to him, life was easier with just her in treatment because he could continue using heroin without having to also pay for her heroin use. However, Flora said it was very difficult being in treatment while he continued using heroin, because it made her want to use heroin, too. She would grow very frustrated that he was usually "loaded and having fun" when she was trying to stay clean and straight.

Respondents reported feeling a great deal of relationship guilt because of the codependency. George felt guilty about influencing his wife, Ruth, by encouraging her to use heroin again, especially after they had been trying so hard to stay clean. He said:

> And then the guy I copped from ended up hanging around my place for a few days and Ruth was there and we both started using again. And we had been staying clean, although I had fixed several times while I was in jail. But she was on the street and staying clean and going to meetings again and everything. It's kind of my fault because I couldn't say no.

The codependent nature of the partnerships often obscured other relationship issues. For example, Ernesto and Gabrielle reported that they had been on heroin so long that they were just now learning whether or not they even liked each other. Ernesto described it: "I've been with Gabrielle for twelve years and we've really only been building a relationship for the past six months. It's scary. I was medicated for so long that now I need to find out if we get along. I'm just learning about her likes and dislikes."

One key finding from this project is the documentation of the centrality of the relationship in the treatment process. Although partners did not always agree about the experience as couples, there was more agreement than I had anticipated. There was substantial gender agreement among the couples that methadone was a means to gain control of their lives and to stabilize in many areas of their lives. For example, initially Curtis and Linda reportedly used methadone as a stopgap measure when they could not find heroin. As Curtis explained:

> Methadone was like our fall-back, our backup. If we couldn't get high, we know we were going to get the juice. We did that for about a year. And then it just, I don't, it just happened that we quit using. We just got sick of throwing the money away or whatever. She quit her job and just focused more on the kids. We basically gave up all our friends that we knew before. A lot of things just became more stable after we'd been on it for a while . . . I managed to keep the same phone number, the same address. So it eliminated a lot of worries. The more worries we eliminated, it just seemed the easier things went along. We just weren't constantly thinking about drugs.

Ernesto was able to feel like a "real person" for the first time that he could remember. He said:

> For the first time in twenty years that I've been on drugs I went on vacation. I got an exception for a take-home from the clinic for a week and went to San Diego for a wedding. We stayed at the Marriott for three days and then we stopped at Disneyland for two days. We went as a family—I felt like I was a normal person. I was with people who were not on drugs and I was away from the clinic and away from drugs.

In general, as in previous research, the couples reported that abstinence from illicit drugs and alcohol increased levels of satisfaction with their relationships. As Frank said, "we both feel better about ourselves 'cause we've gone that much longer being clean and letting methadone do its thing." The couples also generally agreed about the nature of codependency and its influence in treatment outcomes. Specifically, they believed that both partners needed treatment at the same time.

NEGOTIATING TREATMENT

The couples reported a variety of long and complicated pathways to drug use and treatment, with men and women often reporting different roads. Drug use was often a family affair, with multiple generations using at any given time. Motivations for treatment were more often than not tied to conventional family ties. Treatment provided a way for couples to create another source for their codependency, but it was a source that allowed them to stabilize, both as couples and as families.

Ties to conventionality, such as family and children, served as motivations for treatment for the couples. Keeping the family together was without question the most important reason for these couples in seeking treatment. Although both men and women were concerned with family issues, women talked in their interviews at greater length than did their male partners about the impact of the drug use on their children. Women had more responsibility for dealing with issues of family drug use when the children were involved; however, all couples recognized the dangers that alcohol and drug use introduced into the home and worked to minimize them. During the second interview, Gail mentioned that she and her husband, Jack, used to drink occasionally together. But she claimed they were stopping "because we just fight, we're trying to have fun, but we fight—and our twelve-year-old son gets upset with us, so who needs it. We can go to a show instead. He even threatened us that he was going to start drinking too."

Getting older and having the responsibility of taking care of kids prompted Curtis to get into treatment. He explained:

> The kids, you got to feed them and all that. So we're just a lot more stable, the children made us more stable. I got more than just myself to think about. You can't feed them on a song and dance. And then they go to school and you got to deal with that. I'm just older. I'm almost forty and it's about time I started thinking about somebody other than my own personal whims.

Most respondents had children, but it was when the couples had kids together that parenting served as a primary motivating factor for treatment and abstinence. For Rita and Marshall, commitment to each other and to their fifteen-month-old daughter got them through the forced detoxification from methadone after they lost funding for treatment. As Marshall said:

> Things had gotten out of control and my wife got pregnant and I knew I had to make some changes. We were staying in a two-bedroom

apartment and I had two daughters at home and I was trying to provide, 'cause I'd always tried to keep my drug use away from affecting my family, which had been impossible but I'd always managed to do it where it wasn't that noticeable. I didn't take away from them, from at least the necessities. I might not have provided all the extra stuff that they would have liked to have.

Many of the couples spoke in terms of their perceived mutual goals. For example, Frank explained that he and Sherry were counting on the outcome of mutual plans. He said, "We have plans that we are putting money to. I don't think about using drugs. It's going to be a long haul but we're going to do it." For Helen and Donny, it was the hope of regaining health and employment. Helen said:

I see myself cleaning up really and getting my health back. I see him doing the same thing. I see him going back to work. I see me going—I've had little jobs now, off and on for—since I started using, little waitress jobs, cashier jobs. I don't have any professional skills, but I could find a job, I'm sure, if I tried.

Finally, for Gail, making plans and sticking to them made it possible for her and her Jack to stay away from drugs. She explained:

We're looking at twenty-five years together in September. We've been doing couples counseling at the clinic. We don't fight now. We do better when we're together . . . We bought a twenty-foot beautiful sailboat. It's a world-class sailboat and we're learning how to sail. We'll be taking classes at the community college and learning about navigation. It's nice because we are working towards a common goal.

Codependency, while obscuring other relationship issues, actually facilitated retention in treatment and stability for these couples. It gave them joint goals and a replacement "ritual." Whether or not the couples agreed about the process and experience of treatment, the most important part of leaving treatment was that both partners were able to do it on the same schedule. Robert explained:

We made up our own schedule so we would be ahead of the detox schedule that they set up because the way they were doing it from what I understand was they were going to start people in November and have them off in six weeks, which is totally out of control. So we made up a schedule and started bringing ourselves down slowly so that we could be as comfortable as possible in dealing with it.

Forced detoxification led to some difficulties when both members of the couple were not on the same schedule. Henry's wife, Clarice, was detoxed because they could not afford the clinic fees. He requested an increase in his dose so he could sneak some out for her. They discussed detoxing with their counselor and they all decided Clarice was the one who should detox because he would probably end up in trouble if he had to leave treatment. Because of a forced detox, Helen and Donny were not on the same schedules. Helen said, "Donny is using more heroin than me. He's not on methadone and doesn't want to get on anymore. It affects my use, I do more heroin 'cause it's around." Relationship stability was complicated by these types of changes in treatment status for one member of the couple.

DISCUSSION

I began this project seeking to understand how drug-using couples experience methadone treatment. What I found was a perfect opportunity to apply the sociological imagination, a chance to look in-depth at how individuals operate within the social structures in place in their lives. The findings, based on the qualitative investigation of the experiences of couples as they moved in and out of treatment, focus on the areas of agreement and disagreement that stem from the codependent nature of the relationships. I found that respondents consistently used codependency to define their relationships, essentially creating a "culture of codependency." There were some differences in how women and men experienced codependency, with women more likely to describe, or "diagnose," themselves as such. Even if the respondents did not have access to clinical diagnoses, the experience of being in a relationship in which both persons are addicted to drugs is currently being defined as a codependent relationship: according to the self-help literature, when living through or for another, attempting to control others, blaming others, and feeling victimized, it is difficult to discern power from powerlessness. Some or all of these elements were at work in the lives of the couples in this study and impacted their treatment experiences.

The culture of codependency was so pervasive that it became difficult for the couples to pinpoint concrete steps toward stability other than to stay in methadone treatment together, where codependency was still a workable lifestyle. In fact, respondents appeared relieved to have some way to understand themselves, and codependency brought them comfort. Their narratives reflected the culture of dependency and contributed to its continuance. They derived a sense of self, and of their illness identity as drug dependent, from being codependent. It was not surprising to find that the drug use was a central organizing aspect of the relationships, but it was surprising to learn how the respondents lived their codependency, even growing to depend on it as an explanation for much of their behavior, whether drug seeking or otherwise. Women were able to draw strength from the culture of codependency to keep their partnerships and their families together and functioning. These relationships were certainly not without problems (for example, when one member "slipped" and used heroin, the other could use this fact as the source of blame for their own indulgence), but the relationships allowed for companionship in the difficult world of illicit drug use. It appeared to be the women's responsibilitys to use the codependency to keep the relationship going, whether in or out of treatment.

A sociological perspective confronts the struggle between individual agency and social structural limitations on our daily choices. Although recognizing that we have choice, such a perspective also recognizes that these choices are inherently limited by one's position in the social structure, whether through race, class, gender, or any number of possible organizational schemes. The women in this sample took what they needed from the medical establishment to make sense of their lives. Although codependency implies limited power and choices, in fact these women used it to demarcate comfortable boundaries for themselves and their significant others. Rather than using the culture of dependency as an excuse for dependency (on drugs, treatment, and others), I believe, these women used it to make some improvements in their lives. Length of time spent in treatment has been shown to be one of the most important predictors of long-term success for drug-using individuals. Success can be defined in many ways; in this case, it means staying in treatment and creating stability in one's family life, rather than becoming methadone-free. Overall levels of harm have been reduced by the couple's use of codependency as a motivating factor for treatment.

The literature reports that it is preferable to unlink codependents, and that to do so it is important to increase self esteem and reduce anxiety. However, in the case of this small sample, respondents used their codependency to negotiate the treatment experience in their favor. The couples were quite successful at staying in treatment, in part because codependency kept them motivated in unique ways. For these couples, treatment was not linked to each other except in that it happened at the same time. That is, the two individuals were not processed together or "forced" into couple therapy. Family life was important to all of the respondents, yet not immune from the consequences of codependency. That is, the intergenerational drug use with older or younger family members was disturbing for the respondents but the links were difficult to break. Respondents also understood that taking care of their own drug use and treatment schedules, in addition to that of partners', could be overwhelming.

These results impact policy in numerous ways. I believe they confirm previous research that supports treatment based on family systems perspectives. In addition, perhaps there are ways to develop dually diagnosed treatment programs for two individuals, but even then some services will need to be individually tailored; at the very least, dually -addicted couples should be in treatment at the same time. An encouraging trend in program curricula is the goal of empowering women in treatment: other important elements of treatment programs for women include consciousness raising, client participation and evaluation, meaningful work, and community network ties. But empowerment models usually view women as victims—and while such a model is intended to increase self-efficacy, it is unclear that its overall effects address the complex areas of need for women.

A relatively new theoretical treatment approach, the "wraparound model," views women as holding a unique position in society (Kelley 2002; Malysiak 1997; Office of Justice Programs 1999; Skiba and Nichols 2000; Wingfield and Klempner 2000). This position is characterized as having distinct needs and unique experiences, and the model is a long-term approach to planning and coordinating the provision of formal and informal services to the woman and her family. Adapted from models used working with delinquent children, it is one in which a network of coordinated local services are "wrapped around" the woman and her family; these services can include such things as family therapy, vocational training for all adults, parenting classes, and other possibilities tailored to the couple in question. Modified to apply to adult women, this model works to help women function in the mainstream, and accentuate the positive individual strengths of each woman. The use of empathy in this model is potentially empowering for women (Morrison-Velasco 2000). Wraparound approaches, their developers claim, could be employed using *natural* models. That is, "many of the roles played by the numerous professionals could be filled by family members," creating a more natural environment for progress and improvement (Northey, Primer, and Christensen 1997, 14); in addition, an approach "utilizing strengths inherent in the family's support systems communicates that the family is competent and the therapist is confident in the family's abilities" (Northey, Primer, and Christensen 1997, 14). Such changes to treating codependent couples would facilitate their empowerment, encouraging them to make difficult decisions about what is best for themselves and their families. Despite the encouraging findings in criminal justices settings with children and with women, wraparound services are expensive and rare.

The results from this study can only suggest elements of policy improvements. Policy experts need to examine the findings on codependency and make research-based decisions on how to improve policies related to dually addicted couples.

The findings I have made are similar to those in research with couples and alcohol use. However, what is unique is the insight provided by the subjects' own perspectives on their culture of codependency, and I have been able to provide rich detail from the respondents' perspectives. There are obvious limitations to generalizing from these findings. This data was collected from a convenience sample in the Bay Area in the early 1990s; the experience of being a drug-using couple may be very different in different regions of the country. The subset of couples were not recruited specifically for a study about couples; rather, they were identified during the course of data collection and organized after data collection was complete. I did not have the ability to probe many of the issues that arose, because codependency was not an expected outcome. However, given these limitations, we can learn a great deal about the experience of being drug users together, in and out of treatment, from the perspectives of both members of the couples. It will be important to compare these results to those of alcohol studies, since there will be some similar treatment and policy implications; however, there are drug-specific experiences that must be taken into account.

Although clearly operating with the structural limitations of codependency, the women in this study were quite resourceful in negotiating gender roles using the resources they had available to keep their families together. Life is a daily negotiation of power between individual agency and social structure. Structures change based on our daily choices, but they usually change slowly and over long periods of time. Given the women's limited choices, codependency provided the context for maximizing their agency and power. It takes courage to face the cards you are dealt in life, which is exactly what these women chose to do.

NOTE

1. The research reported in this article was supported by National Institute on Drug Abuse Grants R01 DA05277 and R01 DA 08982, Marsha Rosenbaum, PhD, Principal Investigator, Bennet Fletcher, PhD, Program Officer. All quoted respondents have been assigned pseudonyms to protect their confidentiality.

REFERENCES

Allen, K. 1994. "Development of an instrument to identify barriers to treatment for addicted women, from their perspective." *International Journal of the Addictions* 29: 429–444.

Asher, Ramona, and Dennis Brissett. 1988. "Codependency: A view from women married to alcoholics." *The International Journal of the Addictions* 23: 331–350.

Bahna, Geraldine, and Norman B. Gordon. 1978. "Rehabilitation experiences of women ex-addicts in methadone treatment." *International Journal of the Addictions* 13: 639–655.

Copeland, J., and W. Wall. 1992. "A comparison of predictors of treatment drop-out of women seeking drug and alcohol treatment in a specialist women's and two traditional mixed-sex treatment services." *British Journal of Addiciton* 87: 883–890.

Cowan, Gloria, and Lynda W. Warren. 1994. "Codependency and gender-stereotyped traits." *Sex Roles* 30: 631–645.

Fals-Stewart, William, Gary R. Birchler, and Timothy J. O'Farrell. 1999. "Drug-abusing patients and their intimate partners: Dyadic adjustment, relationship stability, and substance use." *Journal of Abnormal Psychology* 108: 11–23.

Fals-Stewart, William, Timothy J. O'Farrell, and Gary R. Birchler. 2004. "Behavioral couples therapy for substance abuse: Rationale, methods, and findings." *Science and Practice Perspectives* 2: 30–41.

Ferrari, J. R., L. A. Jason, R. Nelson, M. Curtin-David, P. Marsh, and B. Smith. 1999. "An exploratory analysis of women and men with a self-help, communal-living, recovery setting: A new beginning in a new house." *American Journal of Drug and Alcohol Abuse* 25: 305–317.

Fraser, James. 1997. "Methadone clinic culture: The everyday realities of female methadone clients." *Qualitative Health Research* 7: 121–139.

Gasta, Carl, Robert A. Steer, Eileen Kotzker, and Jacob Schut. 1978. "Relationship between similarity of needs and marital adjustment in dyadic and monadic heroin-addicted couples." *International Journal of Family Counseling* 6: 74–80.

Gemin, Joseph. 1997. "Manufacturing codependency: Self-help as discursive formation." *Critical Studies in Mass Communication* 14: 249–266.

Harkness, Daniel. 2003. "To have and to hold: Codependency as a mediator or moderator of the relationship between substance abuse in the family of origin and adult-offspring medical problems." *Journal of Psychoactive Drugs* 35: 261–270.

Irwin, Harvey J. 1995. "Codependence, narcissism, and childhood trauma." *Journal of Clinical Psychology* 51: 658–665.

Kelley, Margaret S. 2002. "The state of the art in substance abuse programs for women in prison." In *The Incarcerated Women: Rehabilitative Programming in Women's Prisons*, ed. Susan Sharp, 119–148. Upper Saddle River, NJ: Prentice Hall.

———, and Stephen Meersman. 2000. "Gender, Codependence, and Methadone Maintenance Treatment: A Case Study of Eighteen Injection Drug Using Partners. Paper presented at College for Problems on Drug Dependence." Puerto Rico.

Kelley, Margaret S., Marsha Rosenbaum, Kelly Knight, Jeanette Irwin, and Allyson Washburn. 1996. "Violence: A barrier to methadone maintenance treatment for women injecting-drug users." *International Journal of Sociology and Social Policy* 16: 156–177.

Kirby-Green, Gloria, and J. Elton Moore. 2001. "The effects of cyclical psychodynamics therapy on the codependence of families with legally blind children." *Journal of Visual Impairment and Blindness*: 167–172.

Leonard, Kenneth E., and Kinda J. Roberts. 1996. "Alcohol in the early years of marriage." *Alcohol Health and Research World* 20: 192–196.

Leonard, Kenneth E., and Julie C. Rothbard. 1999. "Alcohol and the marriage effect." *Journal of Studies on Alcohol,* supp. 13: 139–146.

Lindley, Natasha R., Peter J. Giordano, and Elliott D. Hammer. 1999. "Codependency: predictors and psychometric issues." *Journal of Clinical Psychology* 55: 59–64.

Loughead, Teri A., Vicki L. Spurlock, and Ting Yuan-yu. 1998. "Diagnostic indicators of codependence: An investigation using the MCMI-II." *Journal of Mental Health Counseling* 20: 64–76.

Lowrance, N. A. 1990. "Domestic violence." In *Women: Alcohol and Other Drugs*, ed. Ruth C. Engs, 165–173. Dubuque, Iowa: Kendall/Hunt Publishing.

Malysiak, Rosalyn. 1997. "Exploring the theory and paradigm base for Wraparound." *Journal of Child and Family Studies* 6: 399–408.

Morrison-Velasco, Sharon. 2000. "Wrapping around empathy: The role of empathy in the Wraparound model." *Ethical Human Sciences and Services* 2: 109–117.

Northy, William F. Jr., Vicky Primer, and Lisa Christensen. 1997. "Promoting justice in the delivery of services to juvenile delinquents: The ecosystemic natural Wrap-Around model." *Child and Adolescent Social Work Journal* 14, no. 1: 5–22.

O'Brien, Patrick E., and Mauricio Gaborit. 1992. "Codependency: A disorder separate from chemical dependency." *Journal of Clinical Psychology* 48: 129–136.

Office of Justice Programs. 1999. *Conference Proceedings: National Symposium on Women Offenders.* Washington, DC: Office of Justice Programs.

O'Gorman, Patricia. 1993. "Codependency explored: A social movement in search of definition and treatment." *Psychiatric Quarterly* 64: 199–212.

Osterman, Franc, and Virginija Novak Grubic. 2000. "Family functioning of recovered alcohol-addicted patients: A comparative study." *Journal of Substance Abuse Treatment* 19: 475–479.

Prest, L. A., M. J. Benson, and H. O. Protinsky. 1998. "Family of origin and current relationshhip influences on codependency." *Family Process* 37: 513–528.

Reed, Beth Glover. 1985. "Drug misuse and dependency in women: The meaning and implications of being considered a special population or minority group." *International Journal of the Addictions* 20: 13–62.

Roehling, Patricia V., Nikole Koelbel, and Christina Rutgers. 1996. "Codependence and conduct disorder: Feminie versus masculine coping responses to abusive parenting practices." *Sex Roles* 35: 603–619.

Root, Maria P. P. 1989. "Treatment failures: The role of sexual victimization in women's addictive behavior." *American Journal of Orthopsychiatrist* 59: 542–549.

Rosenbaum, Marsha. 1981. *Women on Heroin.* New Brunswick, NJ: Rutgers University Press.

———. 1982. "Getting on methadone: The experience of the woman addict." *Contemporary Drug Problems* 11: 113–144.

Rotunda, Rob J., and Kathy Doman. 2001. "Partner enabling of substance use disorders: Critical review and future directions." *American Journal of Family Therapy* 29: 257–270.

Russell, Sue A., and Saron Wilsnack. 1991. "Adult survivors of childhood sexual abuse: Substance abuse and other consequences." In *Alcohol and Drugs are Women's Issues*, ed. Paula Roth, 61–70. Metuchen, NJ: Women's Action Alliance and The Scarecrow Press.

Seidel, John, Susanne Friese, and D. Christopher Leonard. 1995. *The Ethnograph.* Amherst, MA: Qualis Research Associates.

Skiba, Russell J., and Steven D. Nichols. 2000. "What works in Wraparound programming." In *What Works in Child Welfare*, ed. Miriam P. Kluger, Gina Alexander, et al., 23–32. Washington, DC: Child Welfare League of America.

Vannicelli, M. 1984. "Barriers to treatment of alcoholic women." *Substance and Alcohol Actions/Misuses* 5: 29–37.

Wells, Marolyn, Cheryl Clickauf-Hughes, and Rebecca Jones. 1999. "Codependency: A grassroots construct's relationship to shame-proneness, low self-esteem, and childhood parentification." *American Journal of Family Therapy* 27: 63–71.

Wilsnack, S. 1991. "Barriers to treatment for alcoholic women." *Addiction Recovery* 11: 10–12.

Wingfield, Katherine, and Todd Klempner. 2000. "What works in women-oriented treatment for substance-abusing mothers." In *What Works in Child Welfare*, ed. Kluger, Alexander, et al., 113–124.

Woodhouse, Lynn D. 1990. "An exploratory study of the use of life history methods to determine treatment needs for female substance abusers." *Response* 13: 12–15.

Wright, Paul H., and Katherine D. Wright. 1991. "Codependency: Addictive love, adjustive relating, or both?" *Contemporary Family Therapy* 13: 435–454.

Zetterlind, U., and M. Berglund. 1999. "The rate of co-dependence in spouses and relatives of alcoholics on the basis of the Cermak co-dependence scale." *Nordic Journal of Psychiatry* 53: 147–151.

PART III

⟲ Improved Responses to Drug-Related Problems

THE FINAL SECTION of this book addresses how society can improve its responses to female substance abusers by moving away from formal and informal social controls that stymie females' agency and their accrual of power. Hartwell, Malloch, and Berger, as well as Coontz and Griebel, critically evaluate existing efforts and offer ideas for alternative strategies located within an empowerment and agency perspective. These authors focus mostly on instrumental and political advocacy agency with highly stigmatized groups of women—dually diagnosed (mental illness and substance abuse), inmates, HIV-positives, and sex workers. Therefore, the focus of Part III is on the more applied aspects of dealing with the complexities of women substance abusers' lives.

The chapters begin by showing how existing programs, and the people who administer them, often obstruct women in leading better, more conventional lives over the long term, by undermining their empowerment and devaluing their agency. For example, Malloch takes a critical look at the criminalization model used in prisons across the world and especially in the United States. She finds the model hostile to women and notes how it undermines their survival-based agency, especially in prison-based drug treatment programs and even in their routine medical care, something that Berger and Hartwell also illustrate.

How can precious public resources work against female empowerment when many believe they are designed to strengthen it? Consider drug treatment programs, arguably the most heavily funded prison programs and the most relevant for female offenders. The therapeutic community (TC) approach (a dominant model) to drug treatment relies on "breaking down" hardened street attitudes among addicted offenders via peer-to-peer confrontation (DeLeon 2000). Although TCs have been successful with some drug-addicted inmates, research (see, for instance, Messina et al. 2003) shows that they can be problematic for women. Moreover, such spirit breaking presumes that all agency exercised during drug careers is negative even though, as the authors in this book consistently show, much of it is instrumental in promoting the well-being of self and others (family members). For instance, Berger's chapter clearly illustrates that women find street hustling strategies and experiences useful in pursuing abstinence and other conventional goals postintervention. Hartwell's chapter on one of the most problematic groups of female offenders—those who are dually diagnosed—describes how women's agency sustains their social relationships even though it may cause the women to cycle in and out of the criminal justice system. Again, women's illegal drug-world activities have positive and negative aspects. Pigeonholing women as either villains or victims is problematic.

Yet another concern about many prison programs for women, including TC drug treatment, is the often singular focus on restoring women to traditional gender roles, especially mothering, a focus that denies women's desire for greater fulfillment, as mentioned by Anderson and Ettorre in part I of this volume. For example, a study of thirteen correctional substance abuse programs in the United States (LIS Inc. 1994) found that prison-based drug treatment programs dealt with prior abuse and victimization among women and worked to restore these women as effective parents; on the other hand, the study found, the same programs emphasized self-awareness, pro-social dignity, accomplishment, and responsibility among youthful violent offenders (most of whom were males). Thus, many prison drug treatment programs are situated within the pathology and powerlessness paradigm, enforce traditional ideas about gender, and do little to empower women in the many roles and aspects of their lives. Moving toward an empowerment and agency approach would ask that programs meet all these objectives. This shift is part of Malloch's and Hartwell's call for more informal or community-based supports, both instead of incarceration and for successful reentry after a prison term.

Coontz and Griebel also maintain that extant policies, in this case regarding sex workers, impede women's agency and deny their access to structural power. By situating drug-related sex work at the local level into a broader global sex industry and global issue of human trafficking, Coontz and Griebel show that women prostitutes' survival agency benefits themselves and conventional economies (which is also Anderson's point in chapter 1) yet these women are usually who suffer legal and social consequence from it. Coontz and Griebel claim that societies like the United States tolerate the sex industry but not the female prostitute who provides the services. They make provocative suggestions for policy change, including decriminalization of prostitution, harm-reduction approaches to drug use, and increased social supports to improve sex workers' lives. Like Malloch, Berger, and Hartwell, Coontz and Griebel urge more community-based resources outside of the punitive criminal justice system.

One last point pertains to the significance of stigma that also undermines women substance abusers' positive agency and possession of power. The pathology and powerlessness perspective's view of women as either villains or victims is an extremely negative image that can, at times, exact a social death. When researchers, policy makers, practitioners, the media, and the general public perpetuate and endorse these images, they reduce the life chances of those involved. Redefining a negative image, public identity, or stereotype is extremely difficult, especially if it has been uniformly supported over a long period of time.

The social sciences have consistently documented that stigma reduces life chances and disallows the accumulation of power and resources. Still, there has been little success in finding ways to diminish it. So, where Coontz and Griebel and other authors in this book call for the reversal of stigma to improve the lives of women substance abusers, Berger's chapter just may provide a way to achieve that goal.

Berger's chapter on HIV-positive women substance abusers concerns how women confront sexual stigma, as a type of empowerment strategy. This strategy is a fusion of symbolic resistance and political activism/advocacy agency. Berger finds that political activism and advocacy for oneself and others allows women substance abusers to overcome the negative views society has of them. Her respondents confronted practitioners of all kinds, who treated them as undeserving victims or even a type of villain (bad women responsible for contracting HIV), and mobilized resources on behalf of their own and others' medical and social well-being. The result: personal success, changed social attitudes, and improved conditions. In other words, political activism and advocacy yield relational and structural power for even the most heavily stigmatized women in society.

The alternative vision for policy and practice outlined here may be embraced by some and rejected by others. Moreover, some may find the options discussed here compelling and novel, while others may be far less moved or convinced. Something more likely is that women substance abusers may already know about, and have experienced, what the authors here recommend. The opening quotes by Nicole and Kitt, for example, in Berger's chapter indicate that women substance abusers understand that their illicit drug world agency will be of value in the conventional world, a theme consistently stressed throughout this collection. Therefore, whether or not we successfully shift the narrative away from pathology and powerlessness to empowerment and agency, women substance abusers plan to maximize their agency daily, with few demands and little attention from the public and professionals. This was the case with the family that Tracy describes in her epilogue. Think how much better we all could do with a new approach, resources, and action to assist them.

REFERENCES

De Leon, G. 2000. *The Therapeutic Community: Theory, Model, and Method.* New York: Springer Publishing.

LIS, Inc. 1994. *Profiles of Correctional Substance Abuse Treatment Programs: Women and Youthful Violent Offenders.* Longmont, CO: National Institute of Corrections.

CHAPTER 8

A Spoonful of Sugar?
Treating Women in Prison

Margaret S. Malloch

INTRODUCTION

This chapter examines the increasing emphasis on criminal justice policy with regard to drug issues, and the implications and effects of this emphasis for women. In particular, it will focus on the expansion of imprisonment for women and the potential consequences of this expansion for the development of services within prisons. This chapter will consider the issues of agency (action that benefits self and others—see Anderson, this volume) and empowerment (ability and competence to influence and achieve desired outcomes—see Anderson, this volume), as experienced and applied by women in prison, through an examination of penal policies and responses to drug users in prison. The analysis will illustrate the importance of resisting the current emphasis given to criminal justice responses to women drug users, and will outline the need for comprehensive social and public policy initiatives.

This chapter does not set out to give a detailed discussion of program content, but will illustrate the key requirements for effective practice, based on current research and evaluation. While reviewing the developments that have informed responses to women in the criminal justice system, the difficulties of implementing these responses within the prison will be examined.

In particular, it is noted that the emphasis on incarceration and criminal justice leads to systems of punishment and control that fail to address the key issues facing women drug users in society, and that can compound the difficulties these women must overcome on a regular basis.

BACKGROUND

Increasing numbers of women are incarcerated in prisons throughout the world, although the number of women in prison as a percentage of overall prison figures remains relatively small: around 5 percent in Scotland and Canada; 6 percent in England and Wales, and in New Zealand; 7 percent in Australia, and just under 9 percent in the United States of America (International Centre for Prison Studies 2005). In most countries, the number of women in prison has increased dramatically over the last few decades, significantly outstripping increases in the number of male prisoners.

This increase has had notable effects on particular groups. Minority ethnic, black, and indigenous women constitute disproportionate levels of the female prison populations in several countries, notably Canada (Correctional Service Canada 2004), Australia (Goulding 2004), the United Kingdom, and the United States of America (Campbell 2000; Bloom et al. 2003; Sudbury 2005). For example, in Western Australia, women make up less than 3 percent of the prison population but Aboriginal women constitute 48 percent of the female prison population (Taylor 2004). In Canada, although indigenes make up about 3 percent of the general population, over 20 percent of women held in federal institutions are indigenes (Correctional Services Canada 2004). In England and Wales, 29 percent of women in prison in 2004 were from ethnic minority backgrounds; 19 percent of the female prison population were foreign nationals (Prison Reform Trust 2006, 15). In the United Kingdom, foreign national women sentenced for drug trafficking offenses receive some of the longest sentences distributed (even if one includes sentences for violent offenses).

Internationally, more women are being sent to prison for drug or drug-related offenses and for crimes motivated by poverty (Home Office 2004; Taylor 2004). Further, in some countries the introduction of mandatory minimum sentences for specific drug offenses and the overclassification of women as "security risks" has contributed to this increase (Hannah-Moffat 2000). The number of women on some form of criminal justice supervision is also significant, with over one million women in the United States alone being subject to this requirement (McCampbell 2005). There is no evidence that increases in crime can account for the rise in the numbers of women in prison; rather, it appears that women are being sentenced more severely (Home Office 2004; Taylor 2004). This development is linked to women's economic vulnerability and subsequent offending patterns rather than to either increased levels of crime or increases in the seriousness of crimes committed (Owen 2003; Drugscope 2005). Many women disclose that they became involved in crime to fund a drug habit (Drugscope 2005). Indeed, women's offending is often linked to their material and social situation rather than to other inherent risk factors. The "hybridization of risk and need" has serious consequences for women (Hannah-Moffat 2002 and 2005; Hardyman and Van Voorhis 2004).

The number of prisoners with a drug and/or alcohol problem is significant, and the rise has been dramatic in the last two decades. In Canada, up to 93 percent of provincial offenders have serious problems with drug/ alcohol use issues, although admissions for alcohol or drug-related offenses constitute a much lower proportion of direct admissions (Head 2001, 1). The number of women in the United States imprisoned for drug offenses rose 888 percent between 1986 and 1996 (Taylor 2004, 3). In the United Kingdom between 1992 and 2002, the number of women imprisoned after conviction for drug offenses rose by 414 percent (Home Office 2004). The incidence of drug use by women prior to imprisonment is high. In Scotland, 90–100 percent of women prisoners are believed drug users (HM Inspectorate of Prisons for Scotland 2004); similarly, other countries report high rates of illicit drug use among women prisoners prior to sentencing (Department of Correctional Services 2002; Ramsey 2003). Problem alcohol and tranquilizer use is also reported high among women involved with the criminal justice system (Ramsey 2003). Universally, rates of drug use among women prisoners appear to exceed such rates for male prisoners (EMCDDA 2001). Taylor (2004, 3) notes that: "women are imprisoned in much greater numbers, proportionally, for drug-related crimes than for any other. In this sense, drug related crimes could be seen as a 'female crime,' compared to other crimes which are more likely to be committed by men (such as armed robbery, assault, etc.)." It has been suggested that the war on drugs has constituted a war on women, particularly poor women and women from black/ethnic communities (Bloom et al. 2003, 62). Taylor (2004) goes on to suggest that, given the nature and length of sentences for drug offenses, a form of gender discrimination may be operating that results in "women's" crimes being *punished* more harshly than "men's."

CRIMINALIZING DISTRESS

Women in prison throughout the world share many similar background characteristics, in addition to high levels of drug and/or alcohol problems. Repeated research reports and surveys have illustrated that many women in prison have had experiences of poverty and social deprivation; physical, mental and/or sexual abuse; and mental health problems (Task Force on Federally Sentenced Women 1990; HM Inspectorate of Prison 1997 and 2001; Prison Reform Trust 2000; Scottish Executive 2002; Bloom, Owen, and Covington 2003; Home Office 2003; Goulding 2004; Drugscope 2005; McCampbell 2005).[1] Female prisoners have themselves experienced high rates of victimization, and are much less likely to be imprisoned for crimes of violence than are their male counterparts (Scottish Executive 2002; Women in Prison 2004).

The experiences that characterize the backgrounds of many women in prison have led to a shift from the medicalization to the criminalization of distress. A social model of trauma (Herman 1992) is important for the development of resources for women struggling to cope with feelings of shame and stigma and to address the painful emotional damage caused by physical and sexual abuse and the ongoing constraints on relationships with friends and family that imprisonment obviously creates (Task Force on Federally Sentenced Women 1990; HM Inspectorate of Prisons 1997 and 2001; Prison Reform Trust 2000; Hume 2001; Scottish Executive 2002; Bloom, Owen, and Covington 2003; Home Office 2003; Goulding 2004; Drugscope 2005; Pollack 2005). However, prisons have been traditionally charged with containing the imprisoned, and the extent to which they have the capacity to alleviate the problems faced by prisoners—or the ability to do anything other than exacerbate these difficulties—is a significant question.

Internationally, prison services are called upon to provide resources to meet the needs of those incarcerated. Within the context of punishment, help is made available to prisoners, with the overall intention of reducing future offending and supporting prisoners to change their lives—while they are in effect, a captive audience. Ongoing attempts to develop services for drug users within prisons are based on the recognition that problem drug users experience frequent periods of imprisonment (Addaction 2005) and many individuals may be more likely to have contact with criminal justice than with treatment agencies. Evidence that coerced treatment can be effective has been used to increase treatment options as alternatives to custody, but also strengthens arguments for the provision of resources within prisons. However, the success of prison programs in reducing reoffending is mixed. Evidence from Canada suggests that drug treatment programs may have some success in reducing reentry to custody, but Australian experience suggests that treatment in prison is ineffective, partly due to insufficient staffing levels (Cameron 2001). Clearly success rates will depend on many factors, not least the programs themselves. There are significant variations in the content and quality, at national and international levels, of programs for substance users in prisons (EMCDDA 2001; Ramsey 2003; MacDonald 2004).

However, before going on to consider programs for drug users in prison, it is important to consider the broader effects of incarceration and the impact of penal regimes on the prisoners. Many of the controls that the penal system serves to enact are already present in the lives of women (Howe 1994; Malloch 1999). This fact highlights the fundamental necessity of analyzing patriarchal social relations in terms of the imprisonment of women and in the wider penal sphere. For women, imprisonment constitutes punishment, a fact that has regularly been obscured by the rhetoric of therapy and feminization (Howe 1994; Carlen 1998; Malloch 1999). Images of deviance and criminality operate specifically for women, as do measures of control; within prisons, this determines the emphasis given to the prioritization of policies geared toward containment and control or, conversely, toward reform or rehabilitation. Failure to address the realities of the lives of women and to acknowledge the differences between what they, and what men, experience in prison does not constitute equal treatment, but could be considered, rather, as "vengeful equity" (Bloom 2005). Pollack (2005 80) notes: "The dismantling of social welfare systems, increasing privatization of public institutions, a shrinking secure labour market and a rapidly growing prison industrial complex . . . all provide fertile ground for the proliferation of the disciplinary use of therapeutic discourse."

Prison, as previously noted, has a particular impact on specific social groups. Although drug use crosses all social barriers, and individuals from all social classes are imprisoned for drug offenses, the majority of people in prison for *all* offenses are young and working-class, and disproportionately from minority ethnic communities. Policing and prescribing policies as introduced in both prison and the community historically reflects an explicit class basis. Cutbacks in social services, health, and education, alongside the increasing criminalization of women with mental health problems, has seen more people filtering onto the streets as welfare services are either unable or unwilling to cope. Subsequent increases in the criminalization and marginalization of particular social groups have resulted in growing prison populations (Parenti 1999; Campbell 2000; Malloch 2000). The increasing criminalization of drug users and people with mental health problems clearly illustrates the growing complexity of the problems that prisons are required to respond to, with particular effects on women.

The "carceral clawback" defined by Carlen (1998 and 2002) is accompanied by cutbacks in benefits, housing, and other welfare services, paralleled by the "war on drugs" and stringent responses to crime and antisocial behavior, which has had an inordinate effect on the female prison population. At the same time, the penal–welfare complex described by Garland (2001) has led to changes in the community that have an impact on sentencing practices overall. Women are up-tariffed to receive treatment that may be limited in the community but has become more accessible under the auspices of the criminal justice system, and similarly women are up-tariffed by sentencers reluctant to impose financial penalties on those individuals with few visible means of income or support. Underpinning these developments lies the feminization and racialization of poverty (Maher 1997; Boyd 2004; Sudbury 2005).

COMPASSIONATE COERCION?

Prison services, internationally, have attempted to deal with drug users in prison by developing strategies that attempt to combine security and control with the provision of therapeutic and rehabilitative resources. However, when two distinct policy directions are intended to operate simultaneously, it is likely that greater emphasis will be given to one element over another. This is not to suggest that punishment and treatment are incompatible, but, when resources are limited, certain objectives will be prioritized at the expense of others. The emphasis accorded to discipline and security as a prime function of imprisonment is seen by many prison staff as in accord with their main objective. "Empowered" women are unlikely to be well received within this context. Other aims are often considered secondary to the maintenance of order, and this is reflected in the organization and operation of penal regimes (Malloch 2000).

The prison, although having the opportunity to come into contact with more drug users than most treatment services, may not be best place to provide support. The highly discretionary implementation of policies in relation to medical care, and the provision of medication for drug users in prison, are frequently problematic. Also, the limited medical support available and the reluctance of establishments to provide comprehensive detoxification programs are problematic for many prisoners; this can lead women to conceal their drug use from the authorities, believing that it would not be in their interests to disclose this information when they do not perceive any benefits to be gained from doing so (Malloch 2000; Home Office 2003).

The discretionary decision making of medical officers and health-care workers becomes problematic when based on moralistic judgements and beliefs, which is often the case in relation to drug use (Malloch 2000; Boyd 2004; Drugscope 2005). Additionally, the pressure on limited resources and time available to medical staff will infringe on the opportunities available to design individualized programs of care. Short-term medical provision (particularly of opiate substitutes) is often the main form of support for drug withdrawal. Substitute medication for crack withdrawal is often limited or nonexistent, making this group of users even less likely to access services within prison (Home Office 2003).

Attempts to prevent access to drugs in prison seem doomed to fail. Stricter enforcement strategies lead to more covert responses by prisoners and to behavior that poses even greater risks to health (such as sharing injecting equipment). Clampdowns do little to recover drugs and are neither deterrent nor preventative. The emphasis given to measures of security and control highlight the punitive and controlling aspects of the system. As a result of policies focusing on known users, problems associated with drug use in a controlled environment (such as bullying, intimidation, and smuggling) are often displaced onto those least likely to be suspected by staff. The gendered impact of mandatory drug testing (urinalysis) is clearly problematic in its effects on women (Carlen 1998; Bloom et al. 2003; Boyd 2004).

Although prison systems have been developed primarily to meet the needs of men, there has been a growing recognition that the needs of male and female prisoners differ, as do the most effective approaches, for men or for women, to treatment for drug and alcohol use problems (Bloom et al. 2003). This recognition clearly needs to inform the provision of resources in prisons.

Sentencing women to prison to "break their habit" is, although occasionally effective, generally misguided. In a recent Home Office report (Home Office 2003, 2), "over a quarter of the women interviewed said they were still using heroin while in prison, albeit mainly on an occasional basis." Consequently, many women in prison have access to drugs most of the time, but only limited access to resources and counselling. Certainly, the experience of imprisonment is unlikely to persuade most women to end their use of drugs, and, ironically, it often leads to drug use or experimentation. The emphasis given to security and punishment does little to halt the supply and use of drugs in penal establishments; however, it does serve to increase internal tensions, resulting in attempts by prisoners to resist clampdowns and controlling regimes. Further, the violation of human rights by individual prison workers within women's prisons has been identified in a number of countries (Amnesty International USA 1999; Canadian Human Rights Commission 2003; Scraton and Moore 2004).

The difficulties that exist due to the distribution of power and status between prisoners and staff are unlikely to be easily overcome. Prison service in the United Kingdom are returning to the use of outside organizations for the provision of services to prisoners, even while continuing to expand and develop the expertise of their own staff. However, the organization of penal regimes makes communication between prisoners and staff generally difficult. Prisons are not therapeutic environments, and requests for help are often unmet. A recent Home Office study (2003, 2) noted that 43 percent of women in the study who had sought help for anxiety or depression in prison had been prescribed medication, with very few receiving any other intervention. Black/ethnic women were much less likely to seek help for emotional problems in prison.

There are additional problems in the organization of programs for drug users, which are also issues that community-based services need to address. The Prison Service, in its resource provision, has struggled to acknowledge the many types of drug users. This causes particular problems for prisoners who define themselves as recreational users and who are unable to identify with the dominant image of drug users, especially if they were convicted of a supply/trafficking offense. These prisoners' failure to participate (particularly if charged with a drug offense) is viewed by the authorities as a failure to recognize or accept their "problem," and a failure to seek solutions by changing their attitude. In this context, agency is necessarily contingent on "appropriateness," or perceived conformity. Resistance or nonconformity is likely to result in sanctions; noncompliance can lead to individuals being defined as appropriate targets for punishment. Such individuals are seen as untreatable. This reflects an established principle of imprisonment whereby acknowledgement of "wrongdoing" is a necessary prerequisite for rehabilitation.

Agency and empowerment are conditional, and conformity with the prison regime is approved of; challenges will be neutralized or discouraged. Campbell (2000, 42) notes that: "demand-side drug policy reflects a cultural preoccupation with individual accountability, de-legitimating broader forms of social responsibility." Prison programs and correctional policy can dilute structural analysis, reconstructing issues of social exclusion as problems of individual psychological and social functioning. Pollack (2005, 73) points out, "Consequently, technologies of government in the form of mental health treatment are invoked to encourage self-regulation" (emphasis in original). Programs or environments that attempt to foster empowerment may well come into conflict with the traditional medical model of intervention.

Prison may provide prisoners with access to information and advice around drug-related issues and harm reduction. However, there are clear problems in terms of the provision of counseling and support. Difficulties ensue, such as the lack of follow-up treatment during, as well as after, sentence. Care is required as to how information is presented, particularly in an environment where personal opinions and moral judgments often create further distortions.

Policy guidelines emphasize the importance of providing resources directed toward reduction or cessation of drug use; these take the form of counseling programs provided by multidisciplinary teams within the prison, and programs that help the individual to confront her or his drug use and work toward reducing or ending it (National Institute of Justice 2000 and 2003; Bloom et al. 2003; Ramsay 2003). Effective counseling relies on the proposition that the individual wants to cease drug use and is willing to work towards this end. Voluntarism and participation are essential factors in facilitating change. In the prison environment—where choice is clearly reduced or nonexistent—these factors are unlikely to exist; as a result, people who fail to convince the authorities of their desire and motivation to end their drug use (by participating in counseling or programs for drug users) will often become the focus for stricter security measures. Individual agency and opportunities to make desired changes are limited, open for negotiation only within firmly defined parameters and therefore conditional.

TACKLING THE BIG ISSUES

Clearly, given the backgrounds of many women in prison, there is a need for any form of support or resources aiming to support women to reduce or end drug and/or alcohol use, and to go beyond the issue of addiction—to address trauma. Zlotnick (2002) highlights the importance of services related to childhood physical and sexual abuse as well as drug dependency/addiction-related services (as does the Home Office—see Home Office 2003).

The problems that women experience as drug users tend to be different than men's: women are more likely to have a partner who uses (Bloom et al. 2003; Best and Abdulrahim 2005); women may be required to maintain their partner's supply (Taylor 1993; Maher 1997; Druglink 2003); women may be subject to domestic violence in a current relationship[2] (Gilbert et al. 2000); women may have experienced past sexual abuse (Scottish Office 1998; Howard League 2000; Prison Reform Trust 2000; Scottish Executive 2002); and they may be suffering from poor mental health and/or low self-esteem (Najavits et al. 1997; Gilchrist 2002; Cusick et al. 2003). Studies suggest that women are more likely to inject, to share injecting equipment, and to test positive for HIV than are their male counterparts (Best and Abdulrahim 2005). As Bloom et al. (2003, 43) indicate, women drug users tend to have a "greater number of life problems than do most male substance abusers. Such problems may be related to employment, family issues, child care and mental health." It is acknowledged that a woman's role as a mother can impact on the likelihood that she will use services, and the lack of child-care provisions can hinder access. Similarly, fear of children being taken into care, or of encountering judgmental attitudes (especially if pregnant), can prevent women from seeking or responding to support (Howard League 2000; Advisory Council on the Misuse of Drugs 2003; Scottish Executive 2003). These issues are exacerbated when women are drawn into the criminal justice system.

Taking these issues into account, academics and practitioners have identified some key components for effective program content, based on an understanding of women's lives and the extent to which interventions relating to substance use and offending behavior require an acknowledgment of broader contexts. This understanding has enabled the identification of some key characteristics for effective program development (Bloom et al. 2003; Covington and Bloom 2004; McCampbell 2005). These include: the significance of programs that are gender-responsive in design and delivery, from assessment to after-care; use of theoretical knowledge about women's pathways into the criminal justice system, to inform services for women; the necessity of women-only groups as a feature of services, especially for primary treatment. Further, in relation to service provision, it is important that assessments and services be based on multi-agency cooperation (Fowler 2001), particularly in terms of the integration of mental health and substance abuse services, and that treatment is individualized, with care plans developed to meet individual needs, identified through comprehensive assessment. Given the significance of relationships as a component of service provision, staff should be gender-responsive and gender-sensitive, with ongoing training available. As far as possible, women workers should have some shared experiences with, and be capable of taking a holistic approach to, the lives of the women with whom they are working (Koons et al. 1997; Fowler 2001). Therapeutic environments should be created to provide a "safe" environment for service delivery, and after-care should form a key element in service provision (Ramsey 2003; Addaction 2005; Holloway et al. 2005).

The context and delivery of services is important, to provide a response to the wider context of women's lives. This may be crucial, given the low levels of success for more limited responses. For example, recent research for the Home Office (Cann 2006) on the effects of prison-based cognitive skills programs for women in England and Wales showed no statistically significant differences in one- and two-year reconviction rates between participants and nonparticipants in matched comparison groups. Similar findings were evident for adult males and for young offenders. There is little benefit from changing cognitive patterns if the structural realities of an individual's life remain unchanged.

Moreover, the availability of resources is likely to differ between institutions. Fowler (2001, 90) suggests that "problems faced by individual prison services in relation to the provision and delivery of drug services are delineated by local, regional and national issues." Nevertheless, despite disparities in availability and content, when programs are available to support individuals to address problem drug use, levels of uptake are relatively high, with women more likely than male prisoners to self-refer (May 2005). This illustrates the importance of ensuring that treatment is better suited to meet the needs of women, to achieve successful outcomes (Ramsey 2003; Holloway et al. 2005).

However, the main issue for program development is the extent to which such problems can ever be addressed within the confines of a penal institution. As Comack (2000, 121) astutely comments: "Part of the difficulty stems from the fact that the women's troubles have their source and basis *outside* the prison walls. Confined within the prison, women do not have the power or autonomy to attend to these troubles" (emphasis in original). Providing services with a therapeutic emphasis is made more difficult by the prison environment, with its lack of confidentiality and diminished opportunities for supportive counseling. Tackling the wider issues that relate to an individual's use of drugs becomes inherently problematic within this context. In spite of the official rhetoric (which portrays the prison as enabling women to end their drug use) the reality is that prison denies the potential for developing a trusting/supportive environment. In contrast, prominence is given both materially and ideologically to security, control, and punishment. Individual agency and collective empowerment are unlikely to flourish, unless they fit within the existing predefined regimes.

For women drug users, a gender-specific application of rehabilitation is necessary, but not unproblematic, although increasingly recognized and adopted as part of program formats in women's prisons. Rehabilitation programs focus on assertiveness training and enhancement of self-esteem. Although these may be of benefit in some cases, they tend to operate from a theoretical basis that suggests the individual woman is in some way "inadequate" and that this can be "treated." This form of counseling provides an alternative only when underwritten by a feminist analysis in which individuals' experiences are linked to wider structural issues. The impact of addressing self-esteem issues and working to develop assertiveness skills may be significantly limited within the prison environment, which is unlikely to foster the ongoing use of these tools. Change is a recognized condition of recovery, requiring both changes in self-perception (e.g., self-esteem) and the development of new social networks. Again, few of these conditions can be effectively established or maintained during incarceration. Agency is a crucial part of this process, but while it comes from within, there may be few opportunities in the penal environment for a positive change in self-image. Clearly, the opportunity to come off drugs/alcohol and to stop using during the period of imprisonment will assist in this process.

The addict is central to his or her recovery because the change in status
that is entailed in coming off drugs is something that is largely determined by the individual. This is not to say that services have little or no
impact on the recovery process but to recognise that, in a fundamental
sense, it is the individual who has to change his or her life for recovery
to occur. (McIntosh and McKeganey 2002, 160)

It has been suggested that imprisonment provides an important opportunity to "change" the individual or to contain the unchangeable. This suggestion has particular relevance for drug users who, according to policy,
have the ideal opportunity presented by imprisonment to reduce or end
their use of drugs. Yet the likelihood of change is often mere rhetoric,
given the limited resources available in prisons and the impact of the prison
environment and operational regimes; individual agency and empowerment are necessarily limited within the context of the "total institution."
This is not to suggest that prisoners do not resist their circumstances, but
to illustrate that the opportunities for change are restricted. While incarcerated, there is little opportunity to change anything of life outside
the prison, although comprehensive after-care can, where it exists, clearly
provide an ongoing continuum of support. Where coherent services are
available, the tension between the prioritization of care and the emphasis
on security, particularly in prisons working to capacity or overcrowded,
causes significant tensions for both prisoners and staff (Malloch 2000; National Institute of Justice 2003).

The multiple problems associated with illicit drug use are amplified
within the prison system. Drug users, staff, and, often, non-drug-using
prisoners are faced with difficult situations resulting from the complex factors that provide the context of drug use in secure institutions. A significant
conclusion is that prison serves to magnify the problems associated with
drug use, as a result of the operation of custodial regimes and the underlying objectives of imprisonment.

Prisons do not encourage the development of relationships. Clearly,
prisoners will create their own friendships and alliances, and this forms
an underlying feature of agency and empowerment within regimes. However, such relationships are often limited and contested, perceived as problematic for the smooth functioning of the institution. Certainly it appears
a feature of custodial settings that prisoners and guards are required to
maintain their distance. Despite the importance of the relational aspect
of therapeutic interventions, staff training in prisons is geared to respond
to "danger" rather than to the development of effective communication
between prisoners and staff. The creation of positive relationships among
prisoners, and between prisoners and staff, is crucial for the creation of a

"safe" environment (Koons et al. 1997; Bloom et al. 2003; Covington and Bloom 2004; Loucks et al. 2006), yet such relationships are not a readily available feature of prison regimes (Hannah-Moffat and Shaw 2000; Malloch 2000; Carlen 1998 and 2002; Boyd 2004).

Treatment has to be multidimensional in terms of both the intervention and the environment to respond to needs associated with safety, connection, and empowerment (Hume 2001; Home Office 2003). This responsiveness requires a deliberate attempt to create an environment conducive to providing support. Within prisons, constantly underpinned by issues of discipline and control, such support—despite the best will of individual staff—is likely to be infringed. Regimes based on power and control will inevitably create an "atmosphere of distrust" (Comack 2001, 122); in many ways, the use of mandatory drug testing—where available corresponding support is limited—illustrate the ways in which current approaches are often "entrenched in a disciplinary regime" (Head 2001, 3). An examination of the social context requires analysis of the broader social, economic, and political factors, structures, and inequalities leading to disempowerment and low self-esteem.

CONCLUDING POINTS

Broader policies are continually changing, presently moving toward: an expansion of penal institutions; increased numbers of women serving longer sentences; and more austere, security-conscious regimes. Given these developments, an ongoing examination and review of policies is required. At present, the lengthy sentences given for many drug offenses, and the growing tendency to send users to prison, means that drug offenders' numbers in custody will continue to increase unless there is a sharp change in such policies. Resources in the community must be developed to offer realistic alternatives to custody. Limited changes may improve certain aspects of penal regimes; however, an overall commitment to reevaluating the role of prisons, and particularly to reevaluating the imprisonment of women, is urgently required. It is crucial that the limits of empowering women within prisons be recognized, when programs which aim to rebuild self-esteem and promote change are introduced into such a context.

The Howard League (1990) argues that there is a need to develop effective resources for drug users in the community (see also Social Work Services and Prisons Inspectorate for Scotland 1998), rather than to try and develop services in prison, which will be limited in effect but likely to lead to more women being sent there, ostensibly for treatment. The emphasis on the provision of treatment through the criminal justice system has led to the development of a number of initiatives, such as Drug Treatment and Testing

Orders (DTTOs) and Drug Courts, but there is a real problem of relying on coerced treatment when support is not available on a voluntary basis, as a result of the impoverishment of community resources (Malloch 2004a and 2004b). This can lead to a situation where drug treatment is available for the rich, with prison for the poor (Boyd 2004). Drug Courts and DTTOs have been limited in female referrals and, given the mandatory model of treatment, have led to difficulties for a number of women in their ability to comply (D'Angelo 2002; Eley et al. 2002; Malloch et al. 2003; Boyd 2004). Similarly, evidence from the United States on the effects of coerced treatment and use of Drug Courts is mixed, surrounded by uncertainty regarding outcomes, and raising issues of intrusion for "low-risk" offenders. There are a number of innovative developments taking place internationally that attempt to provide a holistic response to women within distinctive prison environments (such as the Ocimaw Ochi Healing Lodge—see Correctional Services Canada 2002) and within local communities (such as the 218 Centre in Scotland and the Asha centre in England—see Rumgay 2004).

At a practical level, it is possible to argue for and support the development of a number of initiatives in prison, including: the integration of mental health and substance abuse services; gender-responsive assessments and treatment; individualized interventions; informed and responsive staff; services that are informed by and reflect the realities of women's lives; an environment that is, as far as possible, therapeutic (Task Force on Federally Sentenced Women 1999; Scottish Executive 2002; Bloom et al. 2003; Home Office 2003). But we need to proceed with caution. As Campbell (2000, 222) points out, "The redefinition of coercion as compassion is a disciplinary mechanism to which women are highly vulnerable because of their responsibility for social reproduction . . . The emphasis on personal responsibility creates an atmosphere of public surveillance and minimizes public responsibility for structural change and redistributive social policy."

There is a very real need to address the broader issue of the imprisonment of women. Rather than emphasizing women's distinctive needs, in isolation, it is crucial that their lesser criminality be made explicit. No matter how supportive prison staff are or what programs are available, at the end of the day prison is prison. Imprisonment becomes another problem the women have to contend with. Unfortunately, many only get linked into the services they need after they have become involved with the criminal justice system—a direct result of the impoverishment of resources in the community. This represents the failure of social and public policy, juxtaposed with an emphasis on criminal justice and the overreliance on imprisonment in our societies.

NOTES

1. In the United Kingdom, 14 percent of suicides in prison in 2004 were committed by women, although women only account for 6 percent of the prison population (Prison Reform Trust 2005, 10).
2. Only one in ten British refuges for women fleeing domestic violence will automatically admit women with drug problems (Drugscope 2005, 26).

REFERENCES

Addaction. 2005. *Aftercare Consultation 2005: The Service User Perspective.* London: Addaction.

Advisory Council on the Misuse of Drugs. 2003. *Hidden Harm: Responding to the Needs of Children of Problem Drug Users.* London: ACMD.

Amnesty International USA. 1999. *Not Part of My Sentence: Violations of the Human Rights of Women in Custody.* New York: Amnesty International.

Best, D., and D. Abdulrahim. 2005. *Women in Drug Treatment Services.* London: National Treatment Agency for Substance Misuse, Research Briefing: 6.

Bloom, B. 2005. "Creating Gender-Responsive Services for Women in the Criminal Justice System: From Research to Practice." Paper presented at conference "What Works with Women Offenders," University of Monash, Prato, Italy, July 2005.

———, B. Owen, and S. Covington, S. 2003. *Gender Responsive Strategies: Research, Practice, and Guiding Principles for Women Offenders.* U.S. Department of Justice: National Institute of Corrections.

Boyd, S. 2004. *From Witches to Crack Moms: Women, Drug Law, and Policy.* Durham, NC: Carolina Academic Press.

Cameron, M. 2001. "Women Prisoners and Correctional programs." *Trends and Issues in Crime and Criminal Justice,* no. 194. Canberra: Australian Institute of Criminology.

Campbell, N. D. 2000. *Using Women: Gender, Drug Policy, and Social Justice.* New York: Routledge.

Canadian Human Rights Commission. 2003. *Protecting Their Rights: A Systemic Review of Human Rights in Correctional Services for Federally Sentenced Women.* Canada: CHRC.

Cann, J. 2006. *Cognitive Skills Programmes: Impact on Reducing Reconviction among a Sample of Female Prisoners.* London: Home Office Findings 276.

Carlen, P. 1998. *Sledgehammer: Women's Imprisonment at the Millenium.* London: Macmillan Press.

———, ed. 2002. *Women and Punishment: The Struggle for Justice.* Cullompton, Devon, UK: Willan Publishing.

Comack, E. 2000. "The Prisoning of Women: Meeting Women's Needs." In K. Hannah-Moffat and M. Shaw, eds., *An Ideal Prison? Critical Essays on Women's Imprisonment in Canada.* Halifax, Nova Scotia: Fernwood Publishing.

Correctional Services Canada (CSC). 2002. *Report on the Evaluation of the Okimaw Ochi Healing Lodge.* CSC on-line report, http://www.csc-cc.gc.ca/text/PA/oohl_eval_e.shtml.

———. 2004. *Women Offenders: Perspectives, Profiles, Programs.* Forum on Corrections Research Featured Issues, vol. 16, no. 1. Ottawa: CSC.

Covington, S., and B. Bloom. 2004. "Creating gender-responsive services in correctional settings: Context and considerations." Paper presented at 2004 American Society of Criminology Conference, November 17–20, Nashville, TN.

Cusick, L., A. Martin, and T. May. 2003. *Vulnerability and Involvement in Drug Use and Sex Work*. Home Office Research Study 268. London: Home Office.

D'Angelo, L. 2002. "Women and addiction: Challenges for drug court practitioners." *Justice System Journal* 23, no. 3: 385–400.

Department of Correctional Services. 2002. "Illicit Drugs and Correctional Services." Issues Paper for South Australian Drugs Summit. Unpublished.

Drugscope. 2005. *Using Women*. London: Drugscope.

Eley, S., M. Malloch, G. McIvor, R. Yates, and A. Brown. 2002. *Glasgow's Pilot Drug Court in Action: The First Six Months*. Edinburgh: Scottish Executive.

European Monitoring Centre for Drugs and Drug Addiction (EMCDDA). 2001. *An Overview Study: Assistance to Drug Users in European Prisons*. Portugal: European Monitoring Centre for Drugs and Drug Addiction.

Fowler, V. 2001. *Drug Services for Youth and Women in Prisons in Europe*. London: ENDSP and Cranstoun Drug Services.

Garland, D. 2001. *The Culture of Control: Crime and Social Order in Contemporary Society*. Oxford: Oxford University Press.

Gilbert, L., N. Bassel, N. Schilling, and T. Wada. 2000. "Drug abuse and partner violence among women in methadone treatment." *Journal of Family Violence* 15, no. 3: 209–228.

Gilchrist, G. 2002. *Psychiatric Morbidity among Female Drug Users in Glasgow*. Report for Greater Glasgow Drug Action Team. Glasgow: Greater Glasgow NHS Board.

Goulding, D. 2004. *Severed Connections: An Exploration of the Impact of Imprisonment on Women's Familial and Social Connectedness*. Perth, Western Australia: Murdoch University.

Hannah-Moffat, K. 2000. "Prisons that empower: Neo-liberal governance in Canadian women's prisons." *British Journal of Criminology* 40: 510–531.

———. 2002. *Governing through Need: The Hybridizations of Risk/Need in Penality*. Paper presented at the British Society of Criminology Conference, University of Keele, UK.

———. 2005. "Criminogenic needs and the transformative risk subject." *Punishment and Society* 7, no. 1: 29–51.

———, and Shaw, M., eds. 2000. *An Ideal Prison? Critical Essays on Women's Imprisonment in Canada*. Halifax, Nova Scotia: Fernwood Publishing.

Hardyman, P., and P. Van Voorhis. 2004. *Developing Gender-Specific Classification Systems for Women Offenders*. Washington, DC: U.S. Department of Justice, National Institute of Corrections.

Head, D. 2001. *Alcohol and Drugs: A Perspective from Corrections in the Province of Saskatchewan*. Correctional Service Canada. http://www.csc-scc.gc.ca/text/pblct/forum/e133/e133d_e.shtml.

Herman, J. L. 1993. *Trauma and Recovery: From Domestic Abuse to Political Terror*. London: Pandora.

HM Inspectorate of Prisons. 1997. *Women in Prison: A Thematic Review*, London: Home Office.

———. 2001. *Follow-up to Women in Prison: A Thematic Review*. London: Home Office.

HM Inspectorate of Prisons for Scotland. 2004. *HMP and YOI Cornton Vale*. Edinburgh: Scottish Executive.

Holloway, K., T. Bennet, and D. Farrington. 2005. *The Effectiveness of Criminal Justice and Treatment Programs in Reducing Drug-Related Crime: A Systematic Review*. London: Home Office, online report 26/05.

Home Office. 2003. *The Substance Misuse Treatment Needs of Minority Prisoner Groups: Women, Young Offenders, and Ethnic Minorities*. Home Office Development and Practice Report 8. London: Home Office.

———. 2004. *Statistics on Women and the Criminal Justice System, 2003*. London: Station-ary Office.

Howard League for Penal Reform. 1990. *Prison Medical Service*. London: Howard League.

———. 2000. *A Chance to Break the Habit: Women and the Drug Treatment and Testing Order*. London: Howard League.

Howe, A. 1994. *Punish and Critique*. London and New York: Routledge.

Hume, L. 2001. *Programming for Substance-Abusing Women Offenders*. Canada: Correctional Services Canada.

International Centre for Prison Studies. 2005. *World Prison Brief*. London: Kings College London. http://www.kcl.ac.uk/depsta/rel/icps/worldbrief

Koons, B., J. Burrow, M. Morash, and T. Bynum. 1997. "Expert and offender perceptions of program elements linked to successful outcomes for incarcerated women." *Crime and Delinquency* 43, no. 4: 512–532.

Loucks, N., M. Malloch, G. McIvor, and L. Gelsthorpe. 2006. *Evaluation of the 218 Centre*. Edinburgh: Scottish Executive.

Maher, L. 1997. *Sexed Work: Gender, Race, and Resistance in a Brooklyn Drug Market*. Oxford: Oxford University Press.

Malloch, M. 1999. "Drug use, prison, and the social construction of femininity." *Women's Studies International Forum* 22, no. 3: 349–358.

———. 2000. *Women, Drugs and Custody: The Experiences of Women Drug Users in Prison*. Winchester: Waterside Press.

———. 2004a. "Women, drug use, and the criminal justice system." In G. McIvor, ed., *Women Who Offend*. Publishers Research Highlights 44. London: Jessica Kingsley.

———. 2004b. "Missing out: Gender, drugs, and justice." *Probation Journal* 51, no. 4: 295–308.

———, S. Eley, G. McIvor, K. Beaton, and R. Yates. 2003. *The Fife Drug Court in Action: The First Six Months*. Edinburgh: Scottish Executive.

May, C. 2005. *The Carat Drug Service in Prisons: Findings from the Research Database*. Findings 262. London: Home Office Research, Development and Statistics Directorate.

McCampbell, S. 2005. *Gender-Responsive Strategies for Women Offenders*. Washington, DC: U.S. Department of Justice/National Institute of Corrections.

McDonald, M. 2004. *A Study of Existing Drug Services and Strategies Operating in Prisons in Ten Countries from Central and Eastern Europe*. Warsaw, Poland: Cranstoun Drug Services, Central and Eastern European Network of Drug Services in Prison.

McIntosh, J., and N. McKeganey. 2002. *Beating the Dragon: The Recovery from Dependent Drug Use*, Harlow: Prentice Hall.

Najavits, L., R. Weiss, and S. Shaw. 1997. "The link between substance abuse and post-traumatic stress disorder in women: A research review." *American Journal on Addictions* 6, no. 4: 273–283.

National Institute of Justice. 2000. *Reducing Offender Drug Use through Prison-Based Treatment*. Rockville, MD: National Criminal Justice Reference Service.

———. 2003. *Residential Substance Abuse Treatment for State Prisoners*. US Department of Justice. Web-only document. http://www.ojp.usdoj.gov/nij

Owen, B. 2003. "Understanding women in prison" In J. Ross and S. Richards, eds., *Convict Criminology*. Belmont, MD: Thomson/Wadsworth.

Parenti, C. 1999. *Lockdown America: Police and Prisons in the Age of Crisis*. London: Verso.

Pollack, S. 2005. "Taming the shrew: Regulating prisoners through women-centered mental health programming." *Critical Criminology* 13: 71–87.

Prison Reform Trust. 2000. *Justice for Women: The Need for Reform*. Report of the Committee on Offending. London: PRT.

————. 2006. *Bromley Briefings: Prison Factfile*. London: PRT.

Ramsey, M., ed. 2003. *Prisoners' Drug Use and Treatment: Seven Research Studies*. Research Study 267. London: Home Office.

Rumgay, J. 2004. *The Asha Centre: Report of an Evaluation*. London: London School of Economics.

Scottish Executive. 2002. *A Better Way: The Report of the Ministerial Group on Women's Offending*. Edinburgh: Scottish Executive.

————. 2003. *Getting Our Priorities Right: Good Practice Guidance for Working with Children and Families Affected by Substance Misuse*. Edinburgh: Scottish Executive.

Scottish Office. 1998. *Women Offenders: A Safer Way*. Edinburgh: The Scottish Office.

Scraton, P., and L. Moore. 2004. *The Hurt Inside: The Imprisonment of Women and Girls in Northern Ireland*, Belfast: Northern Ireland Human Rights Commission.

Sudbury, J. 2005. "Celling black bodies: Black women in the global prison industrial complex." *Feminist Review* 80: 162–179.

Task Force on Federally Sentenced Women. 1990. *Creating Choices*. Ottowa: Correctional Services Canada.

Taylor, A. 1993. *Women Drug Users: An Ethnography of a Female Injecting Community*. Oxford: Clarendon Press.

Taylor, R. 2004. *Women in Prison and Children of Imprisoned Mothers: Preliminary Research Paper*. Geneva: Quakers United Nations Office.

Women in Prison (WIP). 2004. *Annual Report: 2003–2004*. London: WIP.

Zlotnick, C. 2002. *Treatment of Incarcerated Women with Substance Abuse and Post-traumatic Stress Disorder: Final Report*. Rockville MD: NCJRS.

CHAPTER 9

More of a Danger to Myself

COMMUNITY REENTRY OF DUALLY DIAGNOSED FEMALES INVOLVED WITH THE CRIMINAL JUSTICE SYSTEM

Stephanie W. Hartwell

INTRODUCTION

Utilizing social support, social strain, and feminist perspectives, this chapter examines the quantitative and qualitative data on the reentry experiences of dually diagnosed (mentally ill and substance-abusing) females who have returned to the community from prison. Often treated as a sidebar in the analysis on community reentry experiences, females emerging from the criminal justice system have multiple problems. They also have distinct backgrounds from their male counterparts. After release from correctional facilities, they face numerous challenges but attempt to sustain themselves in the community through inhabiting multiple social roles in the context of complex social relationships. This suggests a highly social response to community reentry that is influenced by the quality of their informal and formal social supports and relationships.

The data and case studies presented below suggest that dually diagnosed females have distinct psychological disorders, drug use patterns, criminal justice involvement, and correctional supervision after reentry. They confront multiple barriers, including the stigma of being female ex-offenders, by valuing their social roles (mother, daughter, girlfriend, and sister) and relationships. They are empowered by their ability to "hustle" and survive in the community by linking together networks of formal and informal supports. Ultimately, they describe their sense of being responsible for themselves and their choices regardless of the quality of their supports and the gendered social strain they experience.

BACKGROUND

Although the image of an ex-con has yet to be feminized, the ranks of female ex-inmates are growing. Females commit crime for many of the same reasons (being poor, antisocial, undereducated, and underemployed) as their male counterparts (Daly and Chesney-Lind 1988; Andrews and Bonta 1994; Bloom et al. 1996; Larson and Garrett 1996). However, given their orientation, personal characteristics, and life experiences, they are more likely to commit nonviolent, drug-related crime (Daly and Chesney-Lind 1988; Chesney-Lind 1989; Andrews and Bonta, 1994; Teplin et al. 1996; Broidy and Agnew 1997; Pajer 1998; Veysey 1998). More than 80 percent of imprisoned females are serving sentences related to illicit drug violations or use (Teplin 1994; Larson and Garrett 1996; Teplin 1996; Veysey, 1998). They are also more likely to have a history of trauma. Half report being physically and/or sexually abused during their lives, whereas only 10 percent of men report the same victimization (Seiden 1989; Jacobson 1989; Bureau of Justice Statistics 1994; Morash et al.1998)

Females comprise approximately 15 percent of all inmates. They are usually younger, less educated, and more likely to come from racial or ethnic minority groups than are their male counterparts (Bureau of Justice Statistics 1994). Female offenders have more extensive histories of social service use (Pajer 1998; Veysey 1998). Before incarceration, many were the primary caretakers of children under eighteen and were receiving welfare (Bureau of Justice Statistics 1994). They are also more likely than men to be diagnosed with a serious mental illness (Teplin et al. 1996). Estimates suggest that 16 percent of all males and 24 percent all females in state prisons have a psychiatric disability, whereas 10 percent of male and 18 percent of female inmates are estimated to have an Axis I major mental disorder of thought or mood (Ditton 1999; Pinta, 2001).

Offender characteristics reflect services needed while incarcerated as well as after release (Kruttschnitt and Gardner 2003). Nearly all inmates are released to the community and must manage the shift from long-term correctional custody to an often new, less structured environment, and to daily life (Travis, 2000; Taxman et al. 2002). Coping with the adjustment from prison to the open community presents exceptional challenges for individuals with mental illness and criminal histories (Hartwell 2003). These challenges are variable, in large part, based on gender, social support, and the experience of adjustment or coping with the strain of reentry. The reentry experiences of psychiatrically disabled females, the vast majority of whom also abuse substances, are suggestive of their potential for recovery and for living competently in the community.

FEMINIST PERSPECTIVES

From a feminist perspective, the patriarchy espoused across the criminal justice system does not translate into appropriate reentry services across genders. For instance, transitional services and programs in place to address individuals released from the criminal justice system are not always generalizable to females as well as to males being released (Daly and Chesney-Lind 1988). Supervised release programs, usually "conditional" based on employment and substance-abuse treatment, including probation and parole, sex offender registries, daily reporting, and electronic monitoring may not be equipped to work with females because (1) there are comparatively so few females in relation to the relative services (as, for instance, if a female requires urine testing as part of her probation, when facilities are limited); (2) females are usually charged for different types of crimes than are men (Andrews and Bonta, 1994; Veysey, 1998), and in turn receive different sentence structures (considering the limited relevance of parole for nonviolent offenders or the sex offender registry); (3) the technologies of the programs in place are not suitable for females who, due to limited resources, may need to travel great distances for daily reporting or meetings required as a condition of release; and (4) there is limited understanding of the structural barriers females confront, such as acquiring the education and skills necessary for gainful employment (even without the stigma of a criminal history and/or, in many cases, the responsibility for dependent children). Thus, it becomes apparent when thinking about reentry that females remain tangential to the criminal justice system due to its structural inequalities and the consistent "gender ratio problem" manifest in the structure and daily functioning of that system (Daley and Chesney-Lind 1988).

Alternatively, there is another ramification of the gender ratio problem. That is, females receive "special attention" simply because there are fewer of them involved with the criminal justice system. For example, Framingham State Prison in Massachusetts is the oldest women's prison still in operation and the only female prison in the state. Comparatively, it has an array of excellent services and programs for women. However, enhanced services and increased attention while incarcerated can complicate releases to the community. For some females, returning to the unstructured community without continued attention can prove overwhelming, whereas others (particularly individuals who are paranoid and have drug-use disorders) prefer more freedom and less scrutiny, "I don't need anymore attention than I already got." Simply put, for a variety of reasons including power differentials and inequality, females are treated differently across the spectrum of the

criminal justice system—from arrest to sentencing and incarceration. This
distinct treatment can be both daunting and empowering.

INFORMAL AND FORMAL SUPPORTS

Informal and formal social supports moderate reentry for all ex-inmates.
Social supports, including network resources and levels of social engagement, influence resultant behaviors based on the quality of the support and
the perception of being supported and cared for by others (House 1981;
Wethington and Kessler 1986; Turner 1999; Turner and Turner 2000). As
mentioned above, incarcerated females are more likely to have a history of
service linkages (mental health, welfare, substance abuse), and these linkages offer a precurser network of formal supports at release. Additionally,
females emphasize the importance of their social relationships and roles
in families and other social networks of informal supports. For instance,
female drug users rely on the informal supports of family and partners
as affirmation of their self-worth (Strauss and Falkin 2001). Social roles
provide these females with meaningful social identities and purpose in life
(Thoits 1983; Rumgay 2004). Ultimately, these women describe relying
on social engagement and roles and/or identities such as mother, daughter,
and sister to desist from antisocial or criminal behavior and to empower
themselves to live better or even what some might describe as more conventional lives.

Although the benefits of social support, networks, and social engagement seem clear, they can also have adverse effects. For instance, stigmatized individuals and groups including ex-inmates and individuals with
mental illness have less social support and fewer network ties. Persons
returning to the community after extended periods of incarceration must
confront the consequences of being excluded from the community and the
normal patterns of daily life (Hubert 2000). Perceived or real discrimination can affect the stigmatized individual's quality of life through both
reduced social support and increased social isolation (Link et al. 1987;
Meyer et al. 2002). Psychiatrically disabled female ex-offenders, however,
are less isolated, as a result of their efforts to keep their formal and informal relationships intact during their transition from incarceration to the
community. They often engage in multiple roles (mother, drug dealer,
prostitute, girlfriend) that can be conflicting, discrepant, and overwhelming, but this strategy offers an important survival strategy within the
confines of extremely limited resources that may become an untapped
potential strength, and should be noted when considering the reentry
experience and developing related programs for female ex-inmates (Coser
1974; Simon 1995).

SOCIAL STRAIN

Female ex-inmates cope differently with reentry because of socialization differences and their gendered experience of stress and strain (Robbers 2004). These differences occur in the context of power differentials where females experience distinct patterns of strain as a result of their marginalized position and the social context of their lives, which revolve around real or perceived social supports and their interpersonal relationships (Broidy and Agnew 1997). One manifestation of gendered variation in strain is that females involved with the criminal justice system are more likely to be mood-disordered than are their male counterparts (Xie 2000; Hartwell 2001), and the higher rates of mood disorders may be related to elevated rates of sexual and/or substance abuse (Gover 2004).

Further, females are more likely to internalize anger and behave in self-destructive ways (Kowalski and Faupel 1990; Oser 2003). This is manifest in their patterns of drug use and crime (Pajer 1998; Hartwell 2001). Certainly, one response to being in a marginalized position with few opportunities is committing "crimes of survival," usually nonviolent property crimes, perpetuating further involvement with the criminal justice system (Chesney-Lind 1989; Steffensmeier and Allan 1995). Ironically, females commit crimes of survival in the context of their social relationships—for instance, to feed their children or their partner's drug habit. A consequence includes cycling in and out of the criminal justice system. Nevertheless, this cycling is itself an act of agency embedded in the women's social relationships. Their instinct to fulfill social roles and be a part of relationships is a linchpin to reentry and recovery that could ultimately empower them to live better and/or more conventional lives.

Utilizing social support, social strain, and feminist frameworks, this chapter examines the quantitative and qualitative data on the reentry experiences of dually diagnosed (mentally ill and substance-abusing) females who have returned from prison to the community in Massachusetts.

METHODS

The quantitative analysis results from a data set of 1,247 individuals identified as being within three months of release, and in need of mental health services, in Massachusetts houses of corrections and prisons between 1998 and 2006. Sixty percent, or 746, of these individuals are dually diagnosed and 20 percent (151) are female. The data collected on these individuals includes (1) demographic information (age, race, gender, ethnicity, and education); (2) clinical information on primary diagnosis and mental health service history; (3) criminal history information including most recent criminal charge; (4) service information, including housing and

treatment needs, relating to substance abuse, sex offenses, vocational training, and social club membership; and (5) outcome information on client
dispositions post-release and three months post-release, such as: engaged in
community services, hospitalized, returned to prison, or disengaged from
treatment. The characteristics of the male and female mentally ill offenders, dually diagnosed males and females, and dually diagnosed females versus their non-substance-abusing female counterparts, were compared using
cross-tabular analysis and chi-square tests of significance.

The qualitative analysis consists of three case studies from a series of
semistructured interviews I completed with mentally ill ex-inmates who
were released from prison. Mental heath staff approached individuals, and
individuals who agreed to meet to be interviewed were briefed on the project and completed consent protocols. Twenty-two individuals (eleven in
prisons and eleven in hospitals) were approached to be interviewed and
twenty consented and completed the interview protocol (one male and one
female refused). Four of these interviews, lasting about 2.5 hours in length,
were completed with females who were dually diagnosed.

An interview script was used to guide the open-ended interviews,
which covered each individual's understanding of her or his social supports
and service needs in the present and in relation to the individual's community integration efforts. Case studies were developed from extensive notes
taken during the interviews, and the narratives were transcribed and coded
using the qualitative analysis tool *Nvivo*. The data reports included the
identification of key reentry variables and respondent narratives. Although
the qualitative data is limited, due to small number of interviews with dually diagnosed females, the identification and selection of the ex-inmates,
and the interview style of the investigator, this bias was reduced somewhat by the standardized interview procedures and the analysis utilized
throughout the course of the study. All the data is limited to the experience of ex-inmates with psychiatric disabilities in Massachusetts.

FINDINGS

In general, psychiatrically disabled females involved with the criminal
justice system differ from their male counterparts (Hartwell 2001). In Massachusetts, psychiatrically disabled females are more likely to serve shorter
correctional sentences for nonviolent crime, including drug-related, public
order, and property offenses, since they are more likely than their male
counterparts to commit these types of crime. They are more likely to receive probation. Females are incarcerated farther from where they live, but
they are more likely to have a mental health service history in their community, and thus at release are less likely to be homeless, because they are

known and released to a familiar service network. Finally, the females are also more likely to be substance abusers and dually diagnosed.

When isolating the dually diagnosed group, a comparison was made across the dually diagnosed females and dually diagnosed males. Findings included that the differences across genders persist in terms of females being more likely to serve shorter sentences for non–person–related charges (see table 9.1). Additionally, females are less likely to be reviewed as "dangerous" or as sex offenders, at release. Nevertheless, descriptive data suggest that when substance abuse is introduced into the equation, dually diagnosed males and females have similarly somewhat higher rates of homelessness (26 percent) and probation (20 percent). Substance abuse interrupts network ties and merits correctional oversight, often in the form of probation. A large body of research has shown that individuals with mental illness fair poorly on probation (see, for example, Solomon and Draine 1999), often violating their conditions and returning to correctional custody. Dually diagnosed females are more likely to violate probation.

Clinically, the dually diagnosed females have a consistent history of mental health services (table 9.1). They differ from their male counterparts both diagnostically and in regard to the type of substances abused. Females are more likely to have primary mood (bipolar, major depression) or personality (borderline, mania) disorders, whereas the males are more likely to be primarily thought-disordered (schizophrenia) (see table 9.1). Men and women also abuse different drugs. In a separate analysis of a subgroup of this sample, males report more marijuana, amphetamine, and hallucinogen use; females are significantly more likely to report the use of opiates, heroin, and crack. In fact, the dually diagnosed females use multiple substances including alcohol (90 percent), crack (64 percent), marijuana (62 percent), cocaine (54 percent), and/or opiates, including heroin (52 percent). These distinctions in psychological disorders, drugs use trends, criminality/criminal justice involvement, and patterns of reentry based on service histories and correctional supervision provide evidence that gender is a major factor influencing offender reentry. When substance abuse enters the equation, both males and females reduce their informal network ties (one result being more homelessness) while increasing their formal supervision (probation), where, ultimately, dually diagnosed females fare worse.

When examining data on the dually diagnosed females and comparing them to females not dually diagnosed, further interesting findings emerged. As mentioned above, the dually diagnosed females continue more likely to be on probation and homeless. They also have a longer history of mental health services. A more striking finding is that the dually diagnosed group is older (more likely to be forty-six years old or older) and more likely

TABLE 9.1

Significant Comparisons between Dually Diagnosed Males and Females[a]

	Male (n=595)		Female (n=151)		X^2	df	significance
Variable	n	%	n	%			
Primary disorder					49.08	2	★★★
Thought	345	58	44	29			
Mood	224	38	88	58			
Personality	30	5	19	13			
Service history	452	76	135	89	12.56	1	★★★
Probation violation	104	17	39	26	5.6	1	★
Violence review	117	20	12	8	11.66	1	★★★
Sex offender review	102	17	5	3	18.9	1	★
Recidivism					12.77	2	★
1 time	89	15	19	13			
2 or more times	13	2	5	3			
Charge					21.43	2	★★
Public order/ property	254	43	75	50			
Person-related	280	47	53	35			
Drug offense	61	10	23	15			

[a]Percentages may not add up to 100 due to rounding error. All variables in tables are statistically significant.

★ $p<.05$
★★ $p<.01$
★★★ $p<.001$

to be serving a felony sentence (table 9.2). That is, they are likely to be "known," or linked into numerous formal social support services, but have continued escalating involvement in the criminal justice system (Hartwell 2003, 145–158).

In turn, non-substance-abusing female ex-inmates show a better prognosis. They are younger, more likely to be diagnosed with a thought disorder, and more likely to be serving misdemeanor sentences. These findings beg

TABLE 9.2

Significant Comparisons: Dually Diagnosed and Non-Substance-Abusing Females[b]

Variable	Dually Diagnosed (n=151)		Non-Substance-Abusing (n=79)		X^2	df	Significance
	n	%	n	%			
Age					6.23	2	★
18–26	22	15	16	20			
27–46	106	70	60	75			
46+	24	16	4	5			
Primary disorder					18.7	2	★★
Thought	44	29	20	28			
Mood	88	58	37	53			
Personality	19	13	5	7			
Service history	135	89	53	67	17.3	1	★★★
Homeless	39	26	6	8	10.96	2	★★
Offense					5.45	1	★
Misdemeanor	44	29	35	44			
Felony	107	71	44	56			
Short-term release outcome					14.29	4	
							★
Engaged in community	55	36	29	35			
Lost to follow-up	16	11	10	13			
Hospitalized	20	13	10	13			
Reincarcerated	29	19	4	5			
Reajudicated	31	20	26	35			

[b] Percentages may not add up to 100 due to rounding error. All variables in tables are statistically significant.

★ p<.05
★★ p<.01
★★★ p<.001

the question whether substance abuse creates a syndrome among psychiatrically disabled females that perpetuates failure across systems and, ultimately, failed reentry patterns, or whether substance abuse is an alternative manner of coping for females caught in an oppressive system that singles them out as disordered and criminal. The three case studies presented here examine this question in the context of feminist, social support, and social strain frameworks.

Sara

Sara is 23 and diagnosed with Axis I bipolar disorder, and uses heroin intravenously. She was recently released from a second misdemeanor sentence after completing a sentence for "sex for a fee" subsequent to a drug court probation violation. She describes herself as "caught up in the drug court system," and dislikes being on probation. She told me, "Being on probation keeps me here . . . when you are on probation you violate doing drugs or defaulting."

Sara has been in and out of drug treatment programs since she was a juvenile. "I've been to five residential substance abuse treatment programs . . . being high is all I ever think about. All I ever think about is getting messed up, forgetting everything. To me it's all about the drugs and getting over on people. I wouldn't go out and do all this nutty stuff because I am in a hyper mood." She describes herself as manic, "more up than down," and has lived in peril due to her prostitution and drug use, telling me that "johns are nut cases. Sometimes I laugh at them and cannot stop . . . some f'd-up stuff happened to me. I got robbed at knifepoint."

The first time Sara was incarcerated, she was arrested and received nine months probation for soliciting sex for a fee. She told me her first probation officer "really worked with me until I gave my seventh dirty urine and got an eighteen-month sentence." When she is not incarcerated, she lives with her mother, in hotels with friends, or with pimps. "It's so awful to say that, like I am homeless. Well, I was I guess, living in hotels. It's embarrassing. I don't like shelters . . . I work the streets to get some money for a hotel room . . . I never exchanged sex for drugs directly, it was sex for cash for drugs." Sara says she uses drugs to forget hard times, reporting

> Growing up I had all types of abuse . . . my parents were addicts [both are currently in recovery] . . . my dad was in prison. I dunno, I grew up with a massive amount of drugs around me with so many people in and out of the house . . . my mother asking me if people were touching me because I was getting rashes down there . . . I cannot talk like this in front of my family so I just stuff it, stuff it down.

Sara's mom will pick her up when she is released. Sara's goals are "maintaining sobriety, getting a GED, getting a job as a cosmetician or animal handler for a vet and starting over."

Victoria

Victoria is a twenty-eight-year-old black female who is schizophrenic and abuses alcohol, crack, and heroin. She was recently released for shoplifting and larceny over five hundred dollars, but says, "I've been doing time most of my life. I was in DYS [Department of Youth Services] for stealing cars and running away from home." She has held a series of low-paying jobs at Reebok, McDonalds, IHOP, and a senior center, where she was fired for forging checks. She told me, "I like money . . . sometimes it is difficult for me. I don't like being without money and my attitude is I am going to do what I have to for money."

Victoria spent three years in Framingham Prison for armed robbery: "I held up a hair salon with a bat. I was smoking crack then." She participated in many programs while incarcerated. "Disgusted in myself, but I still tried to work on myself, a lot of people in there cared about me. This is when I turned my life around. Framingham has a lot of programs that I participated in." When she was released, she told me, she "met this dude who introduced me to sniffing heroin." She lived between relatives and was shoplifting again, "stealing from stores from 8 to 3 all day, everyday . . . I was paid half price for the merchandise from the fences who sold merchandise to their stores. I lifted twenty-nine pairs of sneakers from Footlocker . . . take my rental car out to the mall, dress real sharp, no one notices you," but she was arrested again.

> I was getting greedy and sloppy . . . I was dope sick. It was 9 p.m. and I was filling my bag when I noticed the security guards watching me. I picked up a box cutter and left everything. They stopped me at the entrance and asked me to go to the back of the store where we got in this whole big thing . . . charged with assault and battery with a box cutter.

Victoria describes her family as supportive and loving. Two of her brothers were incarcerated. "My family loves me. Nobody in my family gets high except me. I just started to get high because the people I hung around with did it." She is closest to her younger sister: "she's wild, but has real high standards. She works and pays for everything." She plans on living with family at release: "Family-wise, I was on the right path, but really I was on the wrong path because of that guy. I choose the wrong men. I don't like squares. I want someone who has been to prison and can relate to me, but they are the wrong men for me. I need a square."

Carla

Carla is Caucasian, forty-five, and suffers from major depression. She is an intravenous heroin user who has been, "addicted to heroin for twenty-five

years." She recently completed a four-month sentence for violating probation, telling me "I had to find an inpatient program, I thought, by myself. I
had no idea probation would have helped if I kept going. I didn't ask for help
and they violated me."

She has no legitimate employment history, and a ninth-grade education. She took some courses while incarcerated, but concedes:

> I never complete anything because I never show up . . . I've been incar-
> cerated ten times in the last five years . . . shoplifting, larceny, receiving
> stolen goods . . . all about the heroin habit—heroin is my medication. It is
> where I want to be. I started medicating myself when I was young, used
> to take my mother's benzos, valium.

For most of her adult life she oscillated among hospitals, homelessness, residential programming, and prisons.

> My previous bid, I went to the nuthouse . . . sometimes I just lose it. I get
> so depressed, I don't make sense. I slit my throat with a razor. I am defi-
> nitely more of a danger to myself. I've lived on the streets . . . homeless-
> ness is the bottom, but I was younger and strung out. Sometimes when I
> am on the streets, I need to get a little respite . . . I was living in a DMH
> house, very nice, had my own room, took my meds on my own. I was
> quite happy until I picked up a case using dope and prostituting . . . After
> that I stayed with a friend in recovery and stayed clean for a year, and on
> my year anniversary, I got high with a friend who knew I had money so
> I went with her.

Carla is the oldest of five siblings, and the mother of two children, the
youngest "I've never had any contact with." She describes growing up: "the
household was mental. My mother had another baby and cracked up. I hated
being in my house, hated being me. My grandmother, mother, sister, niece,
my son, and me all have mental health problems. My son and my brothers
have been incarcerated." Carla has a boyfriend she lives with from time to
time; "he hates it [her prostitution], but he is a drug addict, too. Sex for
a fee—he gets something out of it, too." She plans on living with him at
release: "I am scared because my plan is up in the air. I have to rely on my
boyfriend, and I want to go home . . . tell my boyfriend if he uses [drugs] I
am gone . . . I struggle on a fixed income. I am broke. I need help in a lot of
areas. You'd think I know how to live, but I don't. I've been surviving."

DISCUSSION

The above cases are useful in understanding the reported findings from
the quantitative data and providing insights on empowerment and agency

in the lives of these females. From a feminist perspective it is clear that dually diagnosed females are caught in an oppressive system leaving them with few opportunities to accumulate capital in the areas of education, employment, or finances. Essentially, they are forced to hustle to survive, whether hustling means shoplifting or prostitution—and survival often includes drug use. They describe receiving special treatment because they are female and have multiple needs, and being in "good programs," but are not often motivated to follow through. This lack of follow-through is linked to their lack of capital and the immediacy of their needs (money, housing, drugs). One apparent consequence of their lack of capital is their dependence on social supports or social networks of individuals (men in particular are often cited) who do not encourage pro-social engagement or services follow-up. Additionally, these women's dual diagnosis makes them more vulnerable to antisocial supports and to the perils of navigating social service systems alone.

In terms of social support, these women describe service histories and programs as plentiful. They have formal support networks, including case workers and probation officers, that keep them linked to the criminal justice system through surveillance. They also describe themselves as members of families where their roles as daughter, sister, and girlfriend are important and even influential. Nevertheless, they also recount the adverse effects of both formal and informal supports in their lives—too many programs, too much surveillance, unhealthy family members, and codependent partners. Finally, it is apparent that they internalize their experience of strain, manifest in mood and intractable substance use disorders.

Dually diagnosed females often blame themselves (for their drug use, poor choices, getting caught in illegal acts); internalize anger (manifest most severely in acts of self-harm and/or suicide attempts); and feel shame (about being homeless, disappointing case managers and family). Nevertheless, they continue to attempt to be a part of families that may or may not be helpful or healthy. They also are more likely than their male counterparts to be using heroin—a drug habit that insists on daily attention. For poor females, this means participating in array of illegal activities that puts them at risk of getting "sloppy" and being caught in criminal acts.

Essentially, each of these cases suggests that each female has her own standards (staying clean or sober, making money). Although they have made life far from easy for themselves, they are survivors—in part as a result of their insight, resilience, ability to hustle, and innate need to remain connected to others. Each case reveals that these females are not isolated, but are instead caught up in a web of social network ties that sustain them and provide meaning to their lives. Sara describes her mother, who is in recovery, as a consistent resource; Victoria is particularly close to her sister; and Carla describes her boyfriend, who is also in recovery, as her "insulation." Each describes living with friends. For all psychiatrically disabled female ex-offenders, relationships prior to and following incarceration are instrumental and have the potential to empower them to confront the challenges regarding housing, health, education, employment, finances, and recovery head on, at release.

CONCLUSIONS

In general, female offenders with mental illness tend to be younger and have less education than their male counterparts. They are more likely to be substance abusers or mood-disordered, and have a mental health service history indicating that prior to incarceration they had linkages to community mental health resources or to formal supports in the community (Hartwell 2001). Difficulties in finding meaningful employment post-incarceration, a history of service need and reliance, and the shorter sentences that they receive (committing disproportionately more public order and property crimes) move female offenders through the criminal justice system at a faster rate than men. Confronting and overcoming their difficulties is indicative of the women's endurance and coping capacity, potential strengths to be harnessed in the context of their recovery and reentry efforts. Substance abuse and mental illness are formidable barriers; however, if service providers and community programs can help manage these women's symptoms through medication and supports, they could then rechannel these strengths for survival in the community.

Female ex-inmates structure their lives around relationships and the meaning the women attribute to their social roles. They empower themselves by being responsible to these relationships. Therefore, the key for successful reentry is to align themselves with primary attachments that are strong and trusting, and to distance themselves from negative attachments. Dually diagnosed female offenders also fulfill multiple roles and have complex social relationships. Formal social supports can be helpful at reentry; however, supports linked to the criminal justice system proper should be fashioned to fit the needs of females, emphasizing their pro-social roles in the community. This could be accomplished by tailoring gender-specific support programming to stabilize and enhance these roles. For instance, women's reentry groups in the community could foster friendships, and halfway houses for women and their children could help retain and stabilize the maternal bond and primary social role. Informal supports and pro-social relationships are also essential to living more conventional lifestyles. Females who accumulate more pro-social relationships are more empowered.

Dually diagnosed female offenders are a "special population" and seem to utilize an array of formal social supports available to them across systems. However, these supports cannot overcome the structural inequalities and discrimination that limit the women's opportunities (Hartwell 2001; Hartwell 2005). This problem can make reentry and long-term community extremely challenging. In interviews with the dually diagnosed females about their experience of incarceration and reentry, one responded, "There are things I definitely do better in prison. All my needs are right at my hands. I live better and function better in prison, but do I like it? No."

Dually diagnosed females want to live in the community, in spite of the barriers they confront—mental illness, substance abuse disorders, criminal histories, the inability to make legitimate incomes, and stigma. They are resilient and able to persevere, due to their appreciation of the connections (both bad and good) they have made in their lives. They relish the minor details community living, including, "sleeping in my own bed," "buying candy bars," "having my own soap, lotion, and clothes," "going to movies, eating out, and playing softball," and, perhaps most important, "being able to be with people I care about." Instead of giving up, they confront oppression, difficult family histories, addiction, health deterioration, and past behaviors, and focus on the importance of their roles and relationships. Essentially they cope and carry on with their lives as a result of their connections to others, and these connections are pivotal to their recovery, reentry, and empowerment.

ACKNOWLEDGMENTS

The author would like to acknowledge the Massachusetts Department of Mental Health, Division of Forensic Services, for its support of this work, and the University of Massachusetts at Boston, Department of Sociology, and graduate student Sarah Kuck.

REFERENCES

Andrews, D. A., and J. Bonta. 1994. *The Psychology of Criminal Conduct*. Cincinnati, OH: Anderson.

Bloom, B., M. Brown, and M. Chesney-Lind. 1996. "Women on probation and parole: Community corrections in America, new directions and sounder investments for persons with mental illness and co-disorders." *National Coalition for Mental and Substance Abuse Health Care in the Justice System*: 51–76.

Broidy, L., and R. Agnew. 1997. "Gender and crime: A general strain theory perspective." *Journal of Research in Crime and Delinquency* 35: 5–29.

Bureau of Justice Statistics, U.S. Department of Justice. 1994. *Special Report: Women in Prison*. Washington, DC: U.S. Government Printing Office.

Chesney-Lind, M. 1989. "Girls, crime and a woman's place: Toward a feminist model of female delinquency." *Crime and Delinquency* 35: 5–29.

Coser, R. 1974. *Greedy Institutions*. New York: Free Press.

Daly, K., and M. Chesney-Lind. 1988. "Feminism in criminology." *Justice Quarterly* 5: 497–535.

Ditton, Paula. 1999. *Mental Health and Treatment of Inmates and Probationers.* Washington, DC. U.S. Department of Justice, Bureau of Justice Statistics. July.

Gover, Angela R. 2004. "Childhood sexual abuse, gender, and depression among incarcerated youth." *International Journal of Offender Therapy and Comparative Criminology* 48: 683–696.

Hartwell, Stephanie W. 2001. "Female mentally ill offenders and their community reintegration needs: An initial examination." *International Journal of Law and Psychiatry* 24: 1–11.

———. 2003. "Short-term outcomes for offenders with mental illness released from incarceration." *International Journal of Offender Therapy and Comparative Criminology* 47, no. 2: 145–158.

———. 2005. "The organizational response to community reentry." In *The Organizational Response to Persons with Mental Illness Involved with the Criminal Justice System,* ed. Stephanie Hartwell. Research in Social Problems and Public Policy Series, vol. 12. London: Elsevier Science.

House, J. S. 1981. *Work, Stress, and Social Support.* Reading, MA: Addison-Wesley.

Hubert, J. 2000. "The social, individual, and moral consequences of physical exclusion in long-stay institutions." In J. Hubert, ed., *Madness, Disability, and Social Exclusion: The Archaeology and Anthropology of Difference,* 196–207). London: Routledge.

Jacobson, A. 1989. "Physical and sexual histories among psychiatric outpatients." *American Journal of Psychiatry* 146: 755–758.

Kowalski, Gregory S., and Charles E. Faupel. 1990. "Heroin use, crime, and the 'Main Hustle.'" *Deviant Behavior* 11: 1–16.

Kruttschnitt, Candace, and Rosemary Gartner. 2003. "Women's imprisonment." *Crime and Justice* 30:1–81.

Larson, C., and G. Garrett. 1996. *Crime, Justice, and Society.* 2d ed. New York: General Hall.

Link, B. G., F. T. Cullen, E. Struening, P. Shrout, and D. P. Dohrenwend. 1987. "A modified label theory approach to the area of mental disorders: An empirical assessment." *American Sociological Review* 54: 100–123.

Meyer, P. C., S. Christen, J. Graf, P. Ruesch, and D. Hell. 2002. "Determinants of quality of life of mentally ill persons." *Osterreichische Zeitschrift Fur Soziologie* 27: 63–79.

Morash, M., T. S. Bynum, and B. Koon. 1998. *Women Offenders: Programming Needs and Promising Approaches.* Washington, DC: U.S. Department of Justice, National Institute of Justice. Research in Brief, August.

Oser, Carrie B. 2003. "Strain, depression, and criminal offending across male and female adolescents: Examining general strain theory." Paper presented at the Southern Sociological Society (SSS), March 2003, New Orleans, LA.

Pajer, K.A. 1998. "What happens to 'bad' girls? A review of the adult outcomes of antisocial adolescent girls." *American Journal of Psychiatry* 155, no. 7: 862–870.

Pinta, Emil. 2001. "The prevalence of serious mental disorders among U.S. prisoners." In *Forensic Mental Health: Working with Offenders with Mental Illness,* ed. Gerald Landsberg and Amy Smiley. Kingston, NJ. U.S. Civic Research Institute.

Robbers, Monica L. P. 2004. "Revisiting the moderating effect of social support on strain: A gendered test." *Sociological Inquiry* 74: 546–569.

Rumgay, Judith. 2004. "Scripts for safer survival: Pathways out of female crime." *Howard Journal of Criminal Justice* 43: 405–419.

Simon, R. W. 1995. "Gender, multiple roles, role meaning, and mental health." *Journal of Health and Social Behavior* 36: 182–194.

Solomon, P., and J. Draine. 1999. "Explaining lifetime criminal arrests among clients of a psychiatric probation and parole service." *Journal of the American Academy of Psychiatry and Law* 27: 239–251.

Steffensmeier, Darrell, and E. Allan. 1995. "Criminal behavior, gender, and age." In *Criminology: A Contemporary Handbook,* ed. Joseph F. Sheley. 2nd ed. Belmont, CA: Wadsworth.

Strauss, Shiela M., and Gregory P. Falkin. 2001. "Social support systems of women offenders who use drugs: A focus on the mother-daughter relationship." *The American Journal of Drug and Alcohol Abuse* 27: 65–89.

Taxman, Faye S., D. Young, and J. Byrne. 2002. *Offender's Views of Reentry: Implications for Processes, Programs, and Services.* Report for the U.S. Department of Justice. Washington, DC: U.S. Government Printing Office.

Teplin, L. A. 1994. "Psychiatric and substance abuse disorders among male urban jail detainees." *American Journal of Public Health* 84: 290–293.

———, K. M. Abram, and G. M. McClelland. 1996. "Prevalence of psychiatric disorders among incarcerated women." *Archives of General Psychiatry* 53, 505–512.

Thoits, P. A. 1983. "Multiple identities and psychological well-being: A reformulation and test of the social isolation hypothesis." *American Sociological Review* 48: 174–187.

Travis, Jeremy. 2000. *But They All Come Back: Rethinking Prisoner Reentry.* U.S. Department of Justice, Sentencing and Corrections for the Twenty-First Century. Washington, DC: U.S. Department of Justice, National Institute of Justice. Research in Brief, May.

Turner, R. J. 1999. "Social support and coping." In *Handbook for the Study of Mental Health: Social Contexts, Theories, and Systems,* ed. A. Horwitz and T. Scheid. New York: Cambridge University Press.

———, and J. B. Turner. 2000. "Social integration and support." In *Handbook of the Sociology of Mental Health,* ed. C. S. Aneshensel and J. C. Phelan. New York: Plenum.

Veysey, B. M. 1998. "Specific needs of women diagnosed with mental illness in United States jails." *Women's Mental Health Services: A Public Health Perspective,* 368–389. Thousand Oaks, CA: Sage Publications.

Wethington, E., and R. C. Kessler. 1986. "Perceived support, received support, and adjustment to stressful life events." *Journal of Health and Social Behavior* 27: 78–90.

Xie, Liya. 2000. "Gender difference in mentally ill offenders: A nationwide Japanese study." *International Journal of Offender Therapy and Comparative Criminology* 44: 714–724.

CHAPTER 10

"Hustling" to Save Women's Lives

EMPOWERMENT STRATEGIES OF RECOVERING HIV-POSITIVE WOMEN

Michele Tracy Berger

I know how to "hustle." I know how to do a fast deal. When I was on the streets, I was hustling for all the wrong things. Now, I hustle to save women's lives.
— Nicole,[1] advocate and community worker, forty-two

There's the good hustle and there's the bad hustle. I use what I know to help other women. My connections, my contacts, all of that helps me,

I'm glad I learned something while I was out there.
— Kitt, activist and community worker, thirty-three

INTRODUCTION

A fundamental aim of this book is to situate women's illicit drug economy experiences within a context of agency and empowerment. We know the familiar narrative of the isolated, despairing woman with HIV/AIDS who formerly used crack cocaine (or other illicit substances). Although a great deal has been written about HIV/AIDS, drugs, and prostitution, there exist few studies of stigmatized women from substance-using backgrounds who are politically active. The ongoing community work headed by recovering HIV-positive women has, until recently, escaped the sustained attention of feminists, political scientists, and sociologists.

The respondents I discuss in this chapter offer new examples of what happens to women when they transition out of local drug economies after contracting the HIV virus. They transfer skills and observations from their time in the illicit drug economy and make visible the interconnections of stigma and survival that link recovering women and HIV/AIDS. Not only do the women chronicled here survive, they challenge the language, societal norms, and institutional invisibility that have thwarted them as community actors. These women reveal unique and vital pathways to community power and legitimacy—not by disavowing their past, but by trying to recast to others the meanings associated with female experiences of drug use.

Nicole, an HIV/AIDS advocate, is a recovering HIV-positive substance user. She abused crack as an adult and, at one time, was a drug dealer. During the last ten years, she has become one of the foremost female HIV/AIDS advocates in Detroit, working with policy elites, medical providers, and pastors of local church congregations to change the social and political climate for women living with HIV/AIDS. Her community work[2] spans the spectrum of informal and formal political participation.

Kitt is also HIV-positive and a recovering substance user. Brutally abused as a young girl, she experimented with illicit substances at an early age. She currently conducts street outreach with women who are drug users and street prostitutes. For both of these African American women, transformation from participant in the illicit economy to community worker has been marked with stigma, struggle, and sisterhood.

"Hustling" is an apt metaphor for the women's sustained effort to empower themselves and other HIV-positive people. This term recurred in my interviews with HIV-positive women community workers from backgrounds that included prostitution and drug use. It connotes alacrity, the social dynamics of the street life, sexuality, and even a type of structured and gendered play. The women used this term to convey to myself (and others) how their experiential context as women formerly "in the life" helped them in their community advocacy efforts. Reclaiming a term that has been used against them, and not disavowing their connection to "the street" constitutes one of the many ways my respondents confronted the stigma that they encountered in their ongoing efforts at community leadership. They understood and respond to the sexual stigma facing them and other HIV-positive women. Confronting sexual stigma constitutes a type of empowerment strategy. As a researcher, I became fascinated by the multiple ways women translated their prior life experiences to help them in their new roles tackling HIV/AIDS and other salient issues in their communities (crime, education, housing, community development and empowerment, child welfare, and so on).

All women with HIV/AIDS face discrete and tangible forms of stigma in relation to their health status. For women with HIV/AIDS who are or were substance abusers, these experiences of stigma are heightened, because society often holds them personally responsible for their illness. These women often experience crippling instances of stigma and condemnation from peers, community members, medical providers, and others (Berger 2004; Stoller 1998). Researchers have documented that several distinctive challenges are associated with being an HIV-positive substance abuser, including homelessness, legal and financial problems, limited social resources, and mental health issues.

To date, however, researchers know very little about the potential empowerment strategies that HIV-positive, female, recovering users develop and employ in their battle with multiple and intersecting stigmas. To study only the *victimization* of women who are HIV-positive and recovering users, provides researchers only an incomplete picture of the dynamic ways that women resist and challenge hegemonic oppression.

This chapter explores the individual and collective ways in which sixteen female, HIV-positive, recovering users generated and utilized empowerment strategies. I explore a resource and stigma framework to situate empowerment strategies that are experiential, interconnected, peer-based, and developed in local contexts. I first discuss how women experienced stigma in three key arenas during and after their initial diagnosis of HIV—in substance abuse treatment centers, in their families, and in their neighborhoods. I then discuss their empowerment strategies resulting from the creative utilization of resources gained while in a substance abuse treatment setting. The empowerment strategies include naming and claiming a public voice for HIV, undertaking advocacy work, and confronting sexual stigma. These empowerment strategies enabled the women, over time, to counter the prevailing public negative evaluations of recovering HIV-positive women as "unworthy, sick, crack prostitutes" and as social problems.

Using a feminist contextual qualitative inquiry, I examine both the dynamics of victimization and the agency of recovering HIV-positive women. Although this research is context-specific, it may provide researchers new ways to evaluate and discuss the complexity of responses possible for stigmatized women.

DESCRIPTION OF THE RESPONDENTS AND METHODS

This chapter specifically focuses on sixteen HIV-positive women who were part of a four-year study in 1994–1997 that involved observations, interviews, and oral histories with sixty women in various stages of crack use, recovery, HIV infection, and activism in Detroit. The sixteen respondents discussed here constitute a deep sample of all respondents. The construction of a deep sample is also known as theoretical sampling (Glaser and Strauss 1967). Through theoretical sampling, I was able to continue clarifying my ideas about women's substance use through women's life cycle, and also to investigate community activism for this select group of respondents. In this case, I wished to further understand and witness the struggles of recovering HIV-positive women who worked for change in their communities.

These sixteen women were diagnosed with the HIV/AIDS virus between the years 1986 and 1996. They are the only ones at the time of research known to be HIV-positive. All sixty women had histories of crack cocaine use and prostitution; the sixteen women in the *theoretical sample* were ones who became active in their communities in a range of activities constituting community work and informal participation. I utilized a non-random sample devising multiple access strategies to find respondents (Berger 2004). The ethnicities of the sixteen respondents are: thirteen African American, one European American, one "Other"/Caribbean American, and one Puerto Rican American.

The initial interviews with all sixty respondents were approximately one hour long. The in-depth life histories conducted with the sixteen respondents were from two to four hours. There were also follow-up interviews with the sixteen respondents (of varying lengths). These sixteen respondents maintained their roles as community workers during the time of research and for many years after the conclusion of the study. I spent significant amounts of time becoming embedded in respondents' lives, attending support groups, rallies, marches, and other activities that constituted their informal participation. This research generated a rich data base: a field journal, hundreds of pages of transcribed interviews, and personal effects given to me by respondents: poems, educational material, fliers, memos, letters, organizational notes and minutes, and newspaper clippings.

An institutional review board of the University of Michigan's Committee for the Protection of Human Subjects approved the interview protocol and informed-consent procedures. The research was deemed appropriate in its ethical standards and its participant protection program; all participants provided informed consent.

All interviews were audiotaped and transcribed. Respondents in the deep sample were asked to discuss their community work, efforts in recovery, experiences of stigma and discrimination, coping mechanisms, and relationships with family members and peers. Analysis was governed by the use of traditional grounded theory techniques: in vivo coding, clustering, and theme building (Glaser and Strauss 1967). I used NUDIST (Non-Numerical Data Indexing, Sorting, and Theorizing) to augment my coding. These analytical techniques yielded salient themes about the women's community work, routes to empowerment, and experiences with stigma and discrimination. These themes were explored further in subsequent interviews. The analysis was also guided by feminist principles of inquiry that value examining gender, race, and class as providing insight into women's experiences that have been previously hidden, distorted, or undervalued (Devault 1999). The arguments presented here contain the conceptualization deemed to provide the most parsimonious representation of data.

STIGMA AND RESOURCES

Empowerment strategies are a manifestation of the life reconstruction process that respondents have undergone to transform their lives after their diagnosis (Berger 2004). Life reconstruction is a microlevel process that has enabled respondents to become conscious of the role of gender and its impact on their lives. Life reconstruction also captures the incentive and willingness by respondents to develop a public voice and persona in being "a woman with HIV." This process is facilitated through the resources that the women received in treatment and continued to develop after leaving treatment. In other work, I have tried to fully tease out the framework of stigma and resources that forms a key component in life reconstruction (Berger, n.d.). This framework creates a foundation for the discussion of empowerment strategies.

Stigma

There is a rich literature related to the stigma that HIV-positive women face. HIV-positive people experience a continuum of stigma (pre- and postdiagnosis), as do their caregivers (Stoller 1998; Schneider and Stoller 1995). Regarding my respondents, I have argued that their stigma is intersectional and that it shaped their routes to empowerment in distinctive ways (Berger 2004). The women who comprise this research discovered their HIV-positive status in humiliating and traumatizing ways during the early and mid-1990s. They embodied categories heavily saturated with negative messages about women of color, substance abuse, and HIV/AIDS (Berger 2004; Hammonds 1997, 113–126; Stoller 1998; Zerai and Banks 2002). Women who are drug users have historically experienced high levels of stigma and condemnation (Campbell 2000). The use by women of crack cocaine invigorated and sustained new ideological arguments and representations about *deviance* (Campbell 2000; Maher 1997; Murphy and Rosenbaum 1992, 381–388).

These narratives generally placed the onus of responsibility squarely on the shoulders of HIV-positive women, and helped to maintain toxic levels of silence about prostitution, drug use, and the continued erosion of federal and state programs that have historically provided resources to lower-income people. During their discovery of their illness and initial efforts to deal with being diagnosed with HIV, they found little support or sympathy for their condition. My respondents were blamed for the disease by almost everyone because of their experience with both crack cocaine (and other addictive substances) and prostitution. These early negative experiences reinforced the ideas that: (1) they were undeserving victims; (2) help would not be forthcoming; and (3) they were not to bring additional shame to their family, peers, and community by discussing their condition. Thus my respondents have been constructed as, perhaps, prototypes of what Anderson has, in this volume, called the "pathology and powerless" paradigm.

Resources

Resources that contribute to respondents' empowerment strategies are the tangible and intangible benefits initially gained through recovery and then developed by the respondents. These include advocacy and skills building (reading, literacy, communication, and networking), faith and spirituality, therapeutic work on sexual trauma, and understanding gender as a salient feature of their lives.

The focus on resources brings together sociology, political science, and women's studies theorizing on empowerment (Berger 2004). Explicating the dynamics of agency and empowerment of marginalized women with HIV/AIDS has been limited to a focus on what are called survival skills (Boehmer 2000). This emphasis has resulted in a haphazard and nongeneralizable set of experiences. Empowerment strategies help to make more explicit why and how some HIV-positive women have responded to the challenges of HIV in remarkable ways.

EXPERIENCING STIGMA

In this section I discuss the continuum of behavior that women experienced as stigmatizing and hostile in two areas of their lives, both during and after their diagnosis.

Stigma in Treatment Facilities

For some respondents, it took weeks or years after diagnosis to seek substance abuse treatment, but eventually all did. Several respondents had tried recovery before, but with little lasting success. Being HIV-positive and having found this out in degrading ways, and/or lacking a support system, many respondents used drugs heavily even if they were not frequent users at the time of diagnosis.

Once in treatment, these women faced a lack of guidance or a scarcity of professional staff who understood the challenges of being both HIV-positive and in recovery from substance abuse. During the early 1990s, there were few national programs set up to respond to the needs of HIV-positive women in treatment. Detroit and the state of Michigan's health services were also in infancy with regard to response to the growing HIV/AIDS crisis

In other places, I have extensively detailed respondents' experiences in inpatient treatment programs with both peers and staff (Berger 2004). Here I focus on treatment by professional staff, as such staff have critical and vital importance in setting the tone and environment of a treatment center. Respondents reported experiencing negative treatment regarding their HIV status from counselors, staff support personnel, administrators, and client managers.

Over half of the sixteen women cited stigmatizing remarks from personnel. Incidences of experiences with stigma range from casual observations to direct comments about the respondent's HIV status. Respondents often overheard negative comments about them made by one staff member to another. Sometimes a comment was made about the client's health status and/or appearance (e.g., "she looks sick all the time," said of a rather healthy-appearing individual). Other comments clustered around ideas about the mortality and longevity of HIV-positive people; for instance, one respondent overheard a counselor say to another staff person, "They tend to die." Respondents felt that these comments were often inaccurate (e.g., a staff person saying that some clients did not "look sick").

Respondents indicated that, although staff members frequently remarked about their HIV status, the comments generally did not translate into considerate action or responsiveness toward clients, or into general support around their being HIV-positive. One respondent says, about her experience:

> Although the staff talked about me, I can't say that it ever seemed that they knew anything practical about HIV/AIDS. This came up with food often. People with HIV/AIDS on different types of medications can't eat certain things. You know some people can't have spicy foods or real seasoned foods. They would serve foods that made me sick and when I complained they really didn't seem too upset. And they didn't change the menu.

If the women asked special requests concerning their diet, they were usually met with hostility. One respondent, Robin, thirty-one, typifies the larger group experience:

> We can't eat everything else that a person without HIV can. My stomach was getting real upset from the all the cheese and spices in some of the food. And I asked if they could fix something else not just for me but for everyone . . . They said that it wasn't their concern.

Perhaps one of the most troubling ways that treatment staff dealt with some respondents was by delaying action on, minimizing, or ignoring their health concerns. Five of the sixteen women cited negative experiences in getting treatment staff to respond to HIV/AIDS-related health issues, including scheduling time with doctors or for medical procedures. These respondents sensed that their medical interests were consistently put at the bottom of the priority list of client needs and services. One respondent was forthrightly told, "Your condition and medical problems makes excessive demands on the staff." In interviews, the women discussed how demoralizing it was to be perceived as an additional "nuisance" or as "burdensome" to treatment staff because of their HIV-positive status. Shelly, a thirty-seven-year-old African American, says she was told it was difficult for the treatment staff to, "keep up with scheduling for doctors." She says she wanted to respond that "It's not like I was going to Disneyland—shit, I had to see the doctor two or three times a week because of liver problems. I didn't *want* to have to go that many times."

One outcome of such staff behavior was that respondents frequently missed necessary doctor's appointments and were then forced to wait many weeks or even months to reschedule appointments with primary care providers and specialists. Three of the five respondents discussed above related to me how acute ailments turned into more chronic and serious conditions during the time in substance abuse recovery, in part from the difficulty of obtaining medical care.

Treatment staff frequently violated, and did not respect, respondents' confidentiality regarding HIV status. In six cases, a women's HIV-positive status, after being disclosed confidentially to a staff member, did not remain confidential. Staff members shared the information with other staff members or even other clients, in direct violation of the respondent's wishes. This lack of confidentiality put the women at risk for comments, insults, and in some cases threats from other persons in treatment (Berger, n.d.). One respondent described the shock she felt at having her status disclosed:

> At that time, I didn't know the rules or laws regarding confidentiality. Let me be clear: this was a woman who was an administrative person, above the counselors, who blabbed my information. I came down for dinner later that night and everybody living in the house knew [about me]. One woman came running up to me asking me what it felt like to have HIV. I couldn't believe it! Of course the administrator was not there. She had long gone when her shift was over. I was shaking all over. Two days later, I received a nasty note in my box saying that God was punishing me with this disease. That was a lousy week.

Most respondents reported that they did not say anything to anyone about the negative treatment from staff members. A few respondents who did discuss their experiences with personnel said that their concerns were not satisfactorily addressed. Even if a staff member had been alerted that his or her conduct was inappropriate, respondents often felt that the situation had not been handled adequately (e.g., no apology was offered and it did not appear a warning or reprimand was issued by a staff member's supervisor). One respondent, Shenna, a twenty-five-year-old white woman who reported an incident to a staff member, said, "Nothing—they'd never try to intervene or help. I'd go to my room sometimes and cry. God help me get out of this place."

For the majority of respondents, the often poor and biased treatment by staff members reinforced feelings of inadequacy, invisibility, and marginalization. Some felt that this treatment compromised their health status and created additional stress in their lives. Their experience is a disappointing confirmation of bias, given the already vulnerable position an HIV-positive user faces during her efforts at recovery. Several respondents confided that such treatment had made them more vulnerable to relapsing, which some did during their time in treatment. Others, however, used the experiences as a catalyst to think about how to help other HIV-positive women in recovery, if ever they were in a position to do so.

Stigma from Family Members

Respondents' family members frequently treated them as the physical manifestation of the chaos and challenges ravaging the families' communities during the 1990s. The respondents' participation in illicit markets was seen as the ultimate cause of and justification for their disease. Family perceptions of the types of behaviors that respondents engaged in during their addiction usually contributed to familial opinions. The women faced a general consensus in both private and popular imaginations that "the crack made her do it" and "that's what prostitutes and 'crack 'hos' deserve."

Respondents discussed the many misperceptions of their lives prior to contracting HIV. The women expressed to me that, while on the street, they tried to preserve as much self-worth and dignity as they could. Several respondents expressed how difficult this was, given men's dominant roles in the illicit economy. These women contrasted and distinguished their experiences with those of men who also used drugs and participated in the illicit drug economy. They portrayed male substance users as more violent, uncaring, and uncontrollable. Many of the women were very proud that they had never engaged in violent crimes during the height of their addiction. They noted the irony that, although women substance users were rarely convicted of violent crimes, they still received intense condemnation from many family and community members, yet the community was silent both about *male users* and *male patrons*. Simone, forty-one, said, "Yeah, everyone wanted to talk about what the women did and how we were all crack 'hos, but what about the men?" Anna, a forty-one-year-old Latina, elaborates on this point. "People don't really want to know what goes [on] out there. Men will take your money, they are much more violent on drugs, and, yes, they, too, are often prostitutes, but you never ever, ever hear about them in that way." A constant rhetorical question that respondents would later pose to community members was "What about the men?"

Robin recounted the painful things that her mother shouted at her when Robin finally disclosed that she was HIV-positive: "I told you about being in the street! All those men you've been with, this virus could have been from anywhere! How many men did you sleep with? You are a disgrace. How could you do this to yourself and your family?"

After disclosing their status to parents and family members, some women immediately found themselves in a more vulnerable position concerning their living situations. Billy Jean, a thirty-one-year-old African American woman, provides an example of this pattern among respondents. She was a pregnant substance user when she was diagnosed with HIV/AIDS. When diagnosed, she was in an insecure living situation, moving between boyfriends and the street. Both her family of origin and the child's father refused to accommodate her and told her to find a new place to live. She was told that she had a modern form of "the plague." The child's father also tried to pressure Billy Jean into terminating the pregnancy.

In dealing with the shame of HIV, parents often wanted their daughters to put on a public face for neighbors and community members and lie about their disease, as Cynthia, who identifies as "Other/Caribbean American," indicates: "They wanted me to pretend I had something else, lupus or something else. They were just dying of embarrassment. When I started losing weight and looking real bad, I couldn't even go to the holiday gatherings no more."

Family members initially were unable or unwilling to examine their gendered perception of women, sexuality, and drug use. Their reluctance contributed to respondents feeling judged, humiliated, and isolated. Respondents' challenges with families would later be used as a basis to begin community discussions on sexuality and on how families' negative attitudes thwarted the well-being of women with HIV/AIDS.

Empowerment Strategies

The empowerment strategies discussed in what follows are ones that helped to sustain the respondents' commitment to community work, providing both inspiration and motivation. These strategies were teachable and translatable to other community workers. Empowerment strategies were deployed in both personal and public settings.

Naming and Claiming a Public Voice for HIV

An empowerment strategy used by the majority of the respondents was to claim a "public voice." Respondents decided to live with HIV, and understood that this choice meant to accept the gendered and political ramifications of being "a woman with HIV." Respondents have actualized this understanding in community roles as spokesperson, resource finder, and occasional lobbyist. Naming and claiming HIV promotes visibility and a public identity.

This strategy of naming and claiming a public voice creates the bridge to expanded political activity. The literal and symbolic use of voice has been important to many facets of contemporary feminists' articulation of inequality (Anzaldúa 1990, hooks 1989; Moraga and Anzaldúa 1981; Olsen 1979; Rich 1979). The concept of voice (and visibility) has also been a key theme of HIV/AIDS empowerment and activism (Lather and Smithies 1997; Schneider and Stoller 1995).

Respondents made significant statements about "what it means to be a woman with HIV" over the duration of the research study. The majority of the respondents used the phrase with emotional clarity, urgency, and sincerity. This phrase encompassed a larger set of meanings about the self that the women used in formulating their tasks within their communities. My investigative mapping of public voice suggests that it exists as a manifestation along a continuum in which collective identity can be expressed. These women's public voice is about expressing and acting on the desire to become engaged with HIV/AIDS issues. By becoming open with their HIV status, they suggest to other HIV-positive women (and men) that they too can partake in this collective identity.

Being part of this collective identity carries with it a well-developed sense of responsibility. Responsibility was a key theme in how women understood and utilized their public voice. In the following dialogue, Cherise, thirty-two, and Valerie, thirty-five, reflect on how becoming public as a woman with HIV extends past their personal wants:

CHERISE: For me to stay politically active, I have to remember what it means to be a woman with HIV.

INTERVIEWER: What does that mean, to be a woman with HIV?

CHERISE: It means for me to remember that, for everything I do, there are women who are going to die because they did not get the right services, the right treatment, or who don't know they are infected. I have to stay connected with women's lives, with my own life. I have to stay connected with the reality of the disease for women that I meet who are sick and can't get to support groups, rallies, or meetings. They are still invisible.

VALERIE: There is an old saying that leading by example is the best way to get other people to get on your bandwagon. I'm not a preachy person. I just don't barge into people's lives and say "you do this" and "you do that." I share with them my sense of responsibility. I'm out there organizing and turning up the heat. There are so many of us out there who don't have voices . . . when I get scared to speak about women and HIV, I think of them.

"Going public" as a strategy was consciously used to train peer educators about HIV/AIDS awareness. If you can go public, then you can combat the ways that the media and others portray HIV-positive people. Nicole is a celebrated speaker and visible spokesperson. She places a lot of emphasis on women speaking their different stories about living with HIV/AIDS. At one interview, she expressed to me how elated she felt because she was meeting other HIV-positive women, nationally, who did speak up: "I'm talking especially [about] Georgia and New York. There's some bad sisters out there advocating . . . I like them girls and I like their style because they don't mind speaking their mind—they got their stuff together." At meetings and support groups with HIV-positive women, a common exercise used by Nicole was to ask participants to write down their greatest fears about telling and sharing their stories in a public forum.

I questioned another respondent, Julianna, thirty-seven, about her experience in encouraging women to become more public about HIV in their lives. She has a staff position ("Women's Client Manager and Advocate") in a city agency working with HIV-positive people. Working with immigrant women who are HIV-positive has been a focus of hers. I asked, "How do you know someone is ready to speak about what it means being a woman with HIV?" and she said, "I put the number at three. If they can say their story to three people that they don't know who are sitting down . . . then I know that they are ready. Three is the beginning of three hundred."

A public voice that draws on insights and discussions about what it means to be a woman with HIV allows for respondent visibility and recognition. As a strategy, it transforms the personal and public shame related to HIV/AIDS in their communities.

Undertaking Advocacy

The concept of advocacy grows out of two specific contexts, in relation to HIV/AIDS and substance use. In this regard, advocacy has traditionally meant that a person in recovery or an HIV-positive person works on behalf of herself and others. Advocates can receive a minimal stipend, can volunteer, or can work in a formal salaried position. Advocacy can take place in many locations (in homes, on the street, in city and state agencies, in drug treatment centers, in community centers). Advocacy, in my research, expands to include the ways that respondents broadened the role of the advocate to lead to informal political participation highlighting group concerns. Advocacy covers the whole range of experiences that women have in working on local issues of HIV/AIDS. Highlighting the importance of advocacy as an empowerment strategy makes visible the daily work that many respondents have undertaken to transform their communities.

Advocacy work allowed the respondents to deepen bonds with other women and to work together in ways unimaginable to them prior to contracting HIV. Their experiences with advocacy were significant in that they created a context for rethinking the women's own gendered scripts. Robin's comments illustrate this point:

> I had to examine the ways that I thought about other women, I really did. No one ever taught me to stick up for myself let alone other women. Sisterhood is critical when it comes to HIV. I try to stress that for women who are out on the streets, even though they may not have that mentality now. It's a positive thing to work with other women for me right now.

The women would begin with the concept of self-advocacy—learning how to stay off drugs and learning about living with HIV/AIDS. They then usually sponsored someone else and advocated on their behalf. During treatment and sometimes through educational forums, many of the woman improved their literacy, communication, networking, and civic skills.

For some respondents, advocacy has meant to work outside an agency or state-sponsored program. Advocates who work from their homes do not receive a stipend or any monetary support but work on the basic survival issues related to HIV/AIDS—where to get care, how to get additional health services, the monitoring of how effectively and compassionately support groups and services serving HIV-positive people are run.

Because there was so little information available during the 1990s about women and HIV/AIDS, respondents were initially quite frustrated with the lack of resources available. After investigating self-advocacy for a few years, most respondents wanted to connect with other HIV-positive women to share resources and support. Some respondents became involved, in volunteer roles, at emerging HIV/AIDS programs. Others worked alone and tried to find HIV-positive women in their communities who might be isolated. They found that their efforts were questioned and that it was not easy to build alliances with others in the community. Georgia, fifty years old, is an advocate who uses the arts to educate people about HIV, as reflected on her early efforts:

> So, you know I began investigating all the strange "meningitis and cancer" stories that seem to sprout up all over the place in the last few years. People didn't want to tell me nothing. Even though I told them I changed and had two years clean. It didn't matter. Once an addict, always an addict. This is true from women who thought they got it "the good way," from a man they were married to. At first no one wanted to talk. So, I started leaving my poems as a way to reach out.

Advocacy as a role can also be socially bestowed. Constance, age forty-five and a former nurse, exemplifies this kind of advocacy. Constance attended a HIV/AIDS support group operated by a prominent Latino/a organization. She became critical of how the agency provided support services and used federal resources provided by the Ryan White Act. The group often ignored or dismissed the concerns of its African American participants and focused exclusively on its Latino/a members, in conflict with the way federal monies for HIV support services are allocated. In Constance's estimation, the agency also did a poor job in providing transportation to events for members in support groups, coordinating events with other groups in the area, and providing services for substance-using HIV-positive people. Because of her willingness to speak out and challenge the staff, she began receiving calls from other people (both in her support group and outside it) asking for additional advice about how to handle concerns they had regarding the agency's policies. As a result of her background in the medical profession, she was also sought out to help decipher medical instructions, accompany people to doctor appointments, and occasionally intervene between patient and provider. After a number of these experiences, Constance became known as a woman "who is a good advocate." Although she has received no stipend or salary for her work, she has been afforded a high degree of autonomy.

One area that received significant attention for many respondents was how to help recovering women in treatment programs. Given their prior negative experiences, these respondents refused to ignore the issues of poor treatment in terms of access, childcare, and general support. A thirty-five-year-old African American female respondent illustrates this point: "When I became a counselor I talked with them about that there wasn't any HIV programs to train staff. That was one of the first things I did when I got active." Indeed, as many of the women became active in their communities, their organizing resulted, over time, in more, and better trained, staff dealing with HIV/AIDS issues in substance abuse treatment facilities in Detroit (Berger 2004). These women were also advisors and consultants on the few innovative inpatient, comprehensive programs specifically designed for recovering HIV-positive women.

Confronting Sexual Stigma

The last empowerment strategy of significance is the respondents' focus on confronting sexual stigma. Sexuality has been a powerful route of stigmatization for the majority of the population of women living with HIV (Stoller 1998). Many people used sexuality to discredit and discourage respondents. There were two distinct areas of concern for respondents: prostitution and child sexual trauma. Over half the women in the deep sample had experienced some form of sexual trauma either in their family of origin or as an adult, and all had some experience with street-level prostitution. In recovery, many women were able to explore the legacy of sexual trauma experienced as a child or adult. Therapeutic work on these issues offered a new sense of self and new worldview for some respondents. Because many found the work that they did in recovery so helpful, they brought this theme into their advocacy. In responding to sexual abuse and its possible role in HIV risk, respondents collaborated and sought out others to help bring this issue into the forefront of community discussion.

Daria, a sexual survivor of incest, became fascinated by initial research suggesting links between early sexual trauma and increased HIV risk. Many respondents who suffered childhood sexual trauma felt that they had maintained a high degree of both shame and stigma. She began a newsletter for women who were HIV-positive and sexual survivors:

> I got this idea to do something for women that hadn't been done before. I suggested a newsletter for women in the HIV community that specifically addressed sexual survivor issues. There are a lot of us out there just weighed down with trying to deal with things that happened to us as little girls ... I approached six HIV/AIDS groups and said that I was willing to do all the work for it—if they'd give me seed money and small grants so that I could distribute the newsletter ... I told them I'd get the contributions, learn layout—I already knew how to use a computer. I promised them the world of what I could do on my own. As it turned out, I needed more help with some things related to the newsletter than I thought—but it was still my baby. I got the contributors—mostly from Detroit and Michigan—and edited some of their stories.

Daria's newsletter ran six times during the year. It was a useful tool for other respondents who were facilitating support groups. Respondents also utilized this knowledge to create dialogues with other organizations in the city (e.g., hospitals and churches) that were in contact with HIV-positive women.

Other respondents, who did not have first-hand experience of incest and early childhood sexual abuse, focused on issues of prostitution. At a personal level, when dealing with family members, they would try to explain the realities of women's lives on the street. Cherise explains: "If people understand that we were trying to survive, sometimes that made people think about what they would have had to do. You have to break it down for people." They used information gleaned from the CDC, networking, and even prostitutes' rights organizations to help engage with people in more thought-provoking ways. They also used facts about the physiology of women and prostitution, noting that women were more likely to contract HIV/AIDS from a male partner than to spread it. Kitt said, "You explain that women are more at risk for getting the disease than just spreading it, which is what people always believe about prostitution."

At the community level, they introduced and created forums about sexual stigma for diverse populations in Detroit: high school students, senior citizens, HIV-positive men, incarcerated men and women, patrons of libraries and community centers, and church groups. Questioning how society enforces the idea of the "bad girl" was a core theme to the way respondents framed risk and HIV/AIDS. The women also explored the role of gender and class in how the community thought of men and women in the areas of addiction and prostitution. The titles of these forums included "Protecting Us All," "Beyond Surviving: Women With HIV Talk Back," "Women and Men Facing HIV Together," "No More Shame: Coming Home with HIV." In confronting sexual stigma, the women have often had to put their own experiences on the line. Although respondents have talked about the over-hyped "sex for crack exchanges" and survival sex, they were also clear that women's experiences on the street vary widely. In these community forums, they emphasized what they gained from their experiences on the streets that allowed them to work so hard "hustling" to help women with HIV/AIDS.

The women also spoke about these issues on local radio and television shows. Confronting the role of sexual stigma allowed respondents to focus on how negative attitudes about women and sexuality were inhibiting critical HIV prevention work.

Conclusion

It should not be surprising to discover that women who are HIV-positive and come from backgrounds of drug use and prostitution face stigma in our society. They face negative evaluations from peers, family members, and sometimes medical and human service providers. In this research, I focus on what happens to a select group of women as they take control of their lives after being diagnosed with HIV. For my respondents, agency is exercised through embracing and mining life experiences, using resources gained in other contexts and putting into practice what they have learned. I have labeled their conduits that sustain community work "empowerment strategies." These women use these strategies to save their own lives and the lives of other HIV-positive people, especially women.

This research brings into focus the varied life cycles of marginalized and stigmatized women who have used drugs. Currently, the literature under-theorizes the ways that women who have been a part of the illicit economy continue to make sense, as recovering users, of that network of actors. Given the ways in which HIV affects marginalized women, we may see more women who find untraditional routes to empowerment. There is already evidence that substance users who are HIV-positive can mobilize and become empowered (Friedman and Alicea 2001; Stoller 1998). Recovering users who are "hustling to save women's lives" should inspire more feminist research attention.

NOTES

1. All respondents' names are pseudonyms.
2. I use the term *community work* to refer to informal participation that involves both paid and unpaid labor. This work helps to sustain the women's neighborhoods and channel physical and emotional resources to HIV-positive people. Activities include advocacy work, running support groups, developing educational forums, and challenging formal state power.

REFERENCES

Anzaldúa, Gloria, ed. 1990. *Making Face/Making Soul*. New York: Kitchen Table Press.

Berger, Michele. 2004. *Workable Sisterhood: The Political Journey of Stigmatized Women with HIV/AIDS*. Princeton, NJ: Princeton University Press.

———. 2006. "Women with HIV/AIDS in substance abuse treatment programs: Experiencing and confronting stigma." *Qualitative Health Research*. Under review.

Boehmer, Ulrike. 2000. *The Personal and the Political: Women's Activism in Response to the Breast Cancer and AIDS Epidemics*. Albany, NY: State University of New York Press.

Campbell, Nancy. 2000. *Using Women: Gender, Drug Policy, and Social Justice*. New York: Routledge.

Devault, Marjorie L. 1999. *Liberating Method: Feminism and Social Research*. Philadelphia: Temple University Press.

Friedman, Jennifer, and Marixsa Alicea. 2001. *Surviving Heroin: Interviews with Women in Methadone Clinics*. Gainesville: University of Florida Press.

Glaser, Barney G., and Anselm L. Strauss. 1967. *The Discovery of Grounded Theory*. New York: Aldine De Gruyer.

Hammonds, Evelynn M. 1997. "Seeing AIDS: Race, gender, and representation." In *The Gender Politics of HIV/AIDS in Women,* ed. Nancy Goldstein and Jennifer Manlowe. New York: New York University Press.

hooks, bell. 1989. *Talking Back: Thinking Feminist, Thinking Black.* Boston: South End Press.

Lather, Patti, and Chris Smithies. 1997. *Troubling the Angels: Women Living with HIV/AIDS.* Boulder, CO: Westview Press.

Maher, Lisa. 1997. *Sexed Work: Gender, Race, and Resistance in a Brooklyn Drug Market.* Oxford: Oxford University Press.

Moraga, Cherrie, and Gloria Anzaldúa, eds. 1981. *This Bridge Called My Back; Writings by Radical Women of Color.* New York: Kitchen Table Press.

Murphy, Sheliga, and Marsha Rosenbaum. 1992. "Women who use cocaine too much: Smoking crack versus snorting cocaine." *Journal of Psychoactive Drugs* 24, no.3: 381–388.

Olsen, Tillie. 1979. *Silences.* New York: Delacorte Press/Seymour Lawrence.

Rich, Adrienne. 1979. *On Lies, Secrets, and Silence.* New York: Norton.

Schneider, Beth E., and Nancy Stoller, eds. 1995. *Women Resisting AIDS: Feminist Strategies of Empowerment.* Philadelphia: Temple University Press.

Stoller, Nancy E. 1998. *Lessons from the Damned: Queers, Whores, and Junkies Respond to AIDS.* New York: Routledge.

Zerai, Assata, and Rae Banks. 2002. "Dehumanizing discourse, anti-drug law, and policy in America: 'A crack mother's nightmare.'" Burlington, VT: Aldershot.

CHAPTER 11

Drug Use, Prostitution, and Globalization

A MODEST PROPOSAL FOR RETHINKING POLICY

Phyllis Coontz and Cate Griebel

INTRODUCTION

After almost one hundred years of public debate about the evils of drug use and the immorality of prostitution, our policies remain consistently one-dimensional in their approach: we criminalize both.[1] What accounts for such persistence? Prohibitory legislation tends to grow out of fear, and is favored when a social majority objects on moral grounds to the conduct, value system, or culture of others and imposes regulations upon them (Hunt 1999). The Progressive Era and moral reformers of the early twentieth century led the charge to prohibit drugs and prostitution, because participants were fearful of changes brought about by rapid urbanization and immigration. They believed that prohibition would preserve family values and protect the norms of Anglo-Saxon Protestantism. Notwithstanding the moral justifications used to defend prohibitory approaches to social problems, such approaches, time shows, only succeed in widening existing social and cultural divides.

Criminalization has failed to lessen the flow of drugs coming into the United States or to reduce the number of hardcore drug users; not only has drug trafficking emerged as the dominant criminal market in the underworld, but also the number of hardcore drug users has not decreased since the "war on drugs" began in the mid-1980s As a result of the widening net from the "war on drugs," drug use by females has actually increased over the past several decades (Steffensmeier and Schwartz 2003). Similarly, arrest statistics show that the market for prostitution is thriving, indicating that criminalization has had little impact on its occurrence. In 2004 alone, there were ninety thousand arrests for prostitution and an additional unknown number of prostitutes arrested for the catchall offenses of disorderly conduct, loitering, and vagrancy (UCR 2005).

Nowhere is the failure of criminalization more visible than in our local, state, and federal correctional facilities. The prison population has almost doubled since 1990. During the course of a year, 13.5 million people spend time in jail or prison, and the daily count of people serving time in our jails and prisons is 2.2 million persons (Commission on Safety and Abuse in America's Prisons 2006, 11). Although half of those in state prisons are there for violent offenses, the other half have been convicted of nonviolent and drug-related crimes (especially possession or sale of small quantities of drugs). Beyond the human and social costs of our failed drug and antiprostitution policies are the financial costs of operating our burgeoning correctional system. According to the Commission on Safety and Abuse in America's Prisons, we spend over $60 billion a year on corrections (2006, 11). Enforcing antiprostitution statutes is financially costly to municipalities, too. In a study of sixteen of the country's largest cities, Pearl found that municipalities spent a total of $120 million a year to enforce antiprostitution laws (1987). Of this, $53 million was spent on direct police costs; judicial personnel required $35 million; and correctional costs (at the local level) were estimated to be an additional $31 million (Pearl 1987). Norton-Hawk found that not only is it costly to incarcerate street-level prostitutes, but incarceration actually increases a woman's involvement in street-level prostitution (Commission on Safety and Abuse in America's Prisons 2001, 408). Such exorbitant costs in housing nonviolent and drug offenders for increasingly longer periods of time have led many to ask whether it is not now time to "get smart on crime" and substitute "get tough" and mandatory sentencing laws with methods other than incarceration (see, for instance, California's Proposition 36) (Archer 2004).

The failures of our drug and antiprostitution policies have been especially detrimental to women, who are processed through the criminal justice system in record numbers. The arrest rate for drug use among women has quadrupled since 1990, and there has been a more than seven-fold increase in the number of women incarcerated in prisons across the country. Today, almost a million women are under some form of control by the criminal justice system (Sokoloff 2005 129). The number of women being sent to prison has grown faster than the number of men, and more females than ever are being imprisoned for drug violations (Greenfeld and Snell 1999). Although the crimes for which women are incarcerated today are the same kinds of crimes for which women have historically been incarcerated (typically nonviolent, income-generating crimes such as larceny–theft, forgery, and prostitution), there is one noted change—the addition of drug possession and sales (Sokoloff 2001, 2005). The dramatic increase in the number of women in prison for drug-related offenses is very different from the number of men being sent to prison, half of whom are sent there for violent crime.

Women tend to occupy the lowest rungs in the drug hierarchy and have little knowledge of day-to-day operations. Although some women have built careers in the underground economy that insulate them from the exploitation and destructive behavior characteristic of heavy cocaine and crack use, most women involved in drugs continue to hold positions "skewed toward lower status roles and away from management or ownership status" (Fagan 1994, 210). Because women involved in the illicit drug business hold such low-status positions, their involvement is more conspicuous and public, making them more vulnerable to arrest. Indeed, women are at high risk for arrest. Sudbury notes that the women most likely to be incarcerated for drug offenses are women of color (Sudbury 2003).

Although not all prostitutes are drug users, the evidence overwhelmingly shows that prostitution is a mainstay survival strategy for female drug users, especially if they are heavy users (Hunt 1990). What is ironic about prostitution arrests is that the prostitute, almost always a female, continues to be arrested while the other parties involved in the sex transactions—customers and third parties, such as pimps—go largely unpunished. Like the women incarcerated for drug offenses, the vast majority of the women incarcerated for prostitution are poor minority women—55 percent of the women arrested and 85 percent of those women in jail for prostitution are minority females (Rhode 1989; Alexander 1987; Lucas 1995).

Why do women get involved in prostitution? The simple answer is economic: females face barriers to both the legitimate and underground economies, and so the types of income-generating opportunities available to them are highly gendered. Research on women's and men's crime reflects the role that disadvantage plays in criminal careers, and how gender shapes women's and men's responses to poverty. The pathways to crime and career opportunities for female offenders differ from those for male offenders (Steffensmeier and Schwartz 2003; Miller 1986). Research on women in prison confirms the economic disadvantages they face: women prisoners are more economically disadvantaged than their male counterparts; they are slightly older, less likely to be married, and more likely to be a member of a minority group, to have children under the age of eighteen, to be undereducated, to be underemployed or unemployed, to have experienced economic hardship, or to have been a victim of physical or sexual assault (Greenfeld and Snell 1999).

Although the underground economy has undergone changes in the past few decades that have contributed to increased opportunities for female offending—a reduced supply of male crime partners as a result of increased incarceration rates, the transformation of illegal markets and criminal opportunities, and shifts in the ethnic composition of the inner city—female crime opportunities remain dependent, in part, on whether male criminals find females useful as working partners (Steffensmeier and Schwartz 2003). Because criminalization has made the costs of drug use and addiction a function of supply and demand, heavy drug users must resort to criminal activities to generate enough income to purchase drugs (Anglin et al. 1987). Since female offenders gravitate toward activities that fall within their skill set, the level and nature of female crime is influenced by opportunities that reflect traditional female roles. This means that for females drug use, addiction, and prostitution are inextricably interrelated.

Our prohibitory policies have created the conditions linking drug use and crime. Thus, understanding the connection among gender, drugs, and prostitution within the context of the failure of our prohibitory policies is necessary if we are to change the way we think about current policy prescriptions and the institutional apparatus we use to try to regulate drug use and prostitution. Our aim in this chapter is to provide a context for expanding the discourse about the failure of our outmoded and ineffective drug and antiprostitution policies. We do this in three ways.

First, we review the empirical evidence on the relationship among drug use, gender, and crime, the relationship between prostitution and gender, and the impact of both relationships on economically marginalized women.

Second, we situate both relationships within the context of the global economy. We discuss how globalization has led to the dramatic growth of the commercialized sex industry, and how globalization has created a two-tiered system wherein economically marginalized women are confined to work in the high-risk illegal end of the sex trade hierarchy. Oishi (2005, 3) argues that globalization has started a "race to the bottom" for women around the world, in that there is intense competition to provide the cheapest and most docile labor possible. Women from the third world are now competing with women in the first world for low-paying, dead-end jobs. Since more and more migrant women are being incorporated into "global commodity chains" and "global value chains" that serve the demands of the global marketplace—especially in the legal commercial sex industry—highly marginalized nonmigrant women are more dependent on the underground economy to make ends meet. Regrettably, globalization has implications for income-generating opportunities in both the legitimate and underground economies, such that economically marginalized women will probably find themselves further marginalized. Globalization is likely to keep those involved in prostitution at the bottom of the sex industry hierarchy. Sudbury suggests that the dramatic increase in the number of women in prison serving time for nonviolent drug-related offenses is a barometer of the effects of globalization on economically marginalized nonmigrants (2003, 221). The life of the drug-using street-level prostitute is getting riskier because of the increased risk of arrest and incarceration, accompanied by the "widening of the net" practices associated with the "war on drugs" and by tougher sentencing guidelines.

Third, we offer a modest proposal for changing drug use and prostitution policies. Note that, although we recognize the important contributions of feminist scholarship in expanding the discourse on prostitution over the last thirty years, especially with regard to whether prostitution is an expression of sexual autonomy and a form of work, or a form of violence against women (Baldwin 1993; Bernstein 1999; Fechner 1994; Delacoste and Alexander 1989), this chapter is not intended to be part of this polemic. We would like to avoid the more essentialist confines of what Chapkis (1997) and Kempadoo (2003) characterize as universal moralizing about prostitution and sexual labor, in order to move toward new paradigms for examining the complex realities of women's experiences in sex markets. This is why we locate prostitution within the context of the illegal marketplace. We take the position that it is impossible to separate the work of prostitution from the commodification of human beings and the commercialization of the sex industry. Thus, we argue that by making prostitution illegal, criminalization perpetuates the asymmetrical exchange relationship inherent in the commodification of human beings, and penalizes the prostitute for her services. Moreover, the "prostitute as criminal" stereotype serves as a powerful paradigm for relegating certain groups of women to the bottom of the sex industry hierarchy, and thus plays a determining role in controlling economically marginalized women's behavior. At a broader level, referring to a woman as a whore or a slut is a way to exert control over all women and to remind them of how they are defined and what they can be reduced to within a patriarchal culture—that a woman is a commodity and potentially available for a fee.

DRUGS, CRIME, AND GENDER
The relationship between drug use and crime has been consistently documented in the research literature for almost a century (Terry and

Pellens 1928; Lindesmith 1938; Austin and Lettieri 1976; McBride and McCoy 1993; Dorsey and Zawitz 1999; McBride et al. 2002). One of the most consistent themes emerging from this vast literature is that people who use drugs regularly, especially expensive drugs like heroin and cocaine, are more likely than nonusers to be involved in illegal activities—ranging from violent and property crime to confidence games and sex work (Johnson 1991; Chaiken and Chaiken 1990; Defleur et al. 1969; Hunt 1990).

Although there is a strong relationship between drug use and crime, research also shows that, rather than a single path to drug use and involvement in crime, there are multiple, complex pathways (White and Gorman 2000). The relationship is further complicated by gender. Although males account for the overwhelming majority of arrests for drug use violations, making up 81 percent of arrests in 2003, the number of females arrested for drug use violations has been increasing dramatically since the mid-1990s (Uniform Crime Report 2004). Between 1986 and 1999, the number of women incarcerated in state facilities for drug-related crimes increased by 888 percent, far outpacing the rate of growth in the number of men imprisoned for similar crimes (Mauer et al. 1999). The "war on drugs" now reaches beyond women who are addicted to, or using, drugs, by targeting individuals peripherally involved in drug-related activity. This so-called widening of the net has resulted in more arrests of, and higher incarceration rates for, females (Steffensmeier and Schwartz 2003).

As indicated earlier, females involved in crime are typically involved in petty-income generating activities that fit within their skill set and are available to them. The same holds true for female drug users. Research shows that female and male drug users commit different types of crime. Male drug users dominate the higher rungs of the drug distribution hierarchy—for instance, selling—and are engaged in a range of street crimes. Female drug users, on the other hand, tend to limit their criminal activities to income-generating crime, such as shoplifting and prostitution. Female crack addicts are more likely to engage in prostitution; male crack addicts are likely to engage in panhandling, pimping, and other nondrug income-generating offenses (Anderson and Bondi 1998; Cross et al. 2001; Evans et al. 2002; Erickson et al. 2000).

The data on incarcerated females confirms this trend—females are more likely to use drugs, and use them in greater quantities, than incarcerated males (Greenfeld and Snell 1999). About half of the women in prison report having used drugs or alcohol prior to their arrest; about 40 percent (compared to 32 percent of men) report being under the influence of drugs at the time of their arrest; 60 percent of females report using drugs in the month prior to their arrest; 50 percent report they were daily users; and nearly 30 percent committed a crime to get money for drugs (Greenfeld and Snell 1999).

In summary, more women are using drugs, more women are arrested for drug related offenses, and more women are being sent to prison for drug–related violations. Women who are heavy users of expensive drugs like heroin, cocaine, and crack rely on a diverse repertoire of illicit income–producing activities that are available and fit well with their skills. Women who lack social, economic, and political power and face barriers to entry in either the legitimate or underground economies find that their options for generating income are limited to petty crimes. And for women who use drugs, prostitution is a crime of choice because it requires little skill yet generates the quick cash needed for drug use (Delacoste and Alexander 1998).

In the drug economy, where there are high levels of violence and where men hold both physical and economic advantage, female career trajectories tend to cluster around low-status roles. Research has shown that, in the social context of heavy drug use, especially of crack, prostitution is an important source of income (Bourgois 1989; Fagan 1994). Many women who regularly use expensive drugs favor prostitution over selling because they can maintain some control of their options. Fagan notes: "Consigned by traditional gender inequalities to lower wage earning positions in the formal and informal economies, women logically used their bodies as the primary power and income-generating resource available to them" (Fagan 1994, 211).

Certain points need to be clear about prostitution and gender. Prostitution is legally defined as the exchange of money (or something of value) for indiscriminate sex. It is a crime in every state except Nevada. It is also the only form of consensual adult sexual activity that is systematically subjected to criminalization in the United States (Law 2000, 526). Clements argues that not all prostitutes are subject to arrest: those most likely to get arrested occupy the lowest rung in the commercial sex hierarchy and are also the poorest and most marginalized members of society (Clements 1996, 52–53). Street-level prostitutes make up only about 10 to 15 percent of all commercial sex workers, but account for between 85 to 90 percent of the arrests for prostitution and commercialized vice (Miller et al. 1993).

Although criminal statutes define prostitution specifically as the exchange of money for indiscriminate sex, in practice what distinguishes an illegal sexual service from a legal sexual service requires more than simply the exchange of money, in the former case, for indiscriminate sexual services. The crime occurs through police involvement, because it is the police who make an arrest for prostitution. Although criminalization transformed prostitution,[2] Law (2000) argues criminalization was never intended to eliminate it.[3] Instead it was designed to give police control over prostitution's visibility, and discretion to remove certain classes of women who offended the public. Not surprisingly, the result has been selective enforcement, moving prostitution out of public view and into the back alleyways of marginalized neighborhoods. Of course, such containment is functional in that it confines such activity to certain neighborhoods. However, it serves to further marginalize these neighborhoods and the people living in them, and to normalize criminal activities as a part of everyday life.

Although female arrests generally have been increasing over time, the magnitude of female arrests for prostitution has remained fairly stable. This stability in the pattern of arrests for prostitution has broader implications than what it shows about the crime of prostitution. It reflects how the prostitution paradigm is a prototype for the way that gender is socially constructed (Balos 2001, 712). That is, beyond the crime of prostitution, the prostitution stereotype sets a standard against which all female behavior is judged, especially for women coming into contact with the criminal justice system as either offenders for victims of crime. Women's behavior is scrutinized in terms of their sexual fidelity and innocence (or lack of these virtues) such that the more closely a woman resembles the prostitute stereotype, the less deserving she is considered of our empathy and institutional protection (e.g., rape is an occupational hazard of prostitution and not something the police are inclined to define as a crime) (Balos 2001, 713).

Most street-level prostitution is carried out in what Miller (1986) termed "deviant street networks." Deviant street networks are composed of individuals who work together to generate income from illegal activities. These activities include prostitution, larceny, forgery, credit card fraud, embezzlement, auto theft, drug dealing, burglary, and robbery (Miller 1986, 35). The networks themselves tend to be controlled by males who depend on and encourage the "hustling" activity of women. The social organization of deviant networks provides further evidence of the gendered nature of the criminal world.

Not all prostitutes are drug users, but almost all street-level drug users are, at some time, involved in prostitution. To a large extent this is due to the gendered nature of the drug economy and prostitution and the fact that street-level sex markets are coterminous to drug markets. Of course, the geographical proximity of drug and sex markets is not a new phenomenon. Haller (1990) notes that in the red light districts located in American cities, brothels operated alongside dance hall, night clubs, and gambling houses, and that within these areas drug dealers hawked their wares, thieves fenced stolen goods, and pimps and other disreputable outcasts carried out an assortment of deviant activities. That today's street-level sex markets operate in tandem with crack and cocaine markets creates a set of conditions that make involvement in both symbiotic.

A primary motivator for engaging in prostitution is economic (Overall 1992). Despite the fact that prostitution is low-skill, labor intensive, and female dominated, compared to female workers in the formal economy, prostitutes are well paid. Although reliable data on income generated from prostitution are not readily available (prostitutes do not file tax returns), a RAND study of street-level prostitutes in Los Angeles in 1990–1991 found that the average earnings were $23,845 a year while females in the service sector of the formal economy earned on average $17,192 a year (Lillard et al. 1995). Clearly, for women with limited economic options, the earnings from prostitution are a strong incentive for involvement. Catherine MacKinnon has noted that "hooking is the only job for [which] women as a group are paid more than men" (MacKinnon 1987). In the words of Amber Hollibaugh, a former sex worker, "The bottom line for any woman in the sex trade is economics. However a woman feels when she finally gets into the life, it always begins as survival—the rent, the kids, the drugs, pregnancy, financing an abortion, running away from home, being undocumented, having a 'bad' reputation, incest—it always starts at trying to get by" (Hollibaugh 1988).

In summary, female heavy drug users rely on petty income-generating crime to gain the money to live on and buy drugs. And, although there is no question that female heavy drug users are involved in a broad repertoire of criminal activity because they are marginalized within the formal and underground economies, their criminal opportunities are limited to petty income-generating offenses like prostitution, shoplifting, theft, credit card scams, and drug selling (Faupel 1982; McElrath et al. 1997; Fagan 1994; Anglin and Hser 1987; Steffensmeier and Schwartz 2003). Maher and Curtis (1992) argue that in neighborhoods "where bodegas are at least three to a block, fast food, condoms, and Bic lighters are the only legal commodities that do a roaring trade, there is nothing to boost so women resort to opportunities that are available—their bodies" (230).

GLOBALIZATION AND COMMERCIAL SEX

Although prostitution and slavery have existed throughout human history and both are deeply embedded in the economic structures of many cultures, globalization[4] has changed the face and scale of prostitution.

Travel, migration, unfettered capitalism, consumerism, the commodification of people, and "liberal" economic development policies have all contributed to the globalization of prostitution. The commercialized sex industry is a multibillion dollar industry highly integrated within many sectors of the legitimate economy. According to Weeks, the commercialization of the sex trade and the commodification of people parallel the shift from capitalist accumulation to capitalist distribution and from production to consumption (1993).

In today's commercialized sex market, there are a vast number of products spanning all types of media and venues. Some of these include live sex shows, a full range of pornographic texts, videos, and images in print and online, fetish clubs, telephone and cybersex contacts, drive-through strip stops, escort services, clubs featuring lap and wall dancing, and organized sex tours in developing countries (Bernstein 2001; Kempadoo and Doezema 1998). Evidence shows that a third of those surfing the Internet during the workday will visit a pornography site (Wall Street Journal 1999). The demand for sexual services has grown rapidly and become more diversified; it is now integral to other sectors of the global economy, such as hotel chains, long-distance carriers, cable companies, and information technology (Bernstein 2001).

One of the consequences of liberal economic development policies has been the global expansion of the commercial sex industry. In efforts to modernize[5] their economies, many traditional family and community supports of developing countries have been dismantled. This has left millions of people without viable options for generating their incomes within the borders of their own countries. For many, especially women, migration has been the key to economic opportunities.

Of the world's 120 million people who cross borders each year, over half are female. Even though the aggregate numbers tell us nothing about the jobs these migrating females eventually take, there are good reasons to infer that much of the work females end up performing is traditional female work—as nannies, domestics, food service workers, sweatshop workers, and sex workers; this is because females around the world are relegated to work in the service sectors of the informal and illegal economies. Given the kind of work that females perform and the limited forms of migration available to them, many women are forced to use the services of criminal organizations and brokers to help them find a job. Of course, these third parties are more than willing to take advantage of their situations.

One way that this occurs is through the illegal movement of people, or "trafficking." Trafficking in women is in fact the oldest and most traditional form of procuring women for prostitution (Barry 1995). (This is not to say that prostitution is what has led to trafficking, but rather to point out that, throughout history, women have been trafficked for the purpose of prostitution.) Globalization has changed the scale of trafficking and the nature of the sex industry.

It has been argued that prostitution represents the most dramatic aspect of the growing sex industry because it is interrelated to the global economy (Altman 2001, 106). The International Labor Organization (ILO) estimates that the sex sector of the economies of Indonesia, Malaysia, the Philippines, and Thailand accounts for between 2 percent and 14 percent of GDP, and that the revenues generated from prostitution are critical to the livelihoods and earnings of millions of additional workers (Anker 1998). The economic disparities between source countries and destination countries for trafficked humans are considerable. For example, the average per capita GDP for source countries is $4,455 (with the range from $800 to $16,800) and the average per capita GDP for destination countries is $22,807 (with a range from $12,000 to $58,900).

The majority of prostitutes are women; because they are economically marginalized, the "commercialization" of sex feeds off the basic material needs of women. In short, the sex industry is growing because comparable economic opportunities in the formal economy are not available. Economic development has always depended on the immigration of cheap labor, and historically prostitutes have been drawn from immigrant and poor populations. For example, prostitution played an integral role in the economic development of the United States. Gilfoye's (1992) historical analysis of prostitution in New York City in the nineteenth century estimates that 10–15 percent of all females living in New York City were prostitutes and that prostitution was the second largest business (tailoring was the first), in terms of money generated, in the economy.

Over the last three decades, the sex industry has grown rapidly and diversified into a multibillion dollar global business (Anderson and Davidson 2003). The opportunities to buy sexual services have multiplied and become more varied. Sexual services can be purchased legally or illegally, but the boundaries between the two are increasingly blurred. This has occurred in part as a result of major changes in the nature of the sex industry. According to Brents and Hausbeck (1999), legal sexual services in the United States have been transformed from a set of small, privately owned, entrepreneurial, illegitimate, and almost feudal businesses dependent on local sheriffs looking the other way, to a multibillion dollar legal industry that is now dependent on state/capital interests driven by corporate mobilization.

In theory, the commercialized sex industry is fundamentally an economic enterprise that operates by the laws of supply and demand. As in any business, growth is related to creating and increasing demand. Since demand is socially, culturally, and historically determined, buyers have to be made to believe that buying sexual services is a marker of their social identity ("real man," "not gay," "able to buy entertainment"). So, though there is no quotient for the number of lap dancers or lap dance clubs in a given community, the availability, acceptability, and affordability of lap dancers and lap dance clubs stimulate demand among people who had never thought about consuming lap dancing before (Anderson and Davidson 2003, 41). The bottom line for any business is profit, and making a profit requires cheap labor and a growing demand for the product or service.

Kempadoo (2003, 137) notes that the drive to increase profit margins has led to a proliferation of new products, goods, and services and the cultivation of new desires and needs. And, although the demand for sexual services could be met just as easily by anyone in the labor market, there is good reason to expect that in practice the demand is more likely to be met by needy and vulnerable workers. In part, this is because this market itself is changing—parts of it remain criminalized and all of it is poorly regulated and widely stigmatized. In a study of employers of domestic workers and clients of sex workers in four countries, Anderson and Davidson (2003, 43) found that unregulated markets created conditions where the use of forced/marginalized labor was preferable and highly profitable. Owners and operators of sex service venues can offer low pay and long hours, and even charge a commission for the use of their space, to women seeking to work in the sex sector.

What are the implications of globalization for economically marginalized women? Research on the economic impact of globalization shows that women have been especially affected, because they are increasingly responsible for contributing to the household economy within a context of low wages and long working hours. The illegal movement of people to work around the world has become a very real issue for those who are being "squeezed on all sides and have few options available" (Kempadoo 2003, 159). Sudbury argues that large-scale economic dislocation has been especially hard on poor and minority women, because they tend to be the primary caretakers of children and the elderly and are responsible for providing basic needs such as food, shelter, medical care, and clothing (2003, 222).

Moreover, the movement of capital has diminished opportunities for women to make a living. As wages drop and unemployment increases, people who can move away from economically depressed areas do, and their departure adds to the economic depression of distressed communities. For those left behind, the opportunities available are those associated with the underground economy. Not surprisingly, as capital in the underground economy decreases, so too does the potential income generated through illegal activities. As the legitimate commercialized sex industry establishes itself as a viable form of "entertainment" and "consumption," illegal sex markets, like the neighborhoods in which they operate, become even more depressed. Maher's (1997) research confirms the decreasing economic returns for street-level prostitutes.

Toward a New Paradigm on Drugs and Prostitution

The illegal drug and prostitution markets are multibillion dollar global markets. In both cases, our policy approaches for almost a hundred years have had little impact—abating neither drug use nor prostitution. Despite convincing, publicly available evidence of the deleterious effects of these policies, especially on women, policy makers have consistently refused to engage in a serious reevaluation of strategies. In the case of illicit drugs, the main aim of criminalization has been to limit supply so that drug users cannot find or afford drugs, and a secondary aim has been to discourage use by penalizing users. The evidence shows that, although drug enforcement agents confiscate more drugs each year, they have not been able to stem the tide of drugs coming into the country.

Billions of dollars have been spent to enforce criminalization, but research has consistently documented the growth and expansion of drug markets, the increase in the number of hardcore drug users, the increase in the number of arrests for drug violations, and increases in the number of people sent to prison for drug use. In the case of prostitution, our policies have primarily aimed to deter practicing and would-be prostitutes on moral grounds. The empirical evidence shows that, far from these policies reducing or deterring prostitution, prostitution is thriving, and, through the forces of globalization, the legal commercial sex industry has become integrated with the national economies of the world.

Our aim in this chapter has been to provide a context for reevaluating the effects of criminalization on drugs and prostitution, especially as these policies affect women. We have drawn attention to the relevance of gender in differentially impacting the experiences of female drug users with limited economic opportunities and the experiences of females who depend on prostitution as a source of income. The social organization of drug and sex markets mirrors broader social and cultural forces that legitimate the growing economic marginalization of females. We need a paradigm shift that moves us away from polarizing and further marginalizing women, especially women of color. The dramatic increase in the number of women incarcerated for drug-related offenses requires that we expand our thinking to include an examination of how globalization has affected economic opportunities for women around the world and in the inner-city ghettos and rural communities of the United States (Sokoloff 2005; Sudbury 2003).

We also need to incorporate the vast stock of knowledge about the precursors to drug use and abuse, and how these differentially affect females and males. A viable alternative to criminalization of drug use would be a vision that frames drug use and abuse as a public health problem. A viable alternative to criminalization of prostitution would be a vision that frames it as a form of work—much as it is treated in the legal commercialized sex sector, with the proviso that it be protected by regulations.

The social and cultural conditions present in any environment influence the decisions that individuals make about drugs (whether to try them, how often to use them, what precautions to take when using them, how to afford them, whether to seek treatment for their use, etc.). Thus, a strategy that combines prevention and treatment could transform the conditions that give rise to drug use. We know that the pathways to drug use differ for females and for males (Rosenbaum 1983; Miller 1986; Anderson and Bondi 1998). Females get involved with drug use through a husband, boyfriend, or family member; females are more likely than males to have experienced sexual and physical abuse; females experience more severe economic pressures, because of their economic marginalization from both the formal and underground economies; and females are more likely to use drugs to cope with psychological problems whereas males use drugs for recreation and social status.

We also know that prevention and treatment are more cost-effective strategies for dealing with drug dependency than is incarceration. The same environmental conditions that increase the risk of drug use and abuse shape the availability of economic opportunities for females. We have also tried to show the relevance of gender and gender relations in the crime of prostitution. Prostitution is a petty crime and the majority of prostitutes are women; the reason that prostitution is so heavily gendered is the result of women's marginalization in both the legitimate and illegitimate economies.

The evidence overwhelmingly shows that criminalization has been a failure: it consumes enormous public resources and has little impact on sex markets. By definition, criminal statutes prohibiting prostitution have failed to take into account the effects that globalization has on the sex industry and the myriad ways that sexual services are now integrated within the formal economic structures of national economies around the world.

Criminalization only creates criminals and directs resources toward punishing the most economically marginalized members of society, rather than protecting them from violence and abuse. What is objectionable about the prohibitions against prostitution is the framework in which these occur: criminalization tolerates prostitution but not the prostitute. The prostitution stereotype works to affirm the social construction of the prostitute as undeserving, yet for unskilled or low-skilled women, few economic opportunities can provide the income comparable to prostitution (Vanweenenbeeck 1994).

Interest in prostitution has recently been rekindled in the context of human trafficking, by nations and supranational institutions such as the European Union and the United Nations (Outshoorn 2005). As a result of this renewed interest, a number of nation-states—Australia, Canada, Sweden, Spain, and Finland to name a few—have revised their prostitution laws (Outshoorn 2005). The United States stands conspicuously alone for having not changed its antiprostitution policy since the early twentieth century. Clearly the world has changed dramatically since the early twentieth century and these changes warrant revisiting antiprostitution statutes. In most Western industrialized countries, prostitution is decriminalized. The United Nations endorses decriminalization.

We too believe that prostitution should be decriminalized and treated like other sexual services provided in the broader legal sex industry. Then, sexual services could be regulated by civil and labor laws. Further, decriminalization combined with appropriate social services could improve the lives of prostitutes, as well as the communities in which they work. Prostitutes would not be subject to criminal sanctions or limited to working in abusive state-sanctioned zones and brothels, but would have agency over the conditions under which they work and be protected by civil and labor regulations.

Drawing upon Kuo's policy prescriptions for prostitution, we agree that "what needs to be done for prostitutes is what needs to be done for all women"—implementing a set of policy initiatives directed toward improving the economic opportunities open to *all* women (Kuo 2002, 153). Toward this end, Kuo recommends the establishment of "governance boards" that would identify the appropriate regulatory mechanisms, government services, and legal protections geared toward improving the well-being of prostitutes and the community at large (2002, 154). Central to decriminalization is the need to change the way prostitution is constructed—in other words, to think about prostitution in terms of what it is for those who do it. As Geertz has poignantly noted, if you want to know what something is and what it means, you need to ask those who "do it" (Geertz 1973). When researchers have asked prostitutes about their lived experiences as prostitutes, what these researchers have learned is that most prostitutes view what they do as a form of work to generate income, rather than as recreation (Lucas 2005; Albert 2001).

Defining prostitution as a form of work is a necessary first step for improving the lives of prostitutes. Decriminalizing it would also allow it to be treated like other forms of work. Legitimating prostitution could "promote greater social appreciation of the diversity of sexual experiences and options by clarifying that prostitution represents a commodity context for sex" and exists alongside other contexts (both economic and noneconomic) of sexual expression (Lucas 2005, 263). Subsequently, full or partial commodification would lessen the stigma of prostitution, regulate the conditions under which prostitutes work, and go far toward recognizing involuntary prostitution as a form of "forced labor" (Murray 1998).

NOTES

1. Drawing upon Than-Dam Troung's (1990) and Bidman and Dozema's (1997) contention about the need to take into account the varied forms that sexual labor takes in differing historical contexts and political economies, we use the terms *prostitution* and *prostitute,* throughout this chapter, to refer explicitly to sexual services provided within illegal sex markets subject to criminal sanctions. Thus, for our purposes, *prostitution* is a survival strategy carried out in the context of illegal sex markets. *Sex work* applies to the sexual labor that occurs within the broader legal context of the commercialized sex industry. We believe it is necessary to distinguish between involvement in illegal sex markets and involvement in legal sex markets, to better understand the complex realities of women's experiences in the sex industry.
2. Criminalization stigmatizes women for not meeting the idealized vision of virtuous femininity. Thus women are dichotomized either "good" or "bad."
3. Prostitution is a nuisance offense whose gravamen is not the act itself or the event of the accompanying commercial transaction, but rather prostitution's status as a public indecency (Packer 1968).
4. Globalization has been defined in many ways, but generally means the reconfiguration of geography so that spatial organization of social relations and transactions are transformed for the purpose of generating interregional flows and activities (Giddens 1990, 64; Scholte 2000, 46).
5. By this we mean the use of international monetary institutions and regional trade agreements for purposes of integrating into the world economy by reducing tariffs, privatizing state enterprises, and relaxing environmental and labor standards.

REFERENCES

Albert, Alexa. 2001. *Brothel: Mustang Ranch and Its Women.* NY: Random House.

Alexander, P. 1987. "Prostitution: A difficult iassue for feminists." In *Sex Work: Writings by Women in the Sex Industsry,* ed. Frederique Delacoste and Priscilla Alexander. Pittsburgh, PA: Cleis Press.

Altman, D. 2001. *Global Sex.* Chicago: University of Chicago Press.

Anderson, B., and J. O'Connell Davidson. 2003. "Is trafficking in human beings demand driven? A multicountry pilot study." International Organization of Migration Research Series, no. 15 (December).

Anderson T., and L. Bondi. 1998. "Exiting the drug addict role: Variations by race and gender." *Symbolic Interaction* 21, no. 2: 155–174.

Anglin, M. D., and Y. Hser. 1987. "Addicted women and crime." *Criminology* 25: 359–397.

Anker, R. 1998. *Gender and Jobs: Sex Segregation of Occupations in the World*. Geneva: International Labor Organization.

Archer, D. W. 2004. "It's time to get smart on crime." American Bar Association, Chicago. http://www.abanet.org/media/releases/opedcrime.html.

Austin, G., and D. Lettieri. 1976. "Drugs and crime: The relationship of drug use and concomitant criminal behavior" (DHHS Pub. ADM 77–393). Rockville, MD. U.S. Deparatment of Health and Human Services, NIDA.

Baldwin, M. 1993. "Strategies of connection: Prostitution and feminist politics." *Michigan Journal of Gender and Law* 1, no. 65: 68.

Balos, B. 2001. "Teaching prostitution seriously." *Buffalo Criminal Law Review* 4: 709–753.

Barry, K. 1995. *The Prostitution of Sexuality*. New York: New York University Press.

Bernstein, E. 1999. "What's wrong with prostitution? What's right with sex work? Comparing maarkets in female sexual labor." *Hastings Women's Law Journal* 10: 91.

Bidman, J., and J. Dozema. 1997. *Redefining Prostitution as Sex Work in the International Agenda*. London: Anti-Slavery International.

Bourgois, P. 1989. "In search of Horatio Alger: Culture and ideology in the crack economy." *Contemporary Drug Problems* 16: 619–650.

Brents, B., and Kathryn Hausbeck. 1999. "Bodies, business, and politics: Corporate mobilization and the sex industries." Paper presented at the American Sociological Association, August 1999.

Chaiken, J. M., and M. R. Chaiken. 1990. "Drugs and predatory crime." In M. Tonry and J. Q. Wilson, eds., *Drugs and Crime*, 203–239. Chicago: University of Chicago Press.

Chapkis, W. 1997. *Live Sex Acts: Women Performing Exotic Labor.* New York: Routledge. .

Clement, E. 1998. "Prostitution and community in turn-of-the-century New York City." In J. Elias, V. Bullough, and G. Brewwer, ed., *Prostitution: On Whores, Hustlers, and Johns*. Amherst, NY: Prometheus Books.

Clements, T. M. 1996. "Prostitution and the American health care system: Denying access to a group of women in need." *Berkeley Women's Law Journal* 49: 52–53.

Confronting Confinement: A Report of the Commission on Safety and Abuse in America's Prisons. 2006. New York: Vera Institute. June.

Defleur, L., J. Ball, and R. Snarr. 1969. "The long-term social correlates of opiate addiction." *Social Problems* 17, no. 2: 225–233.

Delacoste, F., and P. Alexander, eds. 1997. *Sex Work: Writings by Women in the Sex Industry*. Pittsburgh, PA: Cleis Press.

Doezema, J. 1998. "Forced to choose: Beyond the voluntary v. forced prostitution dichotomy." In K. Kempadoo and J. Doezema, eds., *Global Sex Workers: Rights, Resistance, and Redefinition,* 34–50. New York: Routledge.

Dorsey, T., M. Zawitz, and P. Middleton. 2005. *Drug and Crime Facts* (NCJ 165148). Washington, DC: Bureau of Justice Statistics. www.ojp.usdoj.gov/bjs/pub/pdf/dcf.pdf.

Erickson, P., J. Butters, P. McGillicuddy, and A. Hallgren. 2000. "Crack and prostitution: Gender, myths, and experiences." *Journal of Drug Issues* 30, no. 4: 767–788.

Evans, R., C. Forsyth, and D. Gauthier. 2002. "Gendered pathways into and experiences within crack cultures outside the inner city." *Deviant Behavior* 23, no. 6: 483–510.

Fagan J. 1994. "Women and drugs revisited: Female participation in the cocaine economy." *Journal of Drug Issues* 24, no. 1/2: 179–225.

Faupel, C. 1991. *Shooting Dope: Career Patterns of Hard-core Heroin Users.* Gainesville: University of Florida Press.

Fechner, H. 1994. "Three stories of prostitution in the West: Prostitutes' groups, law, and feminist 'truth.'" *Columbia Journal of Gender and Law*, no. 4: 26.

Geertz, Clifford. 1973. *The Interpretation of Cultures.* New York: Basic Books.

Giddens, A. 1990. *The Consequences of Modernity.* Cambridge: Policy Press.

Gilfoyle, T. J. 1992. *City of Eros: New York City, Prostitution, and the Commercialization of Sex, 1790–1920.* New York: W. W. Norton and Company.

Greenfield, L., and T. Snell 1999. *Women Offenders.* Washington, DC: U.S. Department of Justice, Bureau of Justice Statistics. December.

Haller, M. 1990. "Illegal enterprise: A theoretical and historical interpretation." *Criminology* 28, no. 2: 207–235.

Hollibaugh, A. 1988. "On the street where we live." *Women's Review of Books* 5 (January): 1.

Hunt, A. 1999. *Governing Morals: A Social History of Moral Regulation.* Cambridge: Cambridge University Press.

Hunt, D. 1990. "Drugs and consensual crimes: Drug dealing and prostitution." In M. Tonry and J. Q. Wilson, eds. *Drugs and Crime*, 154–202. Chicago: University of Chicago Press.

Johnson, B. D. 1991. "The crack era in New York City." *Addiction and Recovery* 13, no. 3 (May/June): 24–27.

Kempadoo, Kamala. 2003. "Prostitution and the globalization of sex workers' rights." In *The Criminal Justice System and Women*, ed. Barbara Raffel Price and Natalie Sokoloff. New York: McGraw-Hill.

———, and Jo Doezema. 1998. . *Global Sex Workers: Rights, Resistance, and Redefinition.* New York and London: Routledge.

Kuo, L. 2002. *Prostitution Policy: Revolutionizing Practice through a Gendered Perspective.* New York: New York University Press.

Law, S. 2000. "Commercial sex: Beyond decriminalization." *Southern California Law Review* 73, no. 3: 523–610.

Lillard, L., S. Berry, D. Kanouse. 1995. "The Market for Sex: Street Prostitution in Los Angeles." Monograph. Santa Monica, CA: RAND Corporation.

Lucas, A. 1995. "Race, class, gender, and deviancy: The criminalization of prostitution." *Berkeley Women's Law Journal* 10: 47.

Lucas, Ann. 2005. "The currency of sex: Prostitution, law, and commodification." In *Rethinking Commodification: Cases and Readings in Law and Culture*, ed. Martha M. Ertman and Joan C. Williams. New York: New York University Press.

———. 2005. "The work of sex work: Elite prostitutes' vocational orientations and experiences." *Deviant Behavior* 26: 513–546.

MacKinnon, Catherine. 1987. *Feminism Unmodified: Discourses on Life and Law.* Cambridge, MA: Harvard University Press.

Maher, L. 1997. *Sexed Work.* New York: Oxford University Press.

———, and Curtis R. 1992. "Women on the edge of crime: Crack cocaine and the changing contexts of street-level sex work in New York City." *Law and Social Change* 18, no. 3: 221–258.

Mauer, M., C. Potler, and Richard Wolf. 1999. *Gender and Justice: Women, Drugs, and Sentencing.* Washington, D.C.: The Sentencing Project. November.

McBride, D. C., and C. B. McCoy. 1993. "The drugs–crime relationship: An analytical framework." Prison Journal 73, nos. 3–4.

McBride, D. C., C. J. Vander-Waal, and Y Terry McElrath. 2002. "The Drugs-Crime Wars: Past, Present, and Future Direction in Theory, Policy, and Program Interventions." Paper for NIJ, Drugs and Crime Research Forum [online]. www.ojp.usdoj.gov/nij/drugscrime/

McElrath, K., D. Chitwood, and M. Comerford. 1997. "Crime victimization among injection drug users." Journal of Drug Issues 24, no. 4: 771–784.

Miller, E. 1986. Street Woman. Philadelphia: Temple University Press.

———, K. Romenesko, and L. Wondolkowski. 1993. "The United States." In Nanette Davis, ed., Prostitution: An International Handbook on Trends, Problems, and Policies. Westport, CT: Greenwood Press.

Mullings, J., J. Pollock, and B. Crouch. 2002. "Drugs and criminality: Results from the Texas women inmates study." Women and Criminal Justice 13, no. 4: 69–96.

Murray, Allison. 1998. "Debt-bondage and trafficking: Don't believe the hype." In Global Sex Workers: Rights, Resistance, and Redefinition, ed. Kamala Kempadoo and Jo Doezema. New York and London: Routledge.

Norton Hawk, Maureen. 2001. "The counterproductivity of incarcerating female street prostitutes." Deviant Behavior 22, no. 5: 403–417.

Oishi, N. 2005. Women in Motion: Globalization, State Policies, and Labor Migration in Asia. Stanford, CA: Stanford University Press.

Outshoorn, J. 2005. "Political debates on prostitution and trafficking." Social Politics 12, no. 1: 141–155.

Overall, C. 1992. "What's wrong with prostitution? Evaluating sex work." Signs 17, no. 3: 705–724.

Packer, H. 1968. The Limits of the Criminal Sanction. Stanford, CA: Stanford University Press.

Pearl, J. 1987. "The highest-paying customers: America's cities and the costs of prostitution control." Hastings Law Journal 38, no. 4: 769–800.

Rhode, D. 1989. Justice and Gender: Sex Discrimination and the Law. Cambridge, MA: Harvard University Press.

Rosenbaum, Marsha. 1981. Women on Heroin. New Brunswick, NJ: Rutgers University Press.

Scholte, J. 2000. Globalization: A Critical Introduction. London: Palgrove Press.

Sokoloff, N. 2001. "Violent female offenders in New York City: Myths and facts. Crime and Justice." In Crime and Justice in New York City, ed. Andrew Karmen. Vol. 1, 132–146). Cincinnati: Thompson Learning.

———. 2005. "Women prisoners at the dawn of the twenty-first century." Women and Criminal Justice 16, nos. 1–2.

Steffensmeier, D. 1980. "Sex differences in patterns of adult crime, 1965–1977: A review and assessment." Social Forces 58: 1080–1108.

———, and J. Schwartz. 2003. "Contemporary explanations of women's crime." In The Criminal Justice System and Women, ed. Barbara Raffel Price and Natalie Sokoloff. New York: McGraw-Hill.

Sudbury, J. 2003. "Women of color, globalization, and the politics of incarceration." In Criminal Justice System and Women, ed. Barbara Raffel Price and Natalie Sokoloff, New York: McGraw-Hill.

Terry, C., and M. Pellens. 1928. The Opium Problem. New York: Committee on Drug Addiction, Bureau of Social Hygiene.

Truoung , Thanh-Dam.1990. *Sex, Money, and Morality: Prostitution and Tourism in Southeast Asia.* London: Zed Books.

U.S. Department of Justice, Federal Bureau of Investigation. *Uniform Crime Reports: Crime in the United States, 2004, 2005.* Washington, DC: U.S. Department of Justice.

Vanwesenbeeck, I. 1994. *Prostitutes' Well-Being and Risk.* Amsterdam: Free University Press.

Wall Street Journal, August 3, 1999.

Weeks, J. 1993. "An unfinished revolution: Sexuality in the twentieth century." In V. Harwood, D. Oswell, K. Parkinson, and A. Ward, eds., *Pleasure Principles: Politics, Sexuality, and Ethics.* London: Lawrence and Whishart.

White, H. R., and D. M. Gorman. 2000. "Dynamics of the drug–crime relationship." *Criminal Justice* 1: 151–218.

Epilogue

Carol E. Tracy

MY FIRST EXPERIENCE in working with women dependent on drugs occurred in 1989 when I was the director of the Mayor's Commission for Women in Philadelphia. One afternoon, I came back from lunch and found a family waiting in my office: a grandmother, two adult daughters (one of whom was six months pregnant), and three grandchildren. The Johnson family had got off the elevator on the wrong floor, intending to go to Women against Abuse Legal Center, a domestic violence center. My secretary listened to their story and sent them on to me, realizing that they might need other assistance.

They told me that they had been living in one of the city's shelters and had "escaped" that morning. The women wore several layers of clothes and dressed the children the same way; they had put the rest of their belongings in trash bags and thrown them out of the window. They left the shelter, one small group at a time. They found a supermarket cart, after walking a few blocks, and the adults put the children in it for their five- or six-mile trek to City Hall. On the way, they made a stop at a supermarket where they stole some food so the children could have breakfast.

They had heard about an organization called Women against Abuse, and that it was located in City Hall. Since it was there, they thought they would have access to the mayor, who they felt should know about what was going on in a city shelter.

As the story unfolded, the women disclosed that they were addicted to crack, but still had some control over the addiction, and also that a loan shark hung out around the homeless shelter where they lived. One of the daughters described how she would ask for a loan of five dollars to buy a sandwich and he would give her twenty dollars. He knew, she said, that she was an addict and with twenty dollars would buy drugs instead of food. This was true of all three of them, so the grandmother and her daughters had assumed a big debt. It was problematic for several reasons, not the least of which was that the homeless system required that some portion of their welfare payments go into a savings account or else they would be thrown out.

Fortunately, the office next-door to mine had just had a luncheon, so we had some food to offer. We also had some toys in our office left over from a toy drive. I learned that the daughter who was pregnant had not received any prenatal care. The children were well behaved and appropriately socially interactive.

I sat listening to them, thinking that they presented several emergencies requiring immediate attention, and not having the faintest idea where to begin to troubleshoot this case. For the previous year, I had been working on a policy level to improve and increase drug treatment programs, particularly residential programs for women and their children. We were two weeks away from opening the first residential program for pregnant and postpartum women and their children.

So I began making calls. Being a member of the mayor's staff had few privileges, but one was that other government officials would answer my call. As I outlined the problems, one response emerged from all of the officials: "Are you okay? Are you in danger—do you need someone to come over?" I presented the story—naively, probably—with the same candor with which it had been presented to me. It never occurred to me that describing women with active crack addictions would provoke anxiety or protectionism on my behalf. As I sat looking out at this family eating lunch and playing with toys, the incongruity of perception with reality could not have been starker.

We finally arrived at an option: housing was the first priority. I accompanied the family to the Adult Services Office because I wanted to make sure they were actually taken care of. We met with the director, who was so outraged at the harassment by loan sharks and drug dealers, and the apparent complicity by the operators of a city shelter, that she contacted the police and the district attorney. She told the women that they would be placed, without penalty, in a shelter immediately, but also proposed that they consider going back to the original shelter to collect evidence against the wrongdoers. I was astonished by this suggestion, and more astonished at the willingness of the women to cooperate. I kept interjecting that they did not have to, and kept getting assurances from the director that there would be no negative repercussions on them. The women really wanted to cooperate, because they wanted to help the other women who were being subjected to the same treatment. Arrangements were made for the grandmother to go to the new shelter with the children, while the two daughters went back to the shelter wearing wires to collect evidence.

Fortunately for this family, I was not sophisticated enough about city bureaucracy to discern their most pressing problem and "refer" them: it could have been addiction, housing, poverty, criminal activity, child abuse and neglect, health care related to prenatal care or childhood immunizations, literacy, or job training. They could have been labeled as criminals, addicts, homeless, bad parents, low literacy, unemployable.

The daughters and their children were eventually admitted to the new residential drug treatment program; the grandmother went to a program for single women. A healthy baby was born; a brother who was on the streets was found and brought into treatment; education and jobs were eventually obtained; and sobriety has been sustained all these years. Interesting enough, the Johnsons weren't even asking for treatment or much help—they only wanted fairness. It has always impressed me that it took so little for a family so troubled to get back on its feet. The only thing unusual about them was that they had each other, unlike many addicted women who experience profound social isolation.

I moved from the mayor's office in 1990 to direct the Women's Law Project—in part to participate in legal challenges concerning the denial of drug treatment to pregnant women, the underrepresentation of women in treatment, and the prosecution of pregnant women with untreated addictions. Along the way, I have met many women like the Johnsons struggling with addiction and recovery. I've talked to women who have been abused and assaulted throughout their lives, women who have fought back and paid the consequences for doing so, women who have lost their children to the child welfare system either because of actual abuse and neglect or simply because they were deemed to be bad moms because of their drug use, women who have prostituted themselves, and women who have engaged in drug dealing and in all sorts of other criminal activity.

The only common theme that I have been able to discern is the extraordinary ability of women to survive. I've learned that it is a mistake to romanticize their victimization or to exonerate their wrongdoing, because they themselves do not. I often say that women in recovery from addiction have been from "here to hell and back." Although their grief at their many losses is often palpable, many possess an uncanny honesty and candor about themselves, their experiences, and their future.

These are women who have defied social norms, are risk-takers and decision makers, have experienced untold violence and hardships, have acted out in dysfunctional ways and suffered serious consequences—and yet many have survived and some have thrived. They possess wisdom and experience that could guide social policy; however, virtually impenetrable social forces want to either victimize or demonize them, and unfortunately ignore them as potential agents for social change and social welfare.

The Women's Law Project issued a report, *Responding to the Needs of Pregnant and Parenting Women with Substance Use Disorders in Philadelphia* (www.womenslawproject.org). Much of what is contained in the report came from listening to the women affected by addictions. We learned that addiction, violence, and trauma are inextricably linked and are endemic in the lives of women in health, social service, and criminal justice systems. The report contains a series of findings and recommendations to improve public policy affecting vulnerable women. These recommendations include: creating trauma-informed, culturally competent, integrated services; making long-term commitments to families affected by addictions and violence; and recognizing and believing in the power of women to heal themselves, their families, and their communities.

NOTES ON CONTRIBUTORS

TAMMY ANDERSON is an associate professor in the University of Delaware's department of sociology and criminal justice. Her areas of research and teaching expertise are in deviance, crime, drugs abuse, race/ethnicity, gender, and popular culture. For more than ten years, she has published numerous articles on drug abuse, gender, race, stigma, and health. Dr. Anderson is currently completing a book based on her ethnographic study of club culture, drugs, crime, and victimization, sponsored by her university and the National Institute of Justice. She is past chair of the Section on Alcohol, Drugs, and Tobacco of the American Sociological Association (2005–2006) and of the Division on Drinking and Drugs of the Society for the Study of Social Problems (2003–2004). Her Web site is www.udel.edu/soc/tammya.

DEBORAH R. BASKIN received her doctorate in sociology in 1984 from the University of Pennsylvania. For the past eleven years, she has been director of the School of Criminal Justice and Criminalistics at California State University, Los Angeles. Dr. Baskin has published on a variety of topics, including female offending, substance abuse and violence, forensic mental health, and community mediation. Most recently, she was the co–principal investigator on a National Science Foundation grant studying methamphetamine use and violence. Dr. Baskin is coauthor of *The Social Consequences of Methamphetamine Use* (2004), *Workin' Hard for the Money: The Social and Economic Lives of Female Drug Dealers* (2000), and *Casualties of Community Disorder: Women's Careers in Violent Crime* (1998).

MICHELLE TRACY BERGER is currently an assistant professor in the curriculum in women's studies and an adjunct professor in the department of political science at the University of North Carolina, Chapel Hill. Dr. Berger's teaching and research interests include multiracial feminisms, qualitative methods, and AIDS activism. Her most recent book is *Workable Sisterhood: The Political Journey of Stigmatized Women with HIV/AIDS* (Princeton University Press, 2004). *Workable Sisterhood* is an ethnographic study about the lives of stigmatized women (former drug users and sex workers) with HIV/ AIDS who became politically active in Detroit.

KIM M. BLANKENSHIP is an associate research scientist of epidemiology and public health and the associate director of the Center for Interdisciplinary Research on AIDS at Yale University. A sociologist, Dr. Blankenship focuses on race, class, and gender analyses of law, public policy, and health. Current research projects include analysis of the implementation and impact of community-led structural interventions to address HIV risk in sex workers in India; a study of the impact of the criminal justice system on HIV risk among drug users in Connecticut, and an analysis of the relationships among incarceration, policing, and race disparities in HIV/AIDS. In general, she seeks to understand policy factors associated with changes in health-related structures and processes, and such factors' impact on behavior and disease patterns.

PHYLLIS COONTZ is an associate professor in the Graduate School of Public and International Affairs (GSPIA) at the University of Pittsburgh, and the director of the PhD program in GSPIA. She also holds joint appointments at GSPIA in sociology and women's studies. She is currently doing research on minority street-level sex workers who are also drug users, focusing on their health needs and adherence to treatment for HIV/AIDS and STDs. She and Cate Griebel have published other articles on trafficking in humans, which have focused on the viability of the UN Trafficking Protocol and the Convention on the Elimination of All Forms of Discrimination against Women (CEDAW). Dr. Coontz has published articles on antiprostitution policy; human trafficking, gambling policy; gender disparities in the legal profession, gender and crime, child abuse, and drug use.

ELIZABETH (BETSY) ETTORRE is currently professor of sociology, University of Liverpool, United Kingdom. She has worked in the United States, United Kingdom, and Finland and holds honorary posts at the Abo Academy University, University of Helsinki, EGenis, Exeter University, and Institute for Scientific Analysis (San Francisco, California). She has developed a consistent interest in the sociology of substance use with special reference to women. She has published widely; her books include: *Lesbians, Women, and Society* (1980); *Women and Substance Use* (1992); *Gendered Moods* (1995), with Elianne Riska; *Women and Alcohol: A Private Pleasure or a Public Problem?* (1997); *Reproductive Genetics, Gender, and the Body* (2002); *Before Birth* (2001), and *Revisioning Women and Drug Use: Gender, Power, and the Body* (2007).

ALISON R. GRAY is a research associate at the Center for Drug and Alcohol Studies at the University of Delaware and a graduate student in the department of sociology and criminal justice. She has served as project director of a study of drug court offenders and is currently project director of a national juvenile reentry study. She has coauthored articles that examine participant satisfaction and gender and mental health issues in drug court.

CATE GREIBEL holds her M.S. degree from the University of Pittsburgh, in international development, and was a U.S. Fulbright Fellow in Santiago, Chile, where she researched antitrafficking policy in the region. She currently works in New York City and provides case management for survivors of human trafficking.

STEPHANIE W. HARTWELL is an associate professor of sociology and criminal justice and the director of the Graduate Certificate Program in Forensic Services at the University of Massachusetts Boston. She completed her doctorate in sociology at Yale University in 1995, and was an assistant professor at the University of Connecticut Medical School in the Alcohol Research Center and the department of psychiatry from 1995 until 1997, when she joined the department of sociology at the University of Massachusetts Boston. She is a research fellow with the Center for Mental Health Services at the University of Massachusetts Medical School's department of psychiatry, and conducts research for the Forensic Division of the Department of Mental Health in Massachusetts.

YASMINA KATSULIS is an assistant professor in the Women and Gender Studies Program, Arizona State University. She teaches about sexuality, HIV/AIDS, and the role of social determinants of health at the local, national, and global levels. Her training as a medical anthropologist is based on field research done in the United States and Mexico on the impact of gender, sexuality, and violence in the HIV/AIDS epidemic. A book manuscript related to her research on occupational health and safety among sex workers in Tijuana, Mexico, has been published through the University of Texas Press in 2007.

MARGARET S. KELLEY is currently an associate professor at the University of Oklahoma. She has done considerable research utilizing both qualitative and quantitative approaches and a variety of data sources to investigate illicit drug use. Dr. Kelley has authored and coauthored numerous refereed articles appearing in journals including *Social Science and Medicine, Journal of Drug Issues, Addiction Research,* and *International Journal of Sociology and Social Policy.* She recently completed an edited manuscript that is forthcoming from Allyn and Bacon, *Readings on Drugs and Society: The Criminal Connection.* Her research interests, in addition to drug studies, include drug treatment, needle exchange programs, HIV/AIDS risk behavior, women and violence, and sports and delinquency.

MARGARET S. MALLOCH is a senior research fellow in the Scottish Centre for Crime and Justice Research at the University of Stirling. Her book *Women Drugs and Custody* was published by Waterside Press in 2000, with subsequent journal publications in the *Howard Journal, Women's Studies International Forum, Critical Social Policy, Probation Journal,* and *Punishment and Society.* Relevant research has focused on the experiences of women drug users in prison, women's experiences of the criminal justice system, and evaluations of recent initiatives for drug users in Scotland.

CHRISTOPHER W. MULLINS is an assistant professor of criminology in the department of sociology, anthropology, and criminology at the University of Northern Iowa. He earned his doctorate from the University of Missouri–Saint Louis in criminology. His research focuses on violence, especially interconnections between street culture, gender, and street violence, as well as violence by corporations and nation-states. His work has appeared in *Criminology, Critical Criminology, Criminal Justice Review, Crime, Law, and Social Change, Humanity and Society,* and several edited research volumes. He is the author of *Holding Your Square: Masculinities, Streetlife, and Violence* with Willan Press (2006), and *The International Criminal Court: Symbolic Gestures and the Generation of Global Social Control* from Lexington Books (2006).

CLAIRE M. RENZETTI is professor of sociology at the University of Dayton. She is editor of the international interdisciplinary journal *Violence against Women,* coeditor of the Interpersonal Violence book series for Oxford University Press, and editor of the Gender, Crime, and Law book series for Northeastern University Press/University Press of New England. She has authored or edited sixteen books, as well as numerous book chapters and articles in professional journals. Her current research focuses on the violent victimization experiences of economically marginalized women living in public housing developments. Dr. Renzetti has held elected and appointed positions on the governing bodies of several national professional organizations and is past president of the Society for the Study of Social Problems.

CHRISTINE A. SAUM is an assistant professor in the department of law and justice studies at Rowan University. She is also a faculty associate with the Center for Drug and Alcohol Studies at the University of Delaware. She served as co–principal investigator of a study of drug court offenders and has worked on studies of treatment barriers for drug-using women, and of juvenile offender reentry strategies; she has also performed evaluations of corrections-based treatment. She has published in the areas of drug courts, women and substance abuse, drug policy, sex in prison, and date-rape drugs, and has coauthored a book on cocaine-exposed infants.

IRA SOMMERS received his doctorate in social work in 1983 from the University of Pennsylvania. He was a NIMH post-doctoral research fellow at the University of Massachusetts–Amherst, department of sociology. Currently, Dr. Sommers is a professor in the School of Criminal Justice and Criminalistics at California State University, Los Angeles. Over the course of his academic career, Dr. Sommers has conducted and published research on a range of topics, including female offending, substance abuse and violence, forensic mental health, and domestic violence. He is coauthor of *The Social Consequences of Methamphetamine Use (2004)*, *Workin' Hard for the Money: The Social and Economic Lives of Female Drug Dealers* (2000), and *Casualties of Community Disorder: Women's Careers in Violent Crime* (1998). Most recently, he completed a National Science Foundation grant studying methamphetamine use and violence.

CAROL E. TRACY is executive director of the Women's Law Project (WLP) in Philadelphia, PA. WLP is a legal advocacy and services group purposed to promote women's rights.

INDEX

activism, 176–177. *See also* advocacy; political activism and social change agency; political activity

addiction, 60, 90, 95; dually addicted couple, 118

Adult Services Office, 213

advocacy, 86, 175, 185, 186, 187

agency, 2, 3, 4, 26, 27–28, 33, 85, 89, 92, 96, 128, 135, 138, 139, 146, 150, 168–169, 174; relational and autonomous, 12, 19, 20, 86

assaultive violence, 66, 72, 76. *See also* violence

binging, 95, 96

biopower, 36–37, 39. *See also* power

bipolar disorder, 166. *See also* mental illness

body, the, 33, 34, 36, 37; communicative, 37; consuming, 40–41; domestic, 39; drug-dealing female, 43; drug-using or -consuming, 39, 41, 44; female, in commerce, xiii, 43; female laboring, 1

capital, 203; accumulation of 18, 27

"carceral clawback" (Clawson), 143. *See also* imprisonment; prison

career criminals, 65

case management, 102

claiming a public voice/going public, 184, 185

cocaine, 53; economy, 51; markets, 53, 55, 62; use, 52

codependency, 86, 119, 121–122, 126, 127, 128, 130

commercial sex, 200–201, 202. *See also* prostitution

conventionality, ties to, 125

core activities, 11, 15, 17–27, 34, 38, 42

crack, 53; markets, 53, 62. *See also* cocaine

crimes of survival, 161. *See also* survival/ instrumental agency

criminal careers, 60, 61, 65

criminal histories, 158

criminalization, 142, 143, 192, 193, 199, 204–205

criminology, 2

deindustrialization, 68

depression, 167. *See also* mental illness

detoxification, 123, 127. *See also* drug treatment

deviance, embodied, 37–38

domestic violence center, 212

drug addict, female, 90, 97

drug court, 87, 104, 107, 109, 152; judge, 104–105, 112; model, 103, 105; movement, 103; participant, 106, 107, 110. *See also* therapeutic jurisprudence

drug dealers, 96; becoming, 54; female, 50

drug dealing: hierarchy, 194; initiation into, 49, 61; lifestyle, 61

drug dependence, 95; subsidizing male, 12, 22–24. *See also* addiction

marketing activities, 12. *See also* illicit drug world

masculinity: challenges to, 76; hegemonic, 67

medicalization, 142

mental illness, 157, 158, 161, 162; bipolar disorder, 166; depression, 167; dually diagnosed, 157, 162, 163–165, 169, 171; schizophrenia, 167

methadone maintenance, 117, 127. *See also* harm reduction

middlemen, 26. *See also* middlewomen

middlewomen, 25–26

moral reformers, 192

misogyny, 66

narrative strategy, xiii, 3, 98, 99

offenders, female, 158

offenses, alcohol- and drug-related, 141. *See also* drugs: and crime

pathology and powerlessness, xiii, 1, 2, 4, 28, 66, 87, 136, 137

pimping, 2. *See also* prostitution

pleasure, pursuit of, 12. *See also* leisure and recreational activities

political activism and social change agency, 4, 7, 135, 137

political activity, 184

power, 3, 4, 11, 15, 36, 85, 135; biopower, 36–37, 39; economic, 22; feminist conceptions of, 15; structural/power over, 16, 20, 26; power, transforma-tive/relational/power to, 16, 26. *See also* empowerment

prison, 144, 145, 146, 150; population, 193, 195; services, 142, 144; women in, 140, 141, 197. *See also* imprisonment

Progressive Era, 192

prohibitory policies, 195

prostitutes, 136, 194, 199, 202. *See also* sex workers

prostitution, 60, 178, 188, 192, 194, 198, 199, 200, 201, 204–205, 207; antipros-titution statutes, 193; policies, 196. *See also* sex work

psychological disorders. *See* mental illness

recreational drug use, 34

reentry, 142, 161, 170

rights and care perspective, 104

risks of violence, 57, 59. *See also* violence

schizophrenia, 167. *See also* mental illness

sentencing, for drug offenders, xiv, 143. *See also* drug court

sex markets, street-level, 200

sex tours, xiv

sexual object, 92

sexual subject, 86, 92

sex work, 20–21, 71, 81, 90, 136. *See also* prostitution

sex workers, 2, 21, 137. *See also* prostitutes

social relationships, 160

social roles, 160, 170

social welfare, 24

sociology, 2

status challenges, 76

stereotypes, 85, 89, 90, 206

stigma, 97, 137, 142, 157, 175, 176, 178–179, 188; from family, 182–183; sexual, 188, 189; in treatment, 179

stigmatized identities, 33

street life, xiv. *See also* life as party

street violence, xiv. *See also* violence

style and empowerment, 25

substance abuse, xiv; dually diagnosed, 157, 162, 163–165, 169, 171; male, 3; problems, 141; studies, 2; treatment, 100. *See also* addiction

subversion, 33

supports, informal and formal, 1, 160

survival, 175, 214. *See also* survival/instru-mental agency

survival/instrumental agency, 4, 5, 66, 86, 125

symbolic resistance agency, 4, 5–6, 86, 137

systemic violence, 72, 78. *See also* violence